LARGE PRINT

Dot-to-Dot

Meditation

MADDY BROOK

SIRIUS

SIRIUS

This edition published in 2024 by Sirius Publishing, a division of
Arcturus Publishing Limited
26/27 Bickels Yard, 151–153 Bermondsey Street,
London SE1 3HA

ISBN: 978-1-3988-0284-1
CH005510NT
Supplier 29, Date 0424, PI 00005873

Printed in China

Created for children 10+

INTRODUCTION

Most of us lead busy lives, with home and work responsibilities that can often lead to constant feelings of stress and anxiety. Meditating is a great way to relieve some of the tension of daily life, but what exactly does 'meditation' mean? Most people think meditation is sitting cross-legged on the floor in silence, but, although that is one method, there are many other ways to have a meditative experience.

Making art can be one of the most fulfilling ways to achieve this relaxed state, as well as being a profoundly enjoyable activity. However, not all of us are natural painters or drawers, or have the time to color in full pages of artwork. That's why this book has been made for people of all skill levels to enjoy, no matter what your artistic ability is. All you have to do is join up the dots.

Dot-to-dots are not nearly as complicated as they look. Each dot is numbered, starting from one up to 200. The first step is finding the first dot, then you simply join one dot to the next, in ascending order.

All of the illustrations here contain between 150 and 200 dots. The best thing is that you won't need to strain your eyes or use a magnifying glass when completing them as they are all in an accessible 'large print' size, meaning they are easier to see than your usual dot-to-dot puzzle. The illustrations vary from patterns and swirls to landscapes, animals, and objects. With so many subjects to discover, there is something in this book for everyone. All you have to do is grab your pen or pencil and get started!

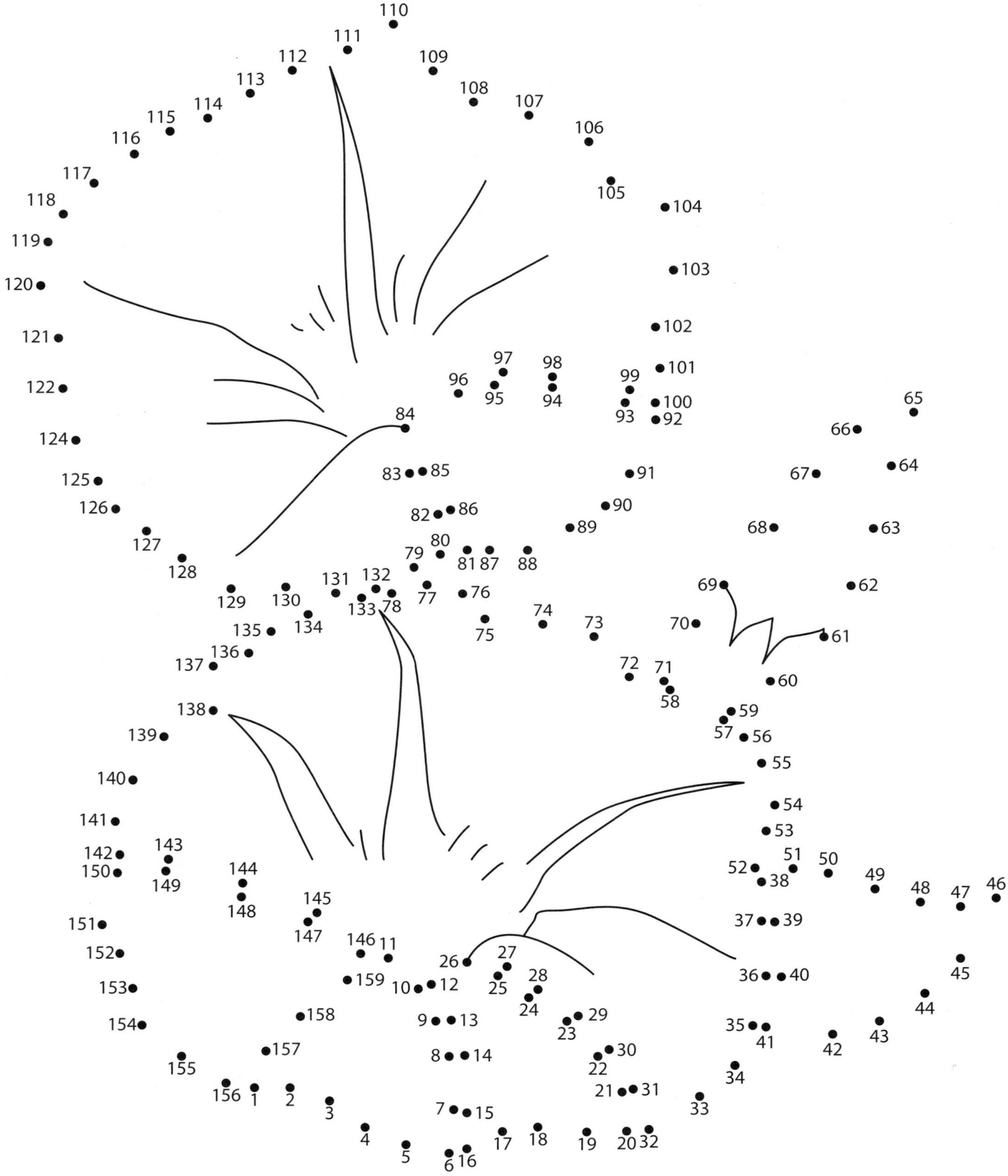

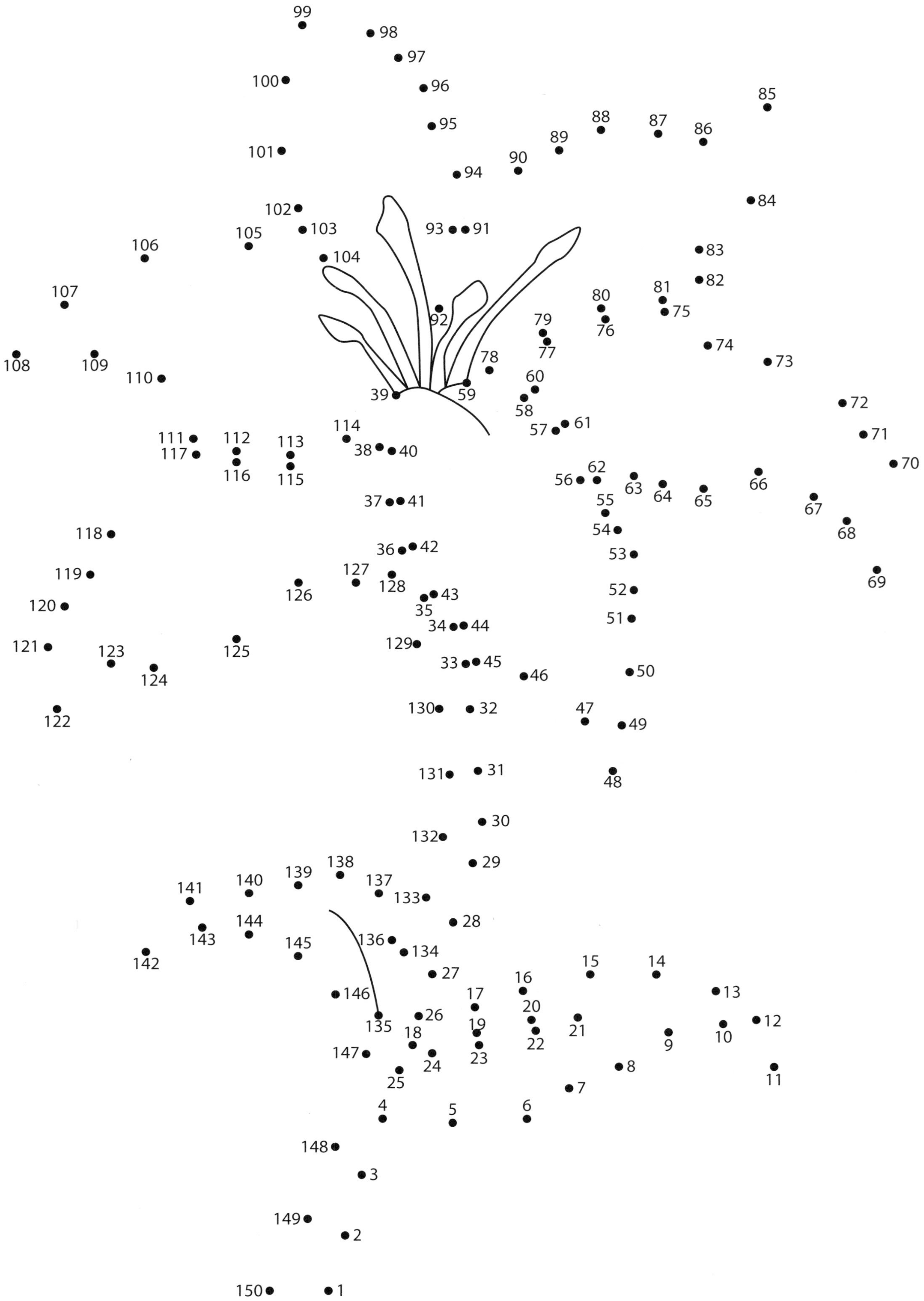

1
2
3
4
5
6
7
8
9
10
11
12
13
14
15
16
17
18
19
20
21
22
23
24
25
26
27
28
29
30
31
32
33
34
35
36
37
38
39
40
41
42
43
44
45
46
47
48
49
50
51
52
53
54
55
56
57
58
59
60
61
62
63
64
65
66
67
68
69
70
71
72
73
74
75
76
77
78
79
80
81
82
83
84
85
86
87
88
89
90
91
92
93
94
95
96
97
98
99
100
101
102
103
104
105
106
107
108
109
110
111
112
113
114
115
116
117
118
119
120
121
122
123
124
125
126
127
128
129
130
131
132
133
134
135
136
137
138
139
140
141
142
143
144
145
146
147
148
149
150

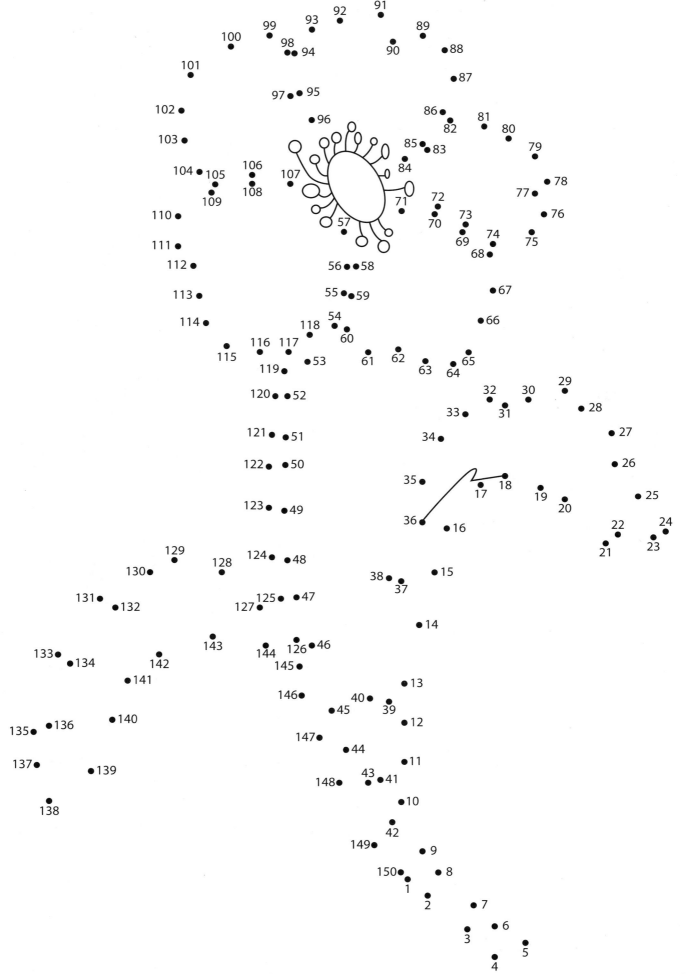

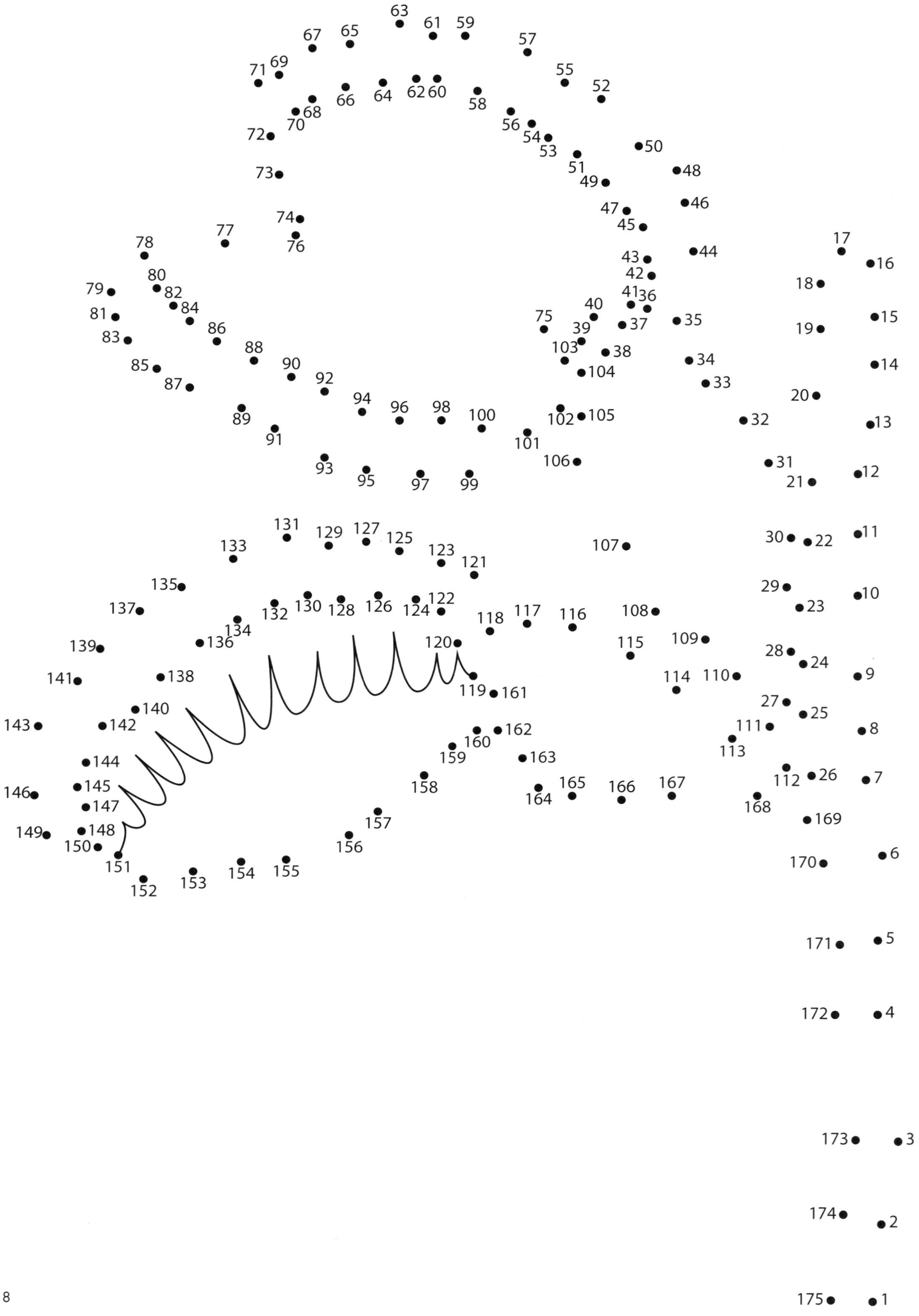

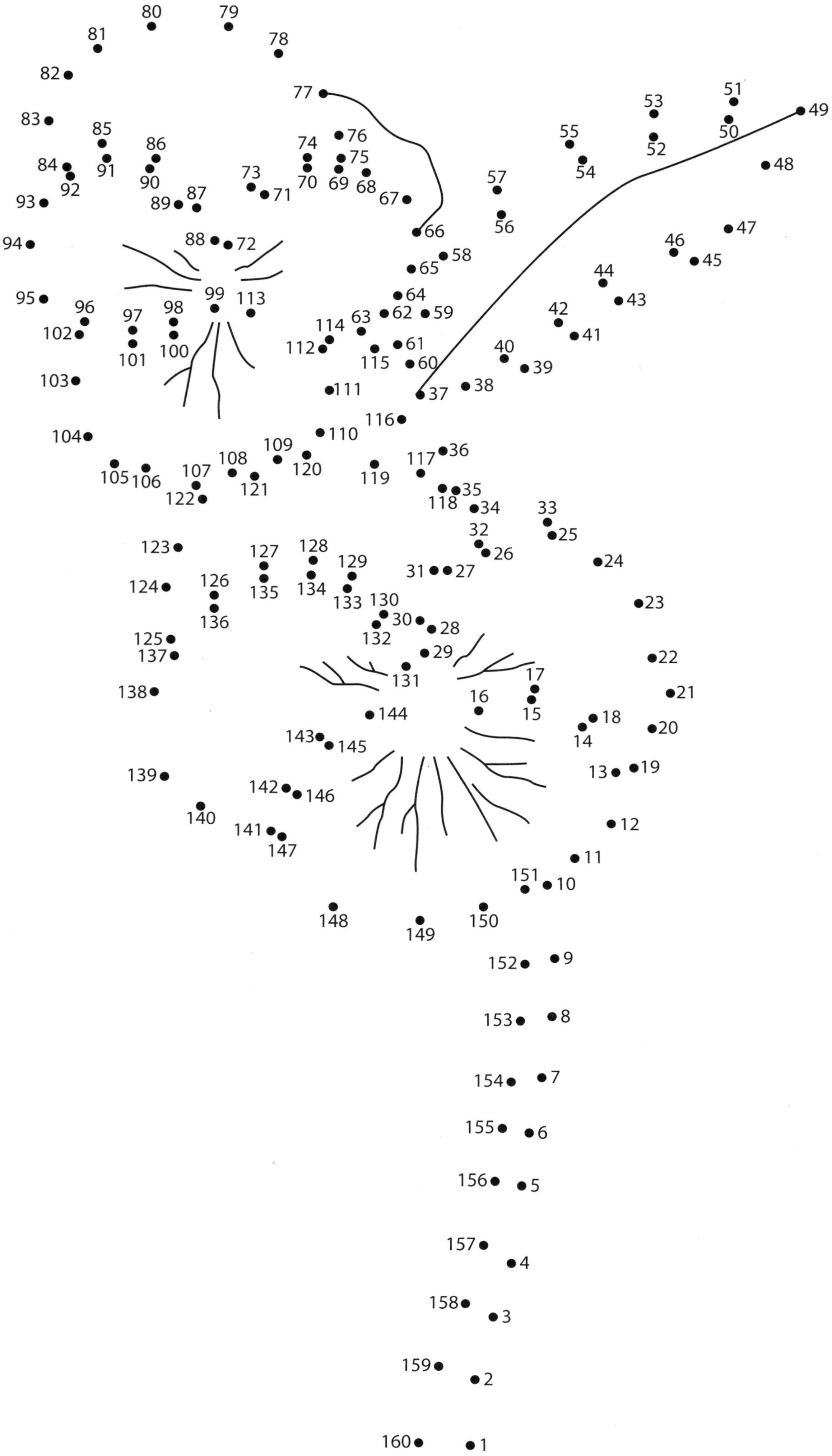

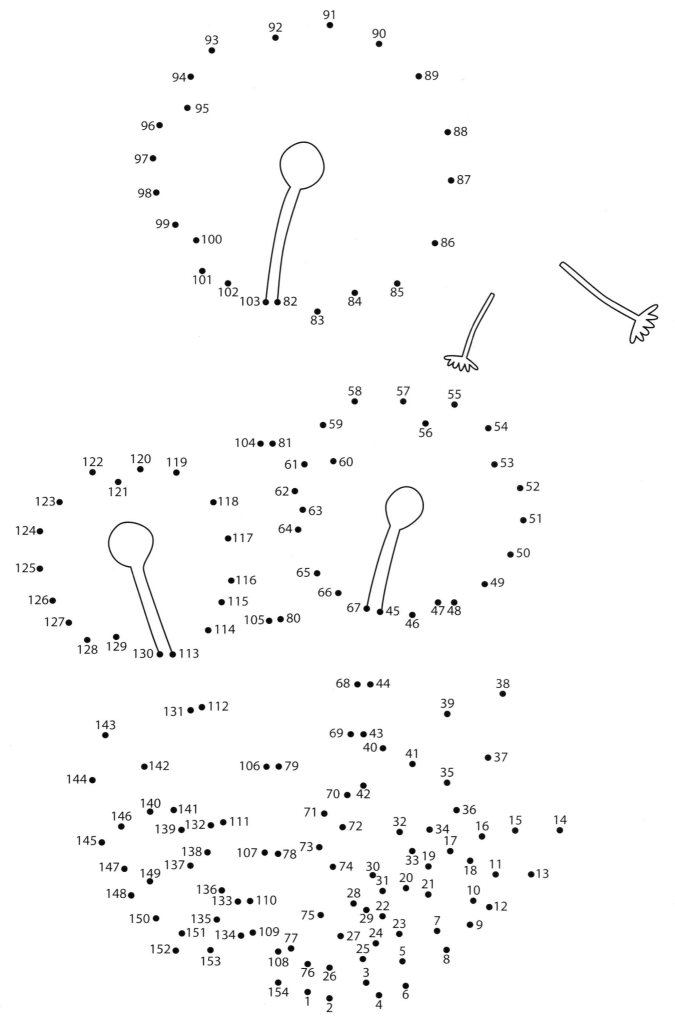

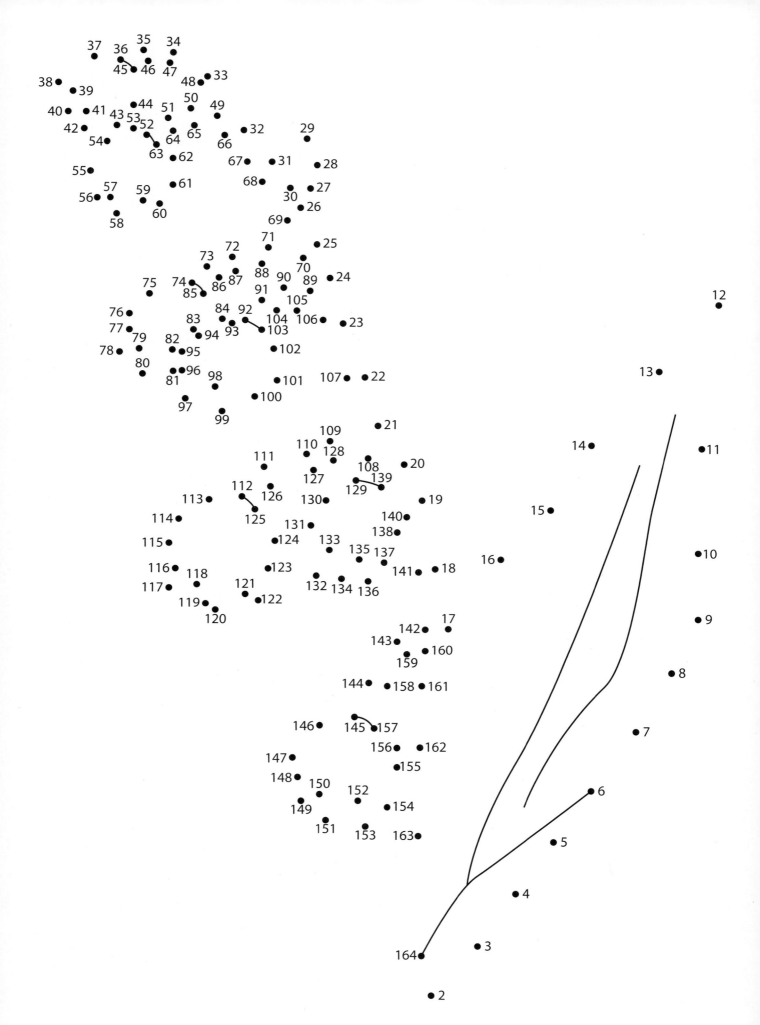

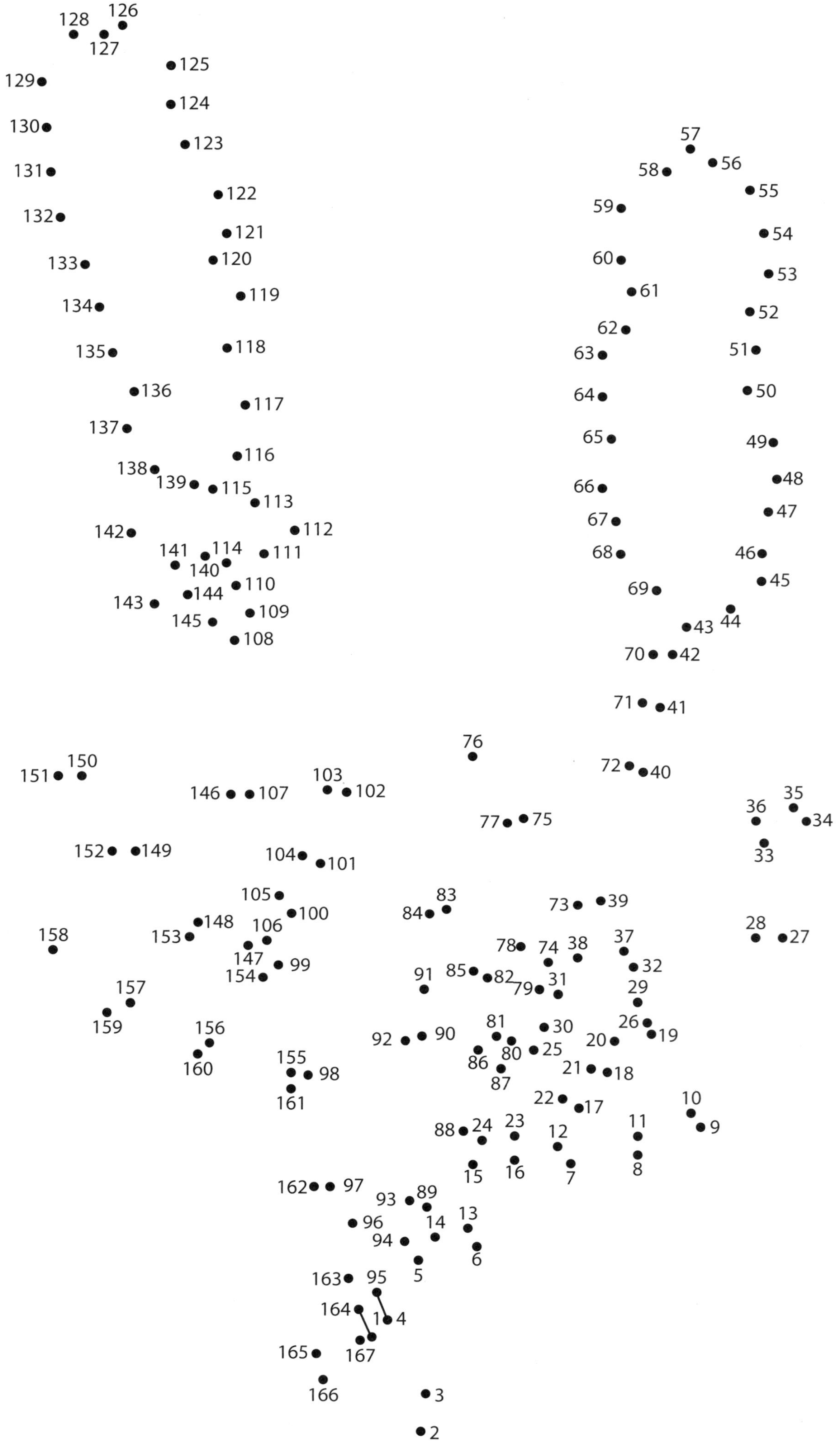

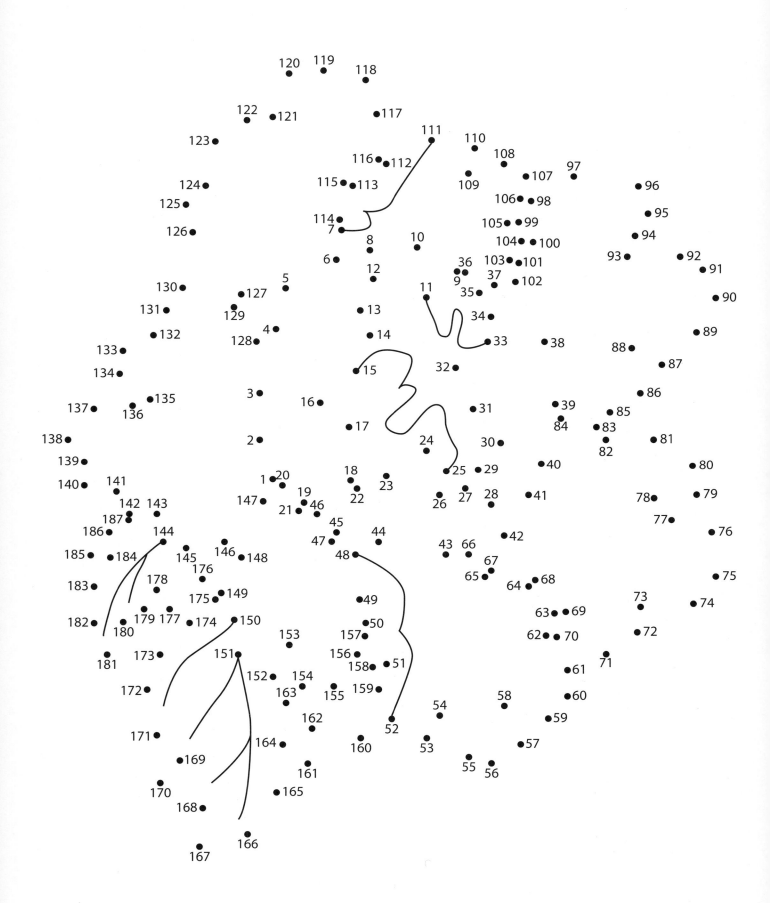

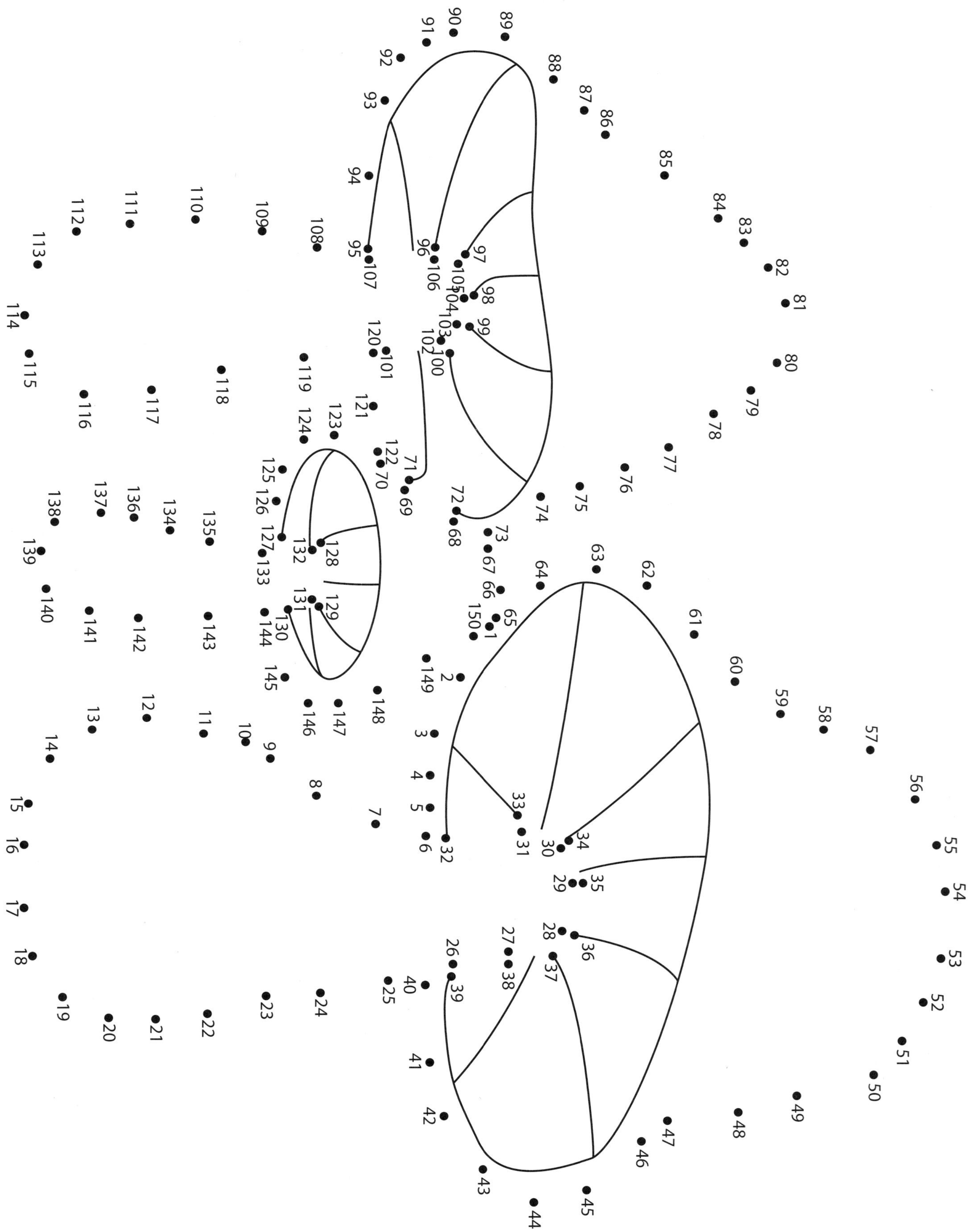

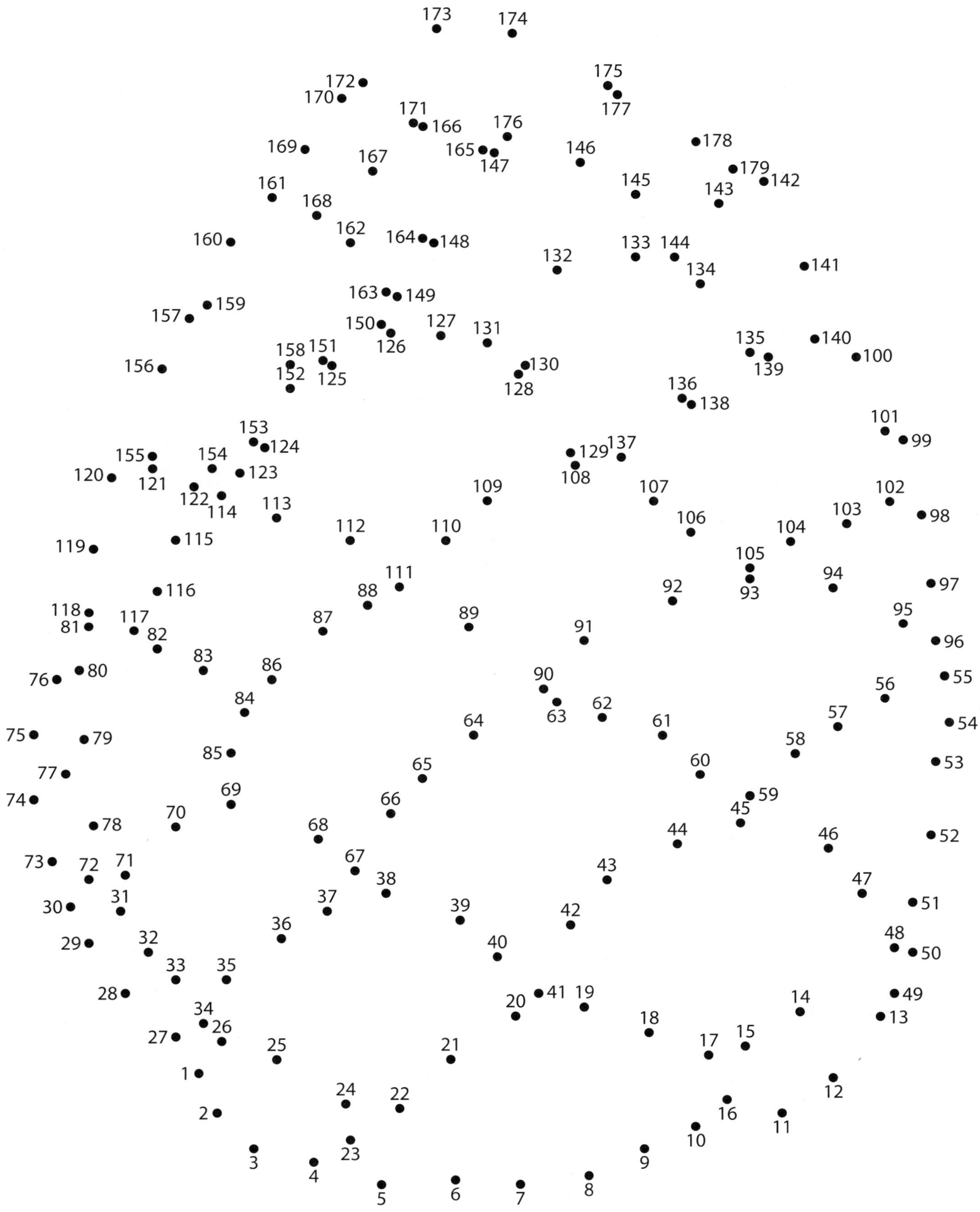

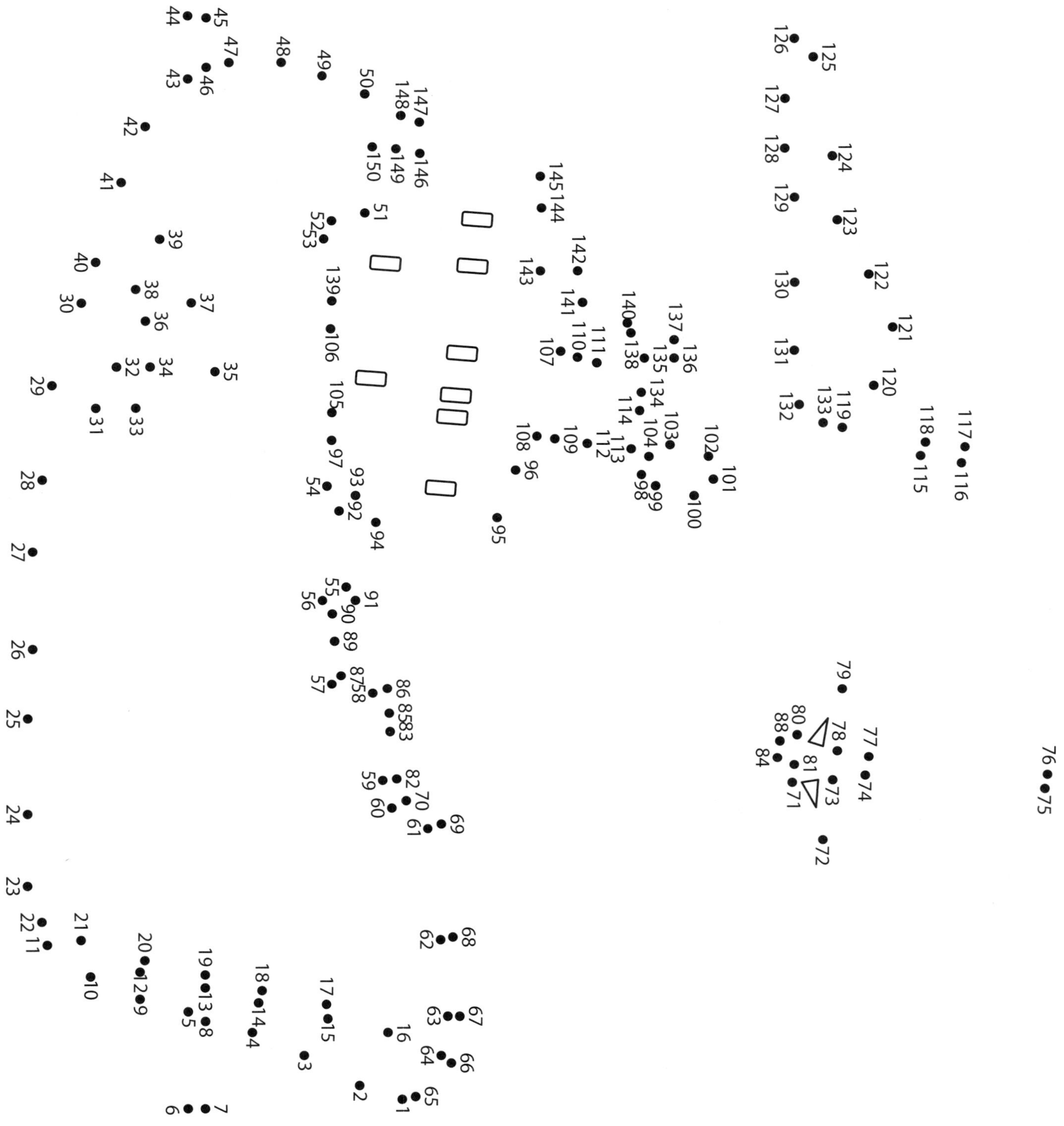

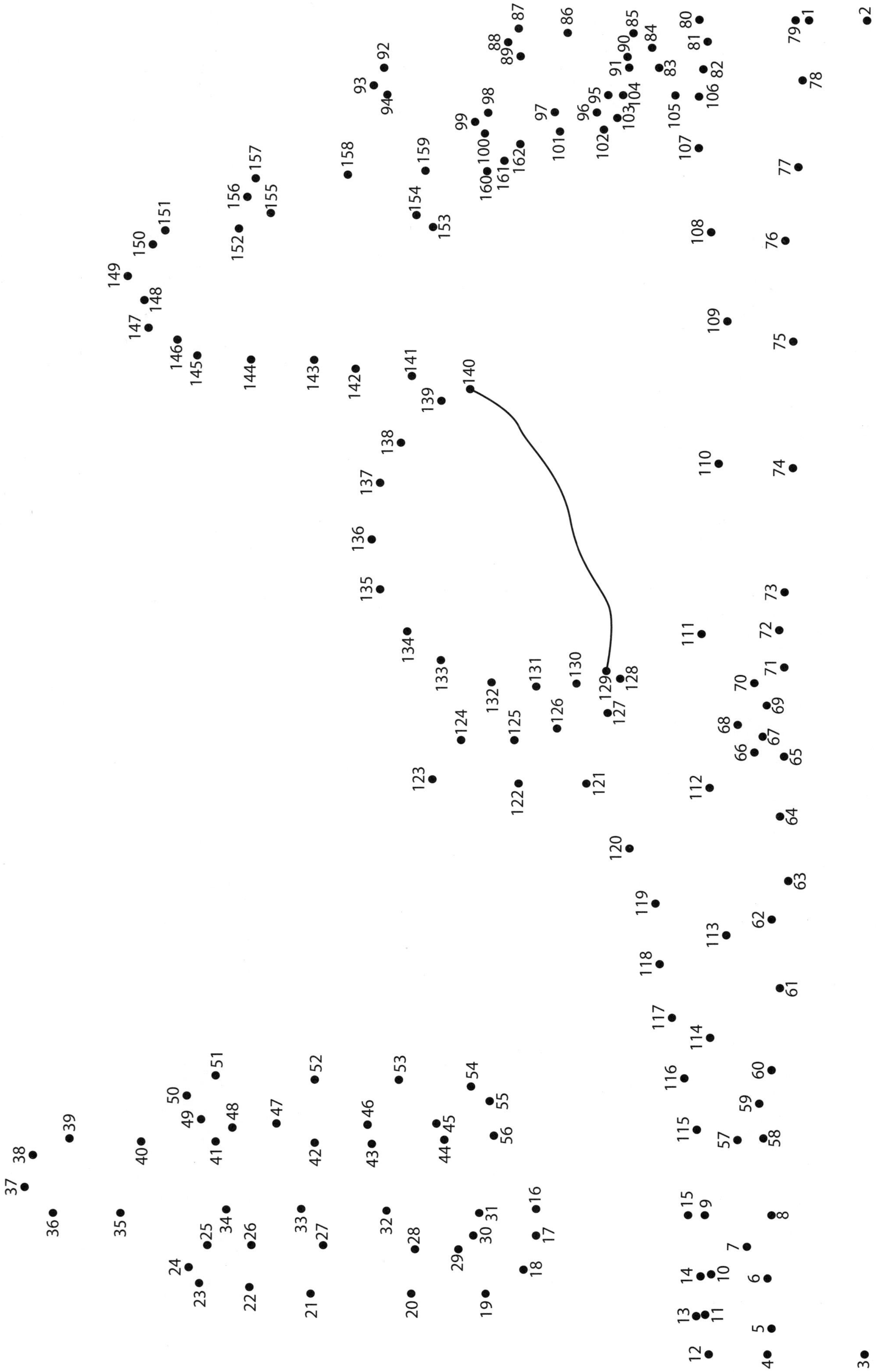

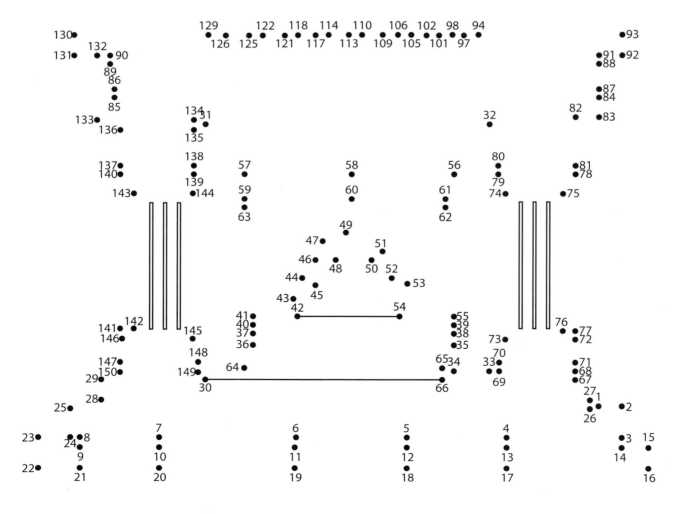

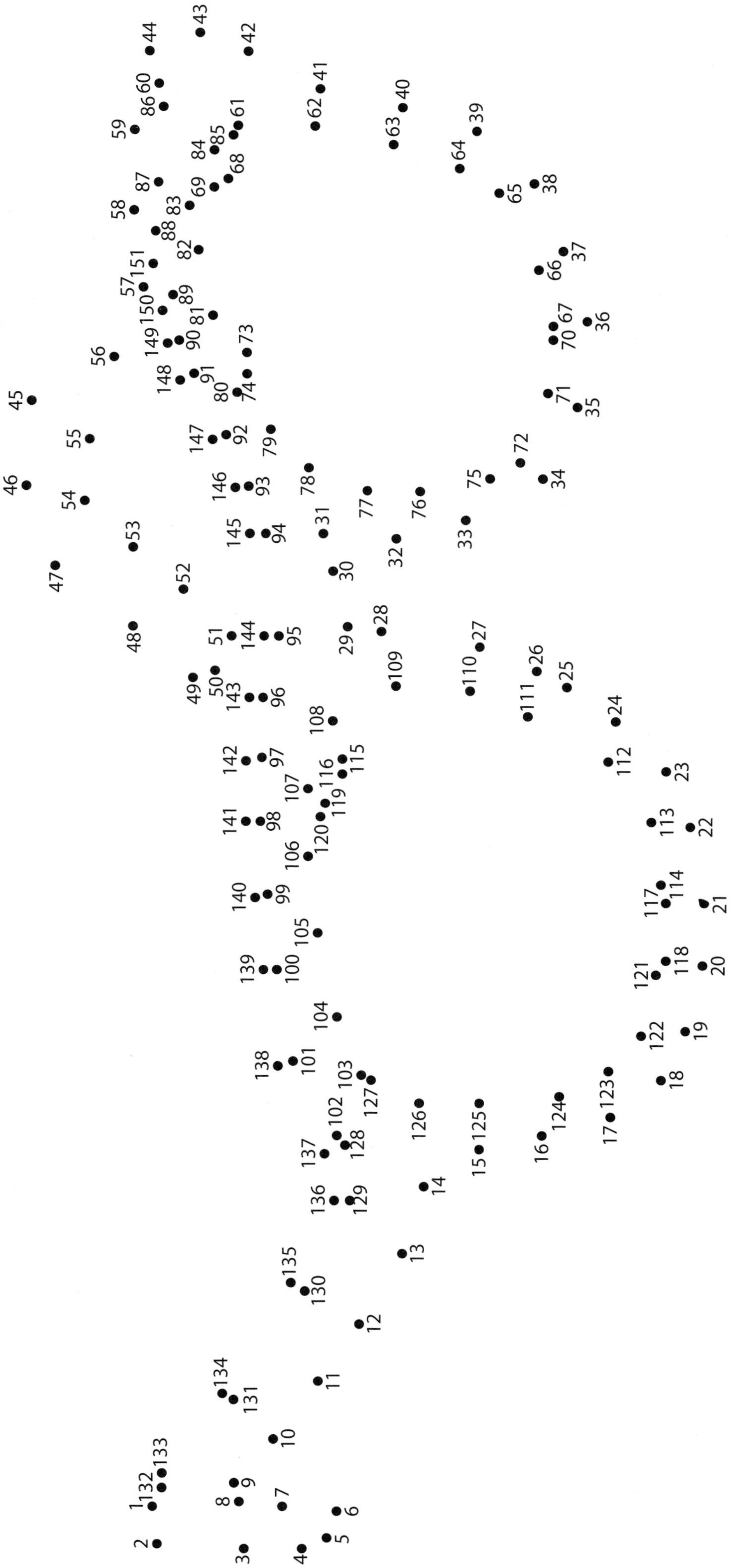

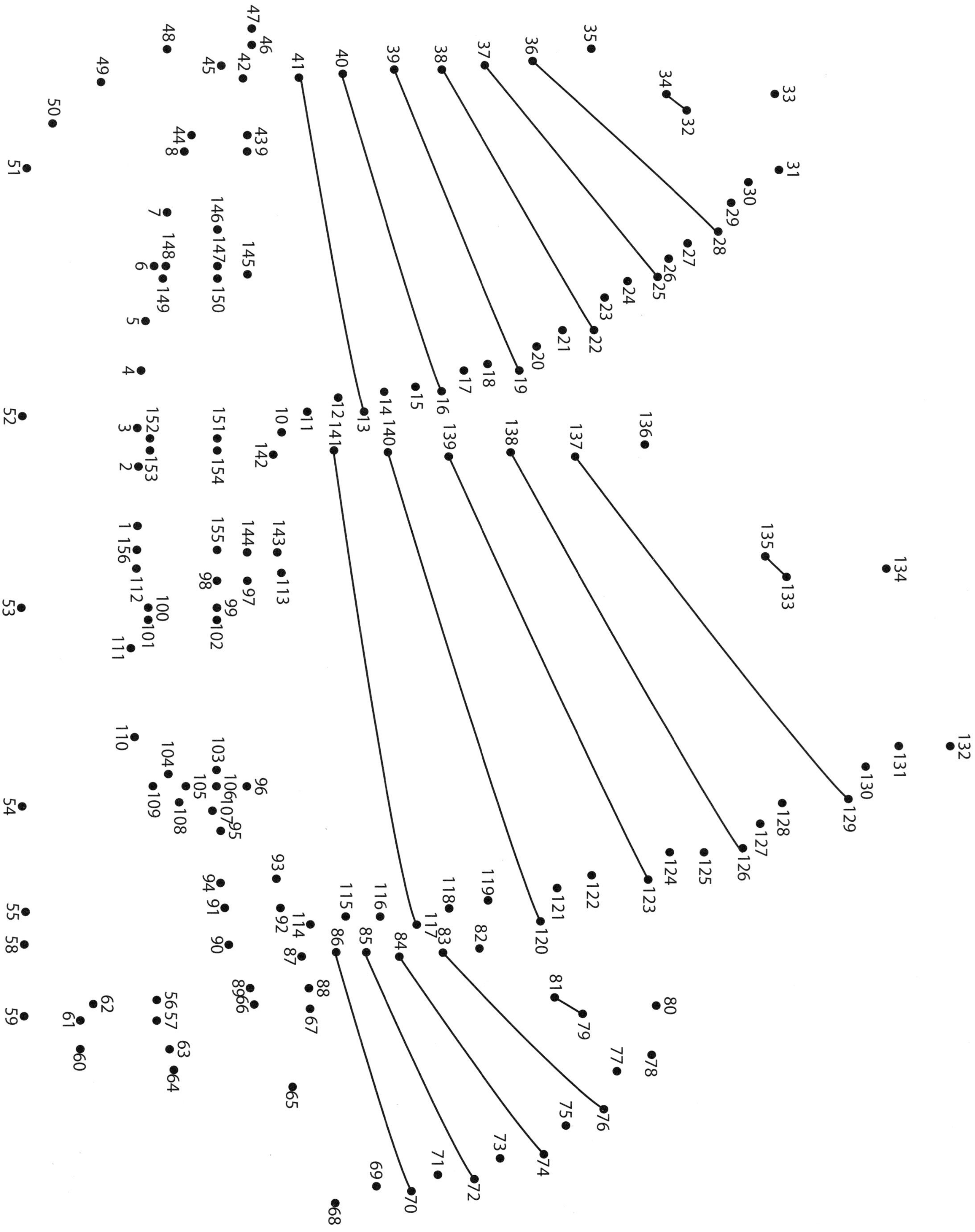

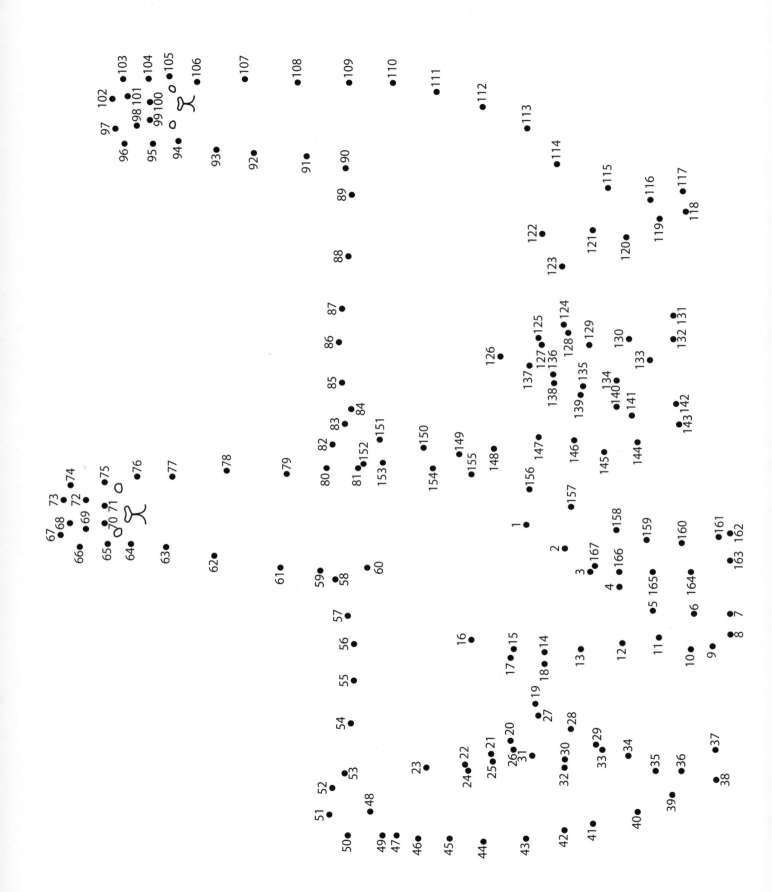

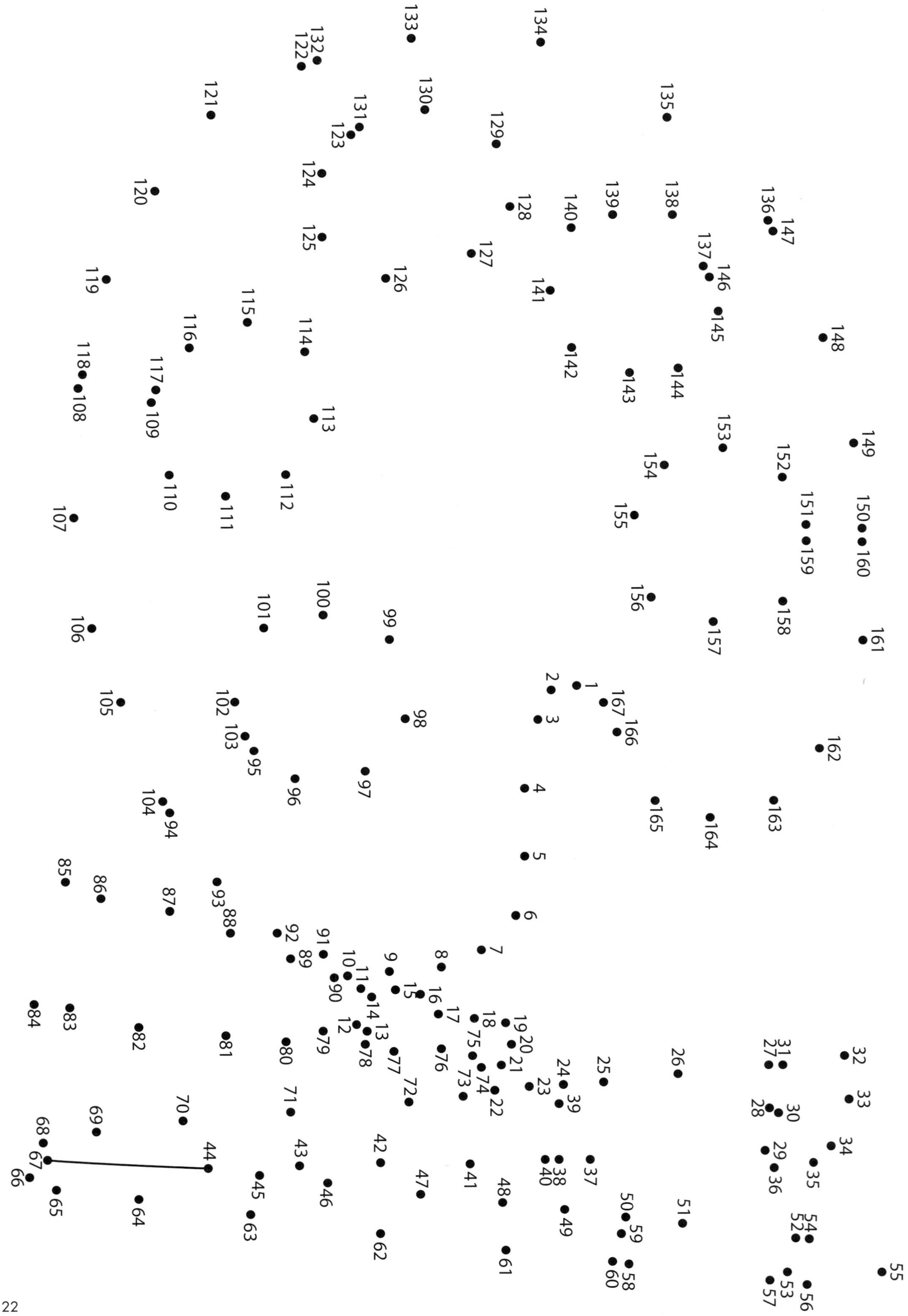

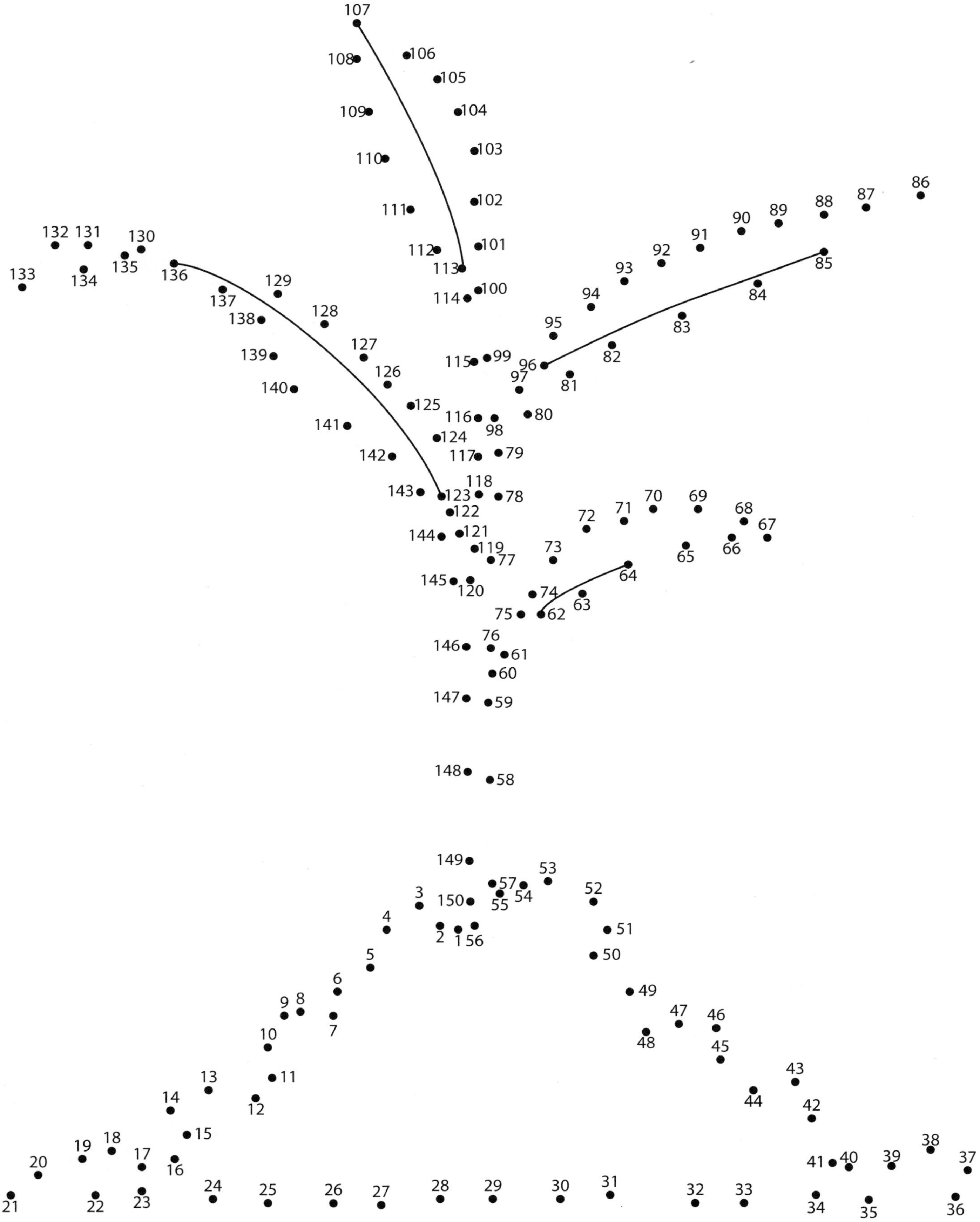

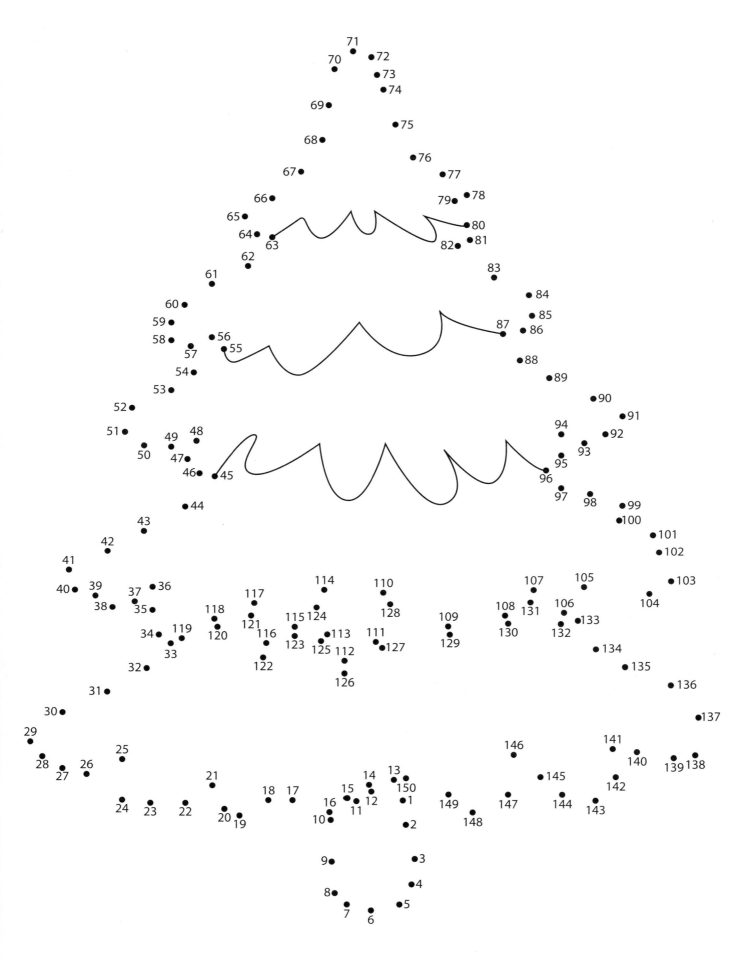

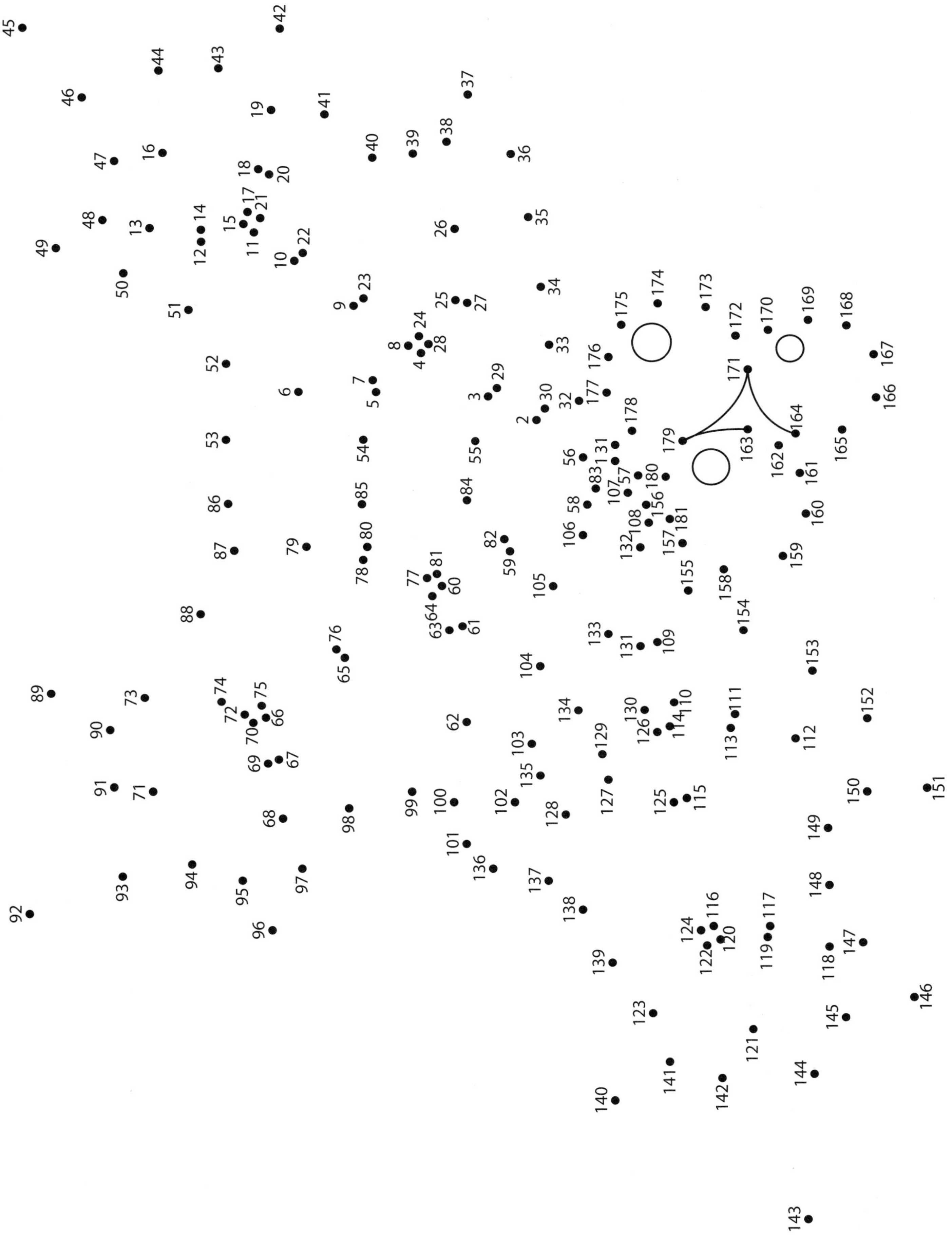

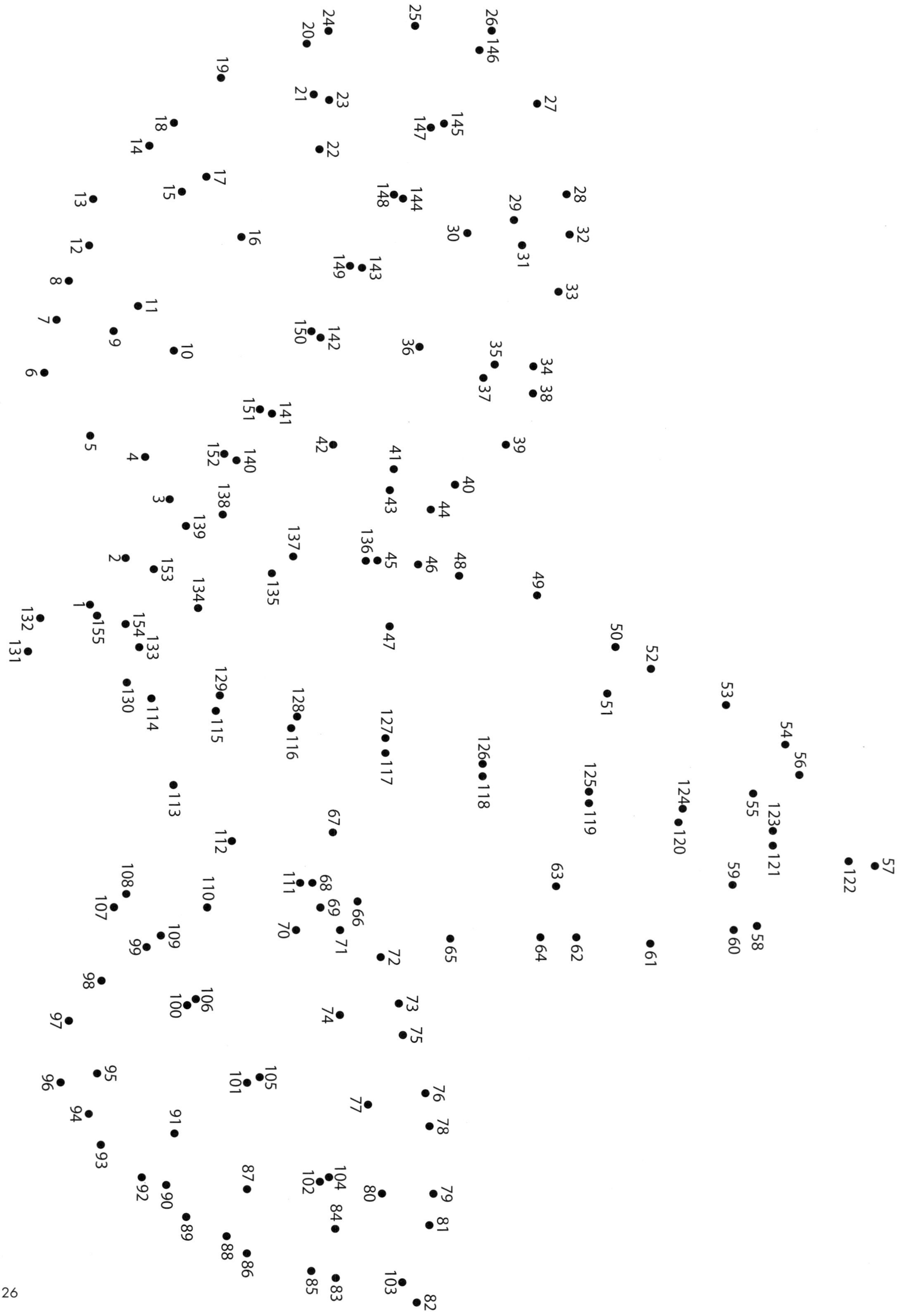

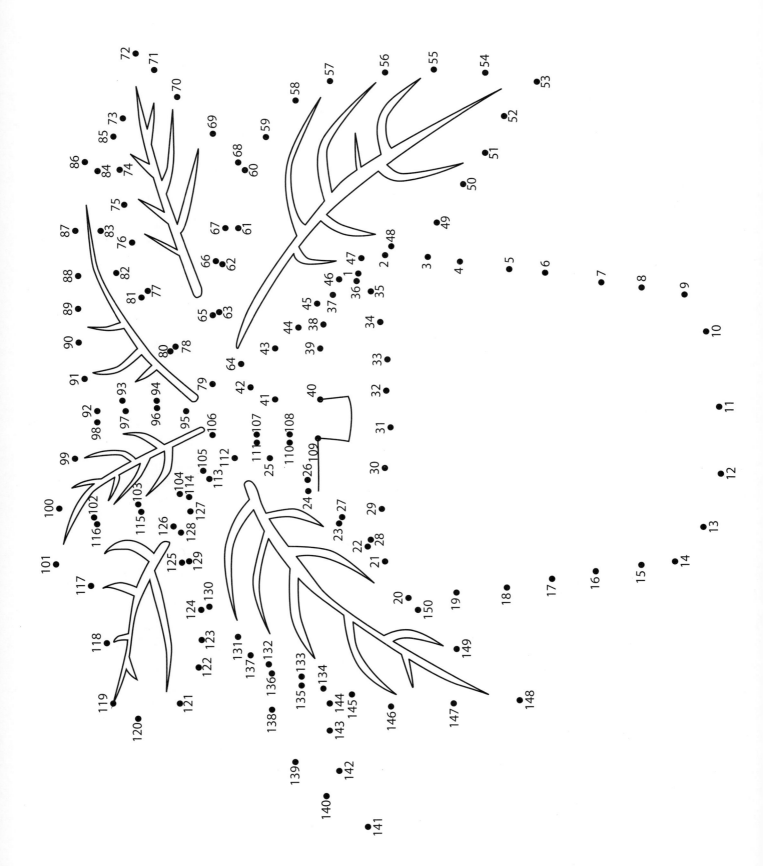

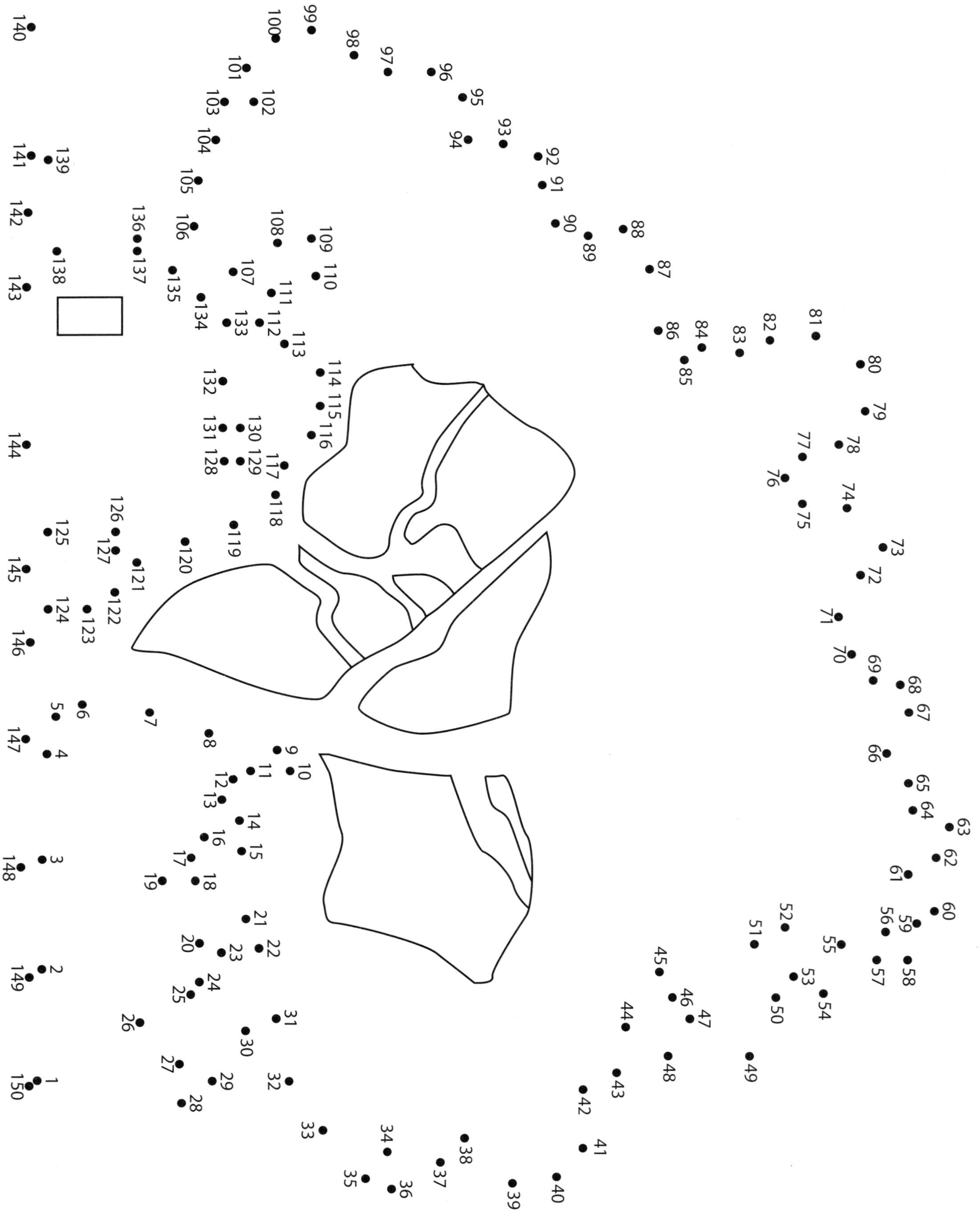

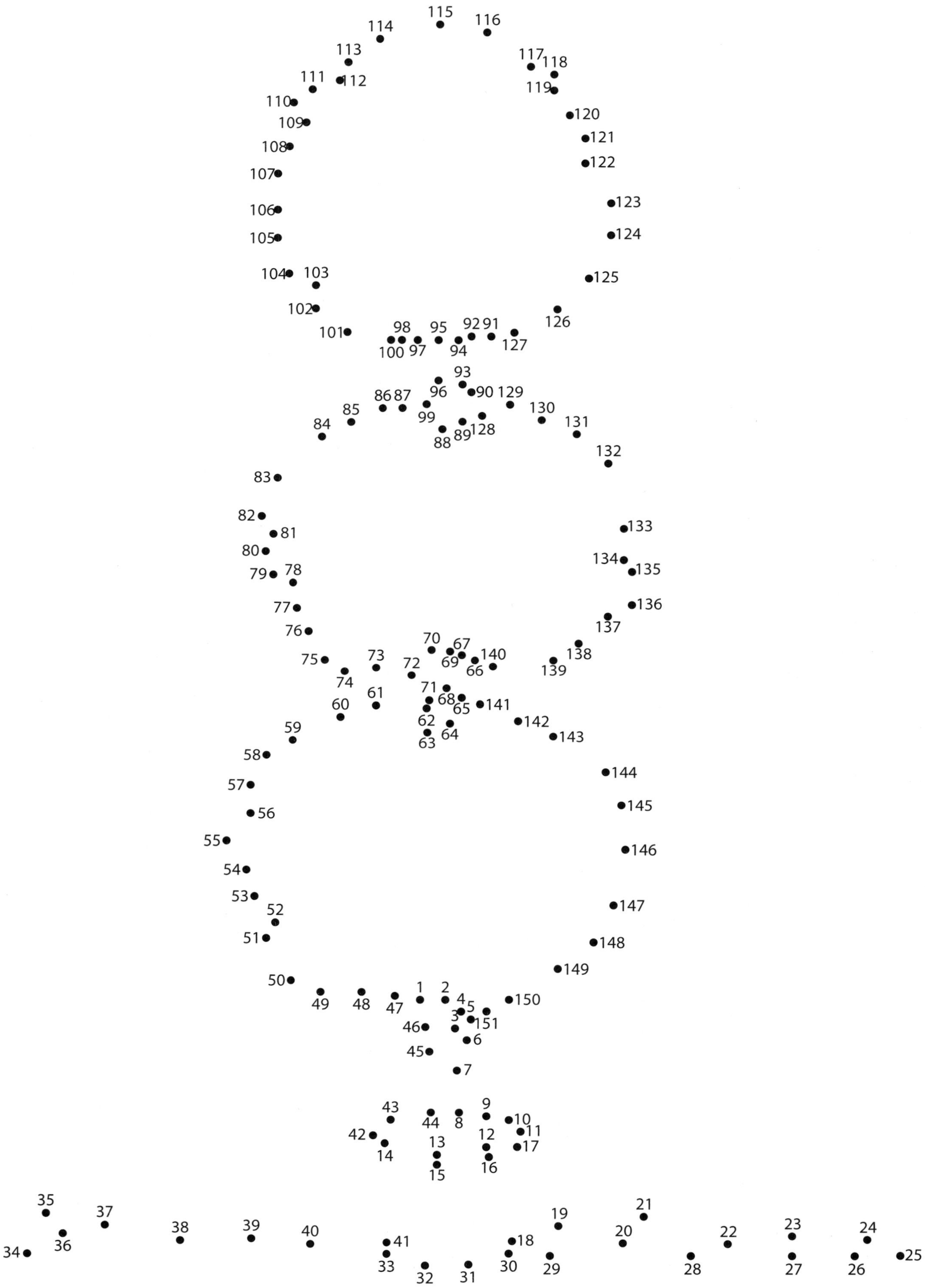

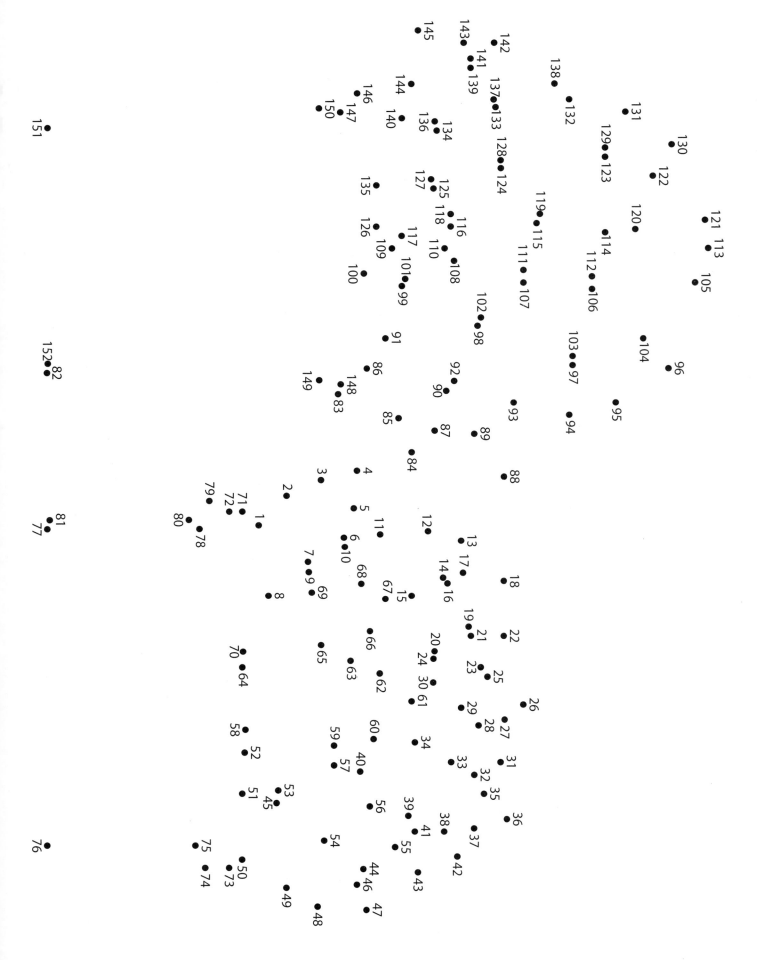

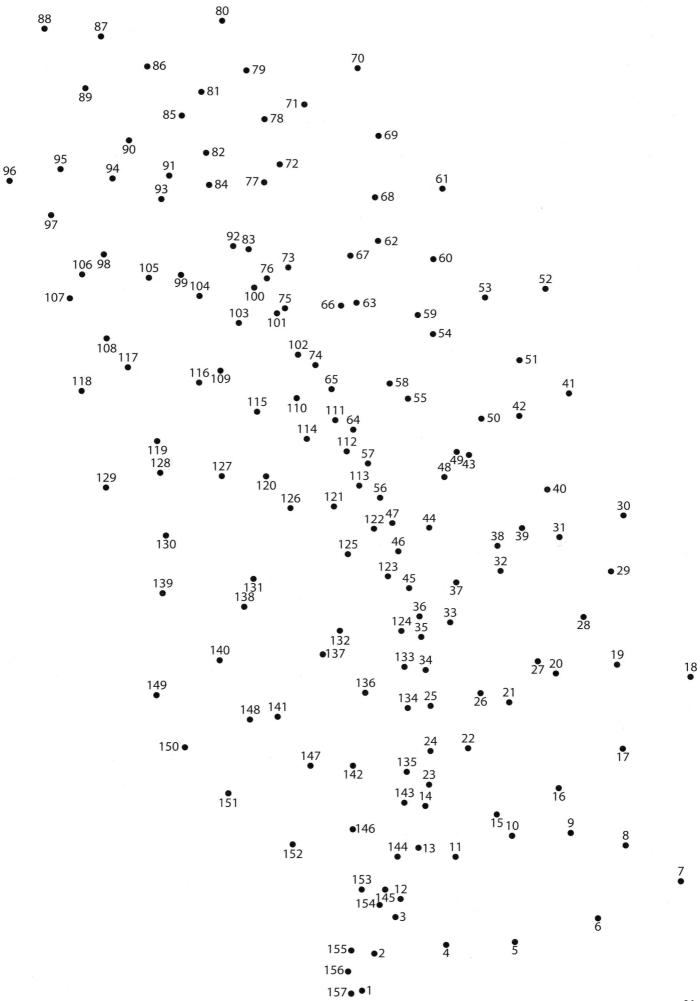

31

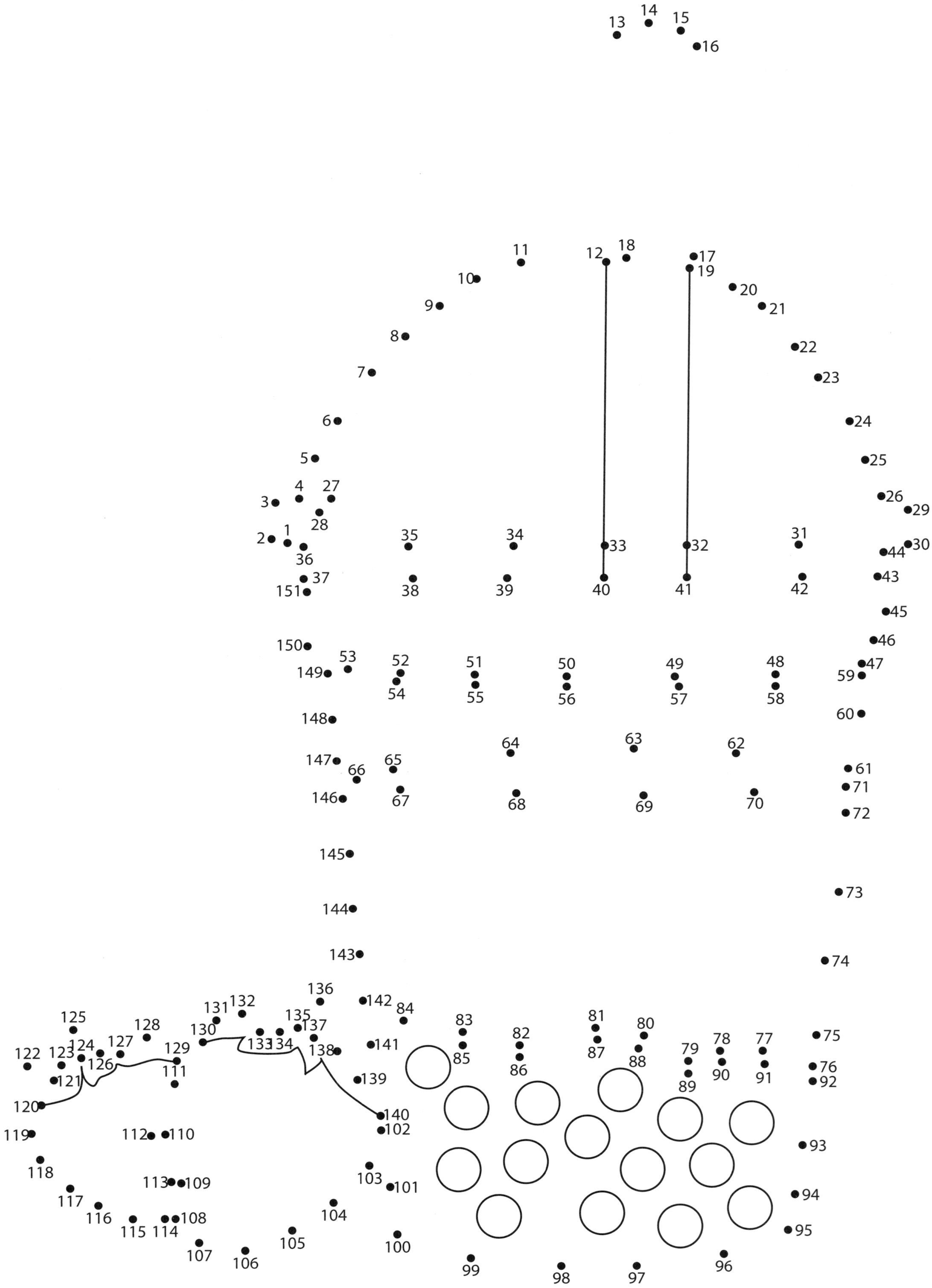

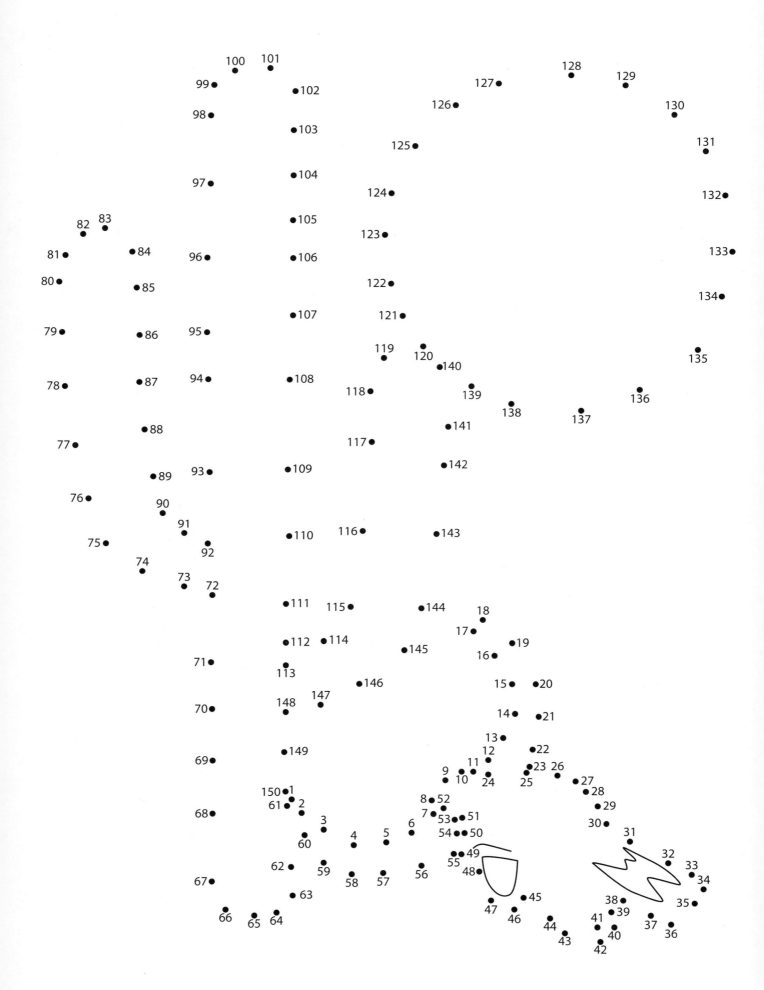

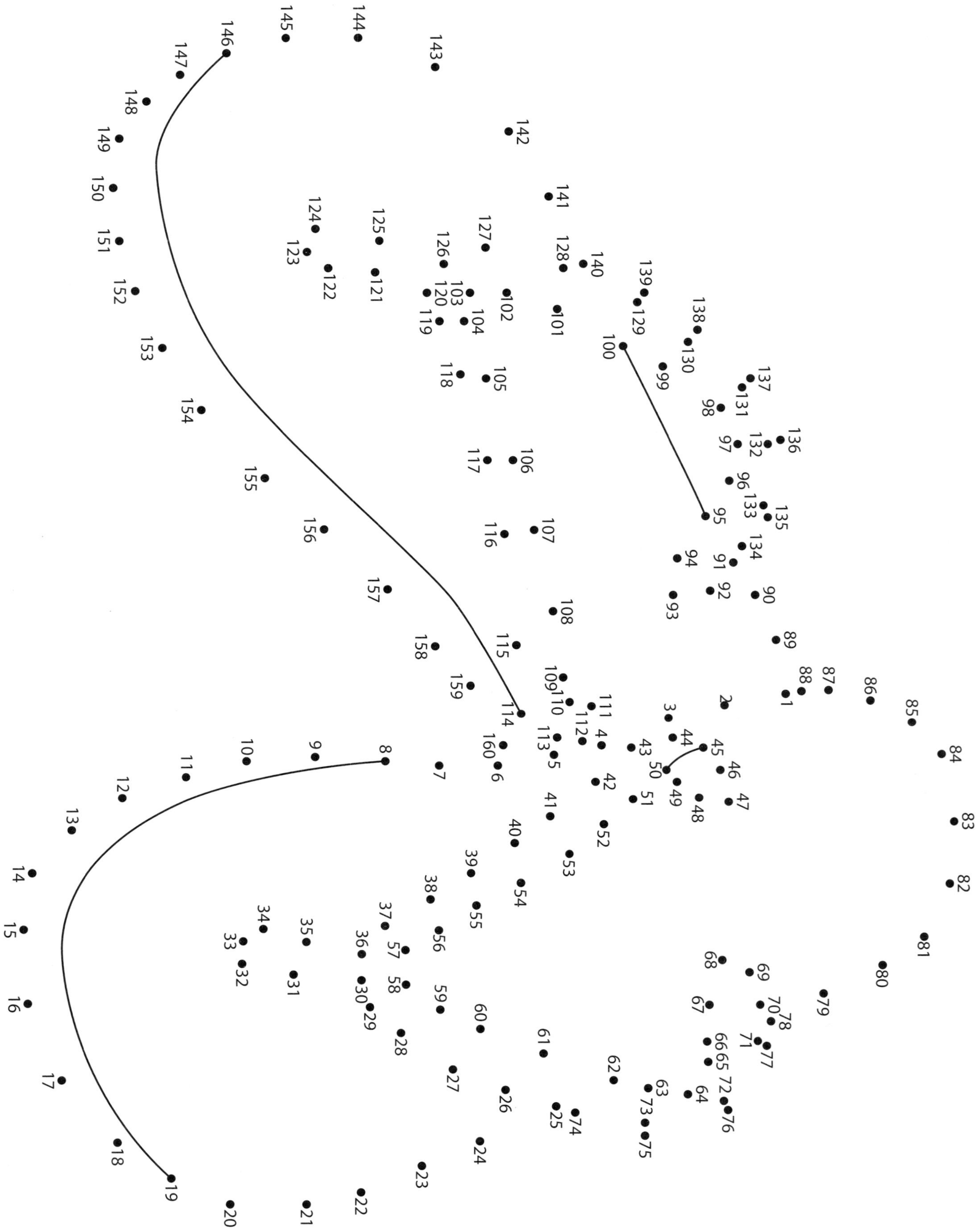

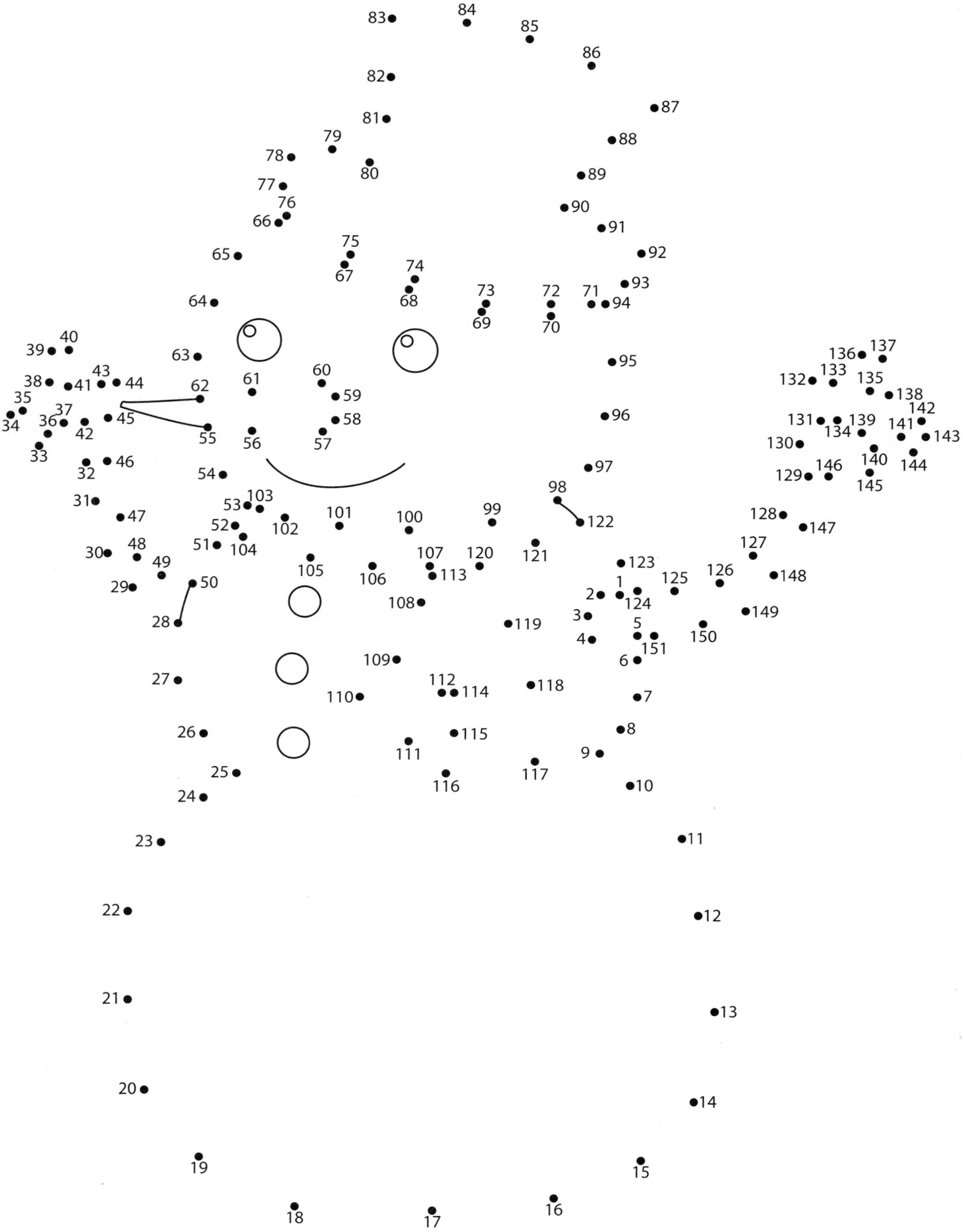

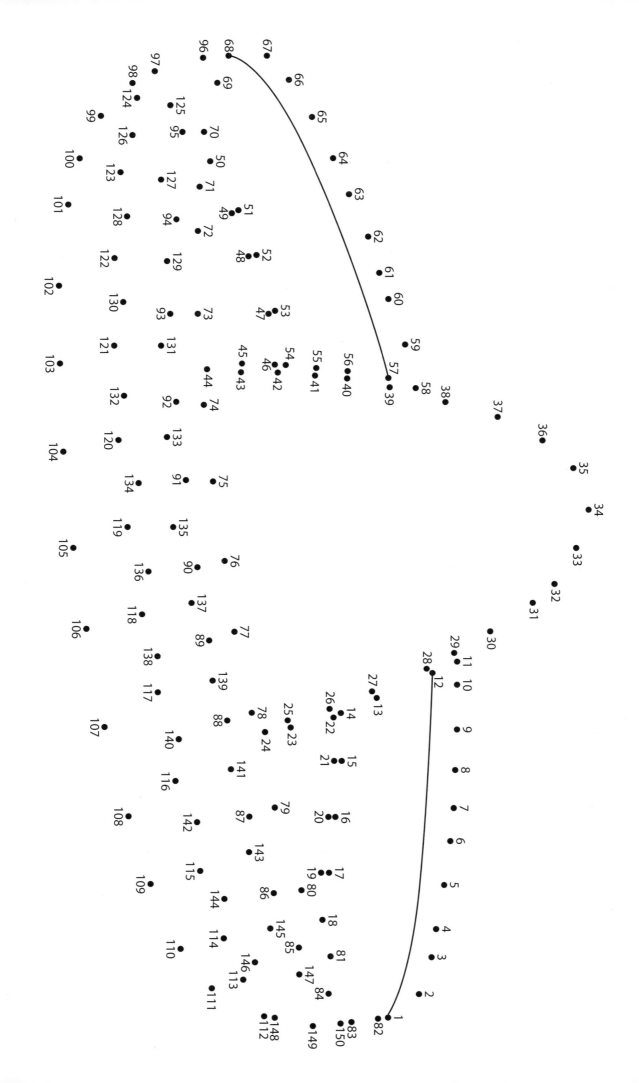

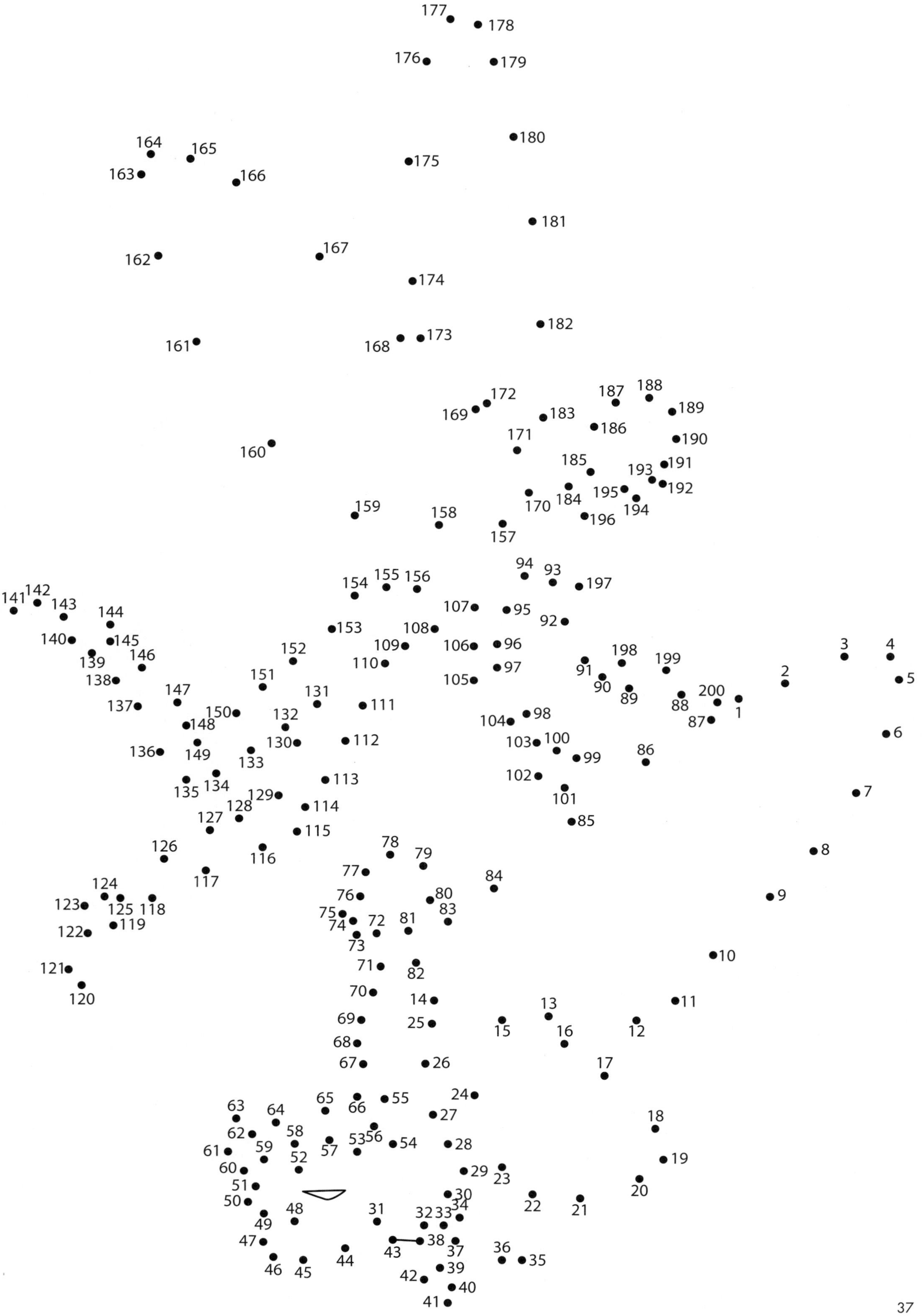

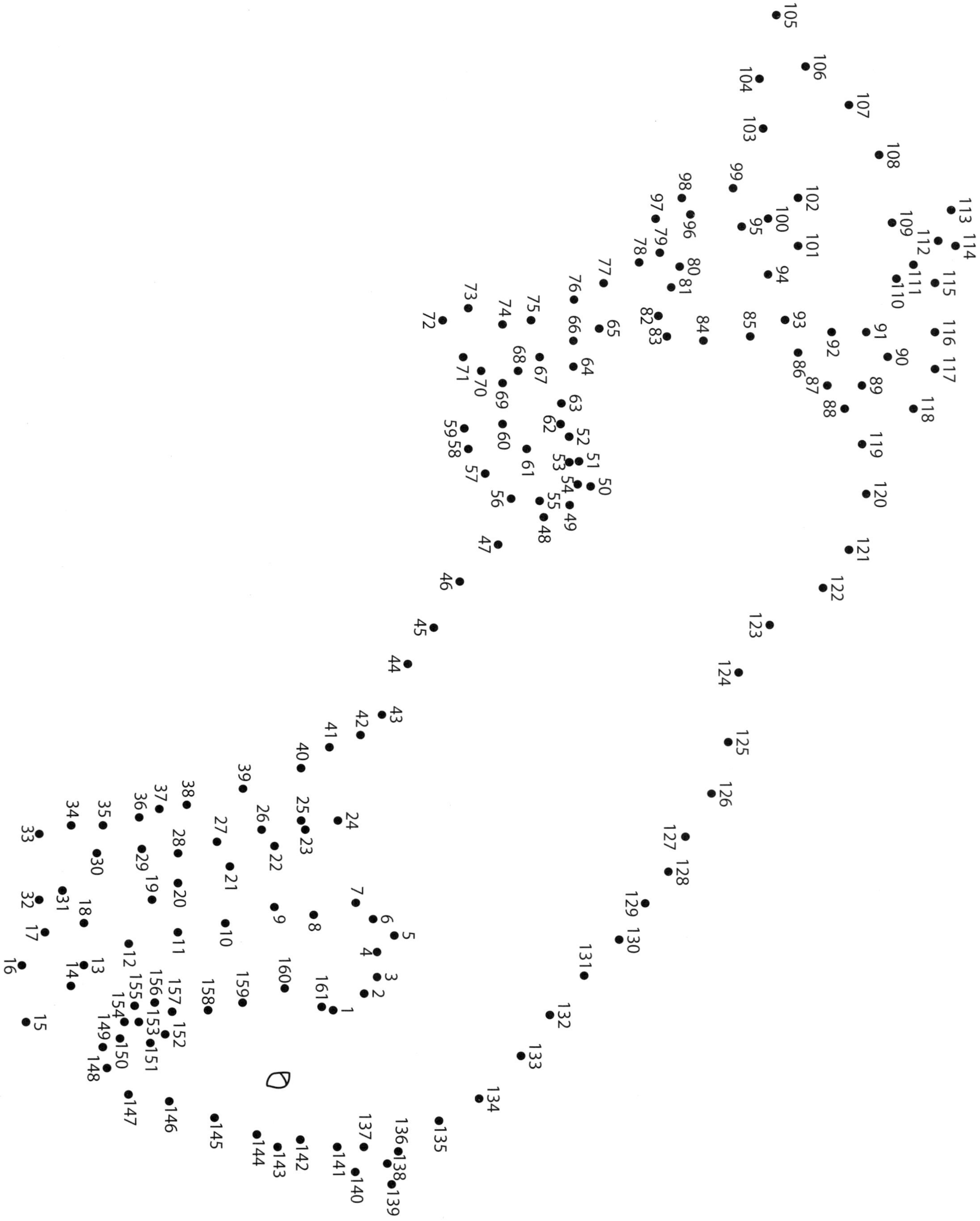

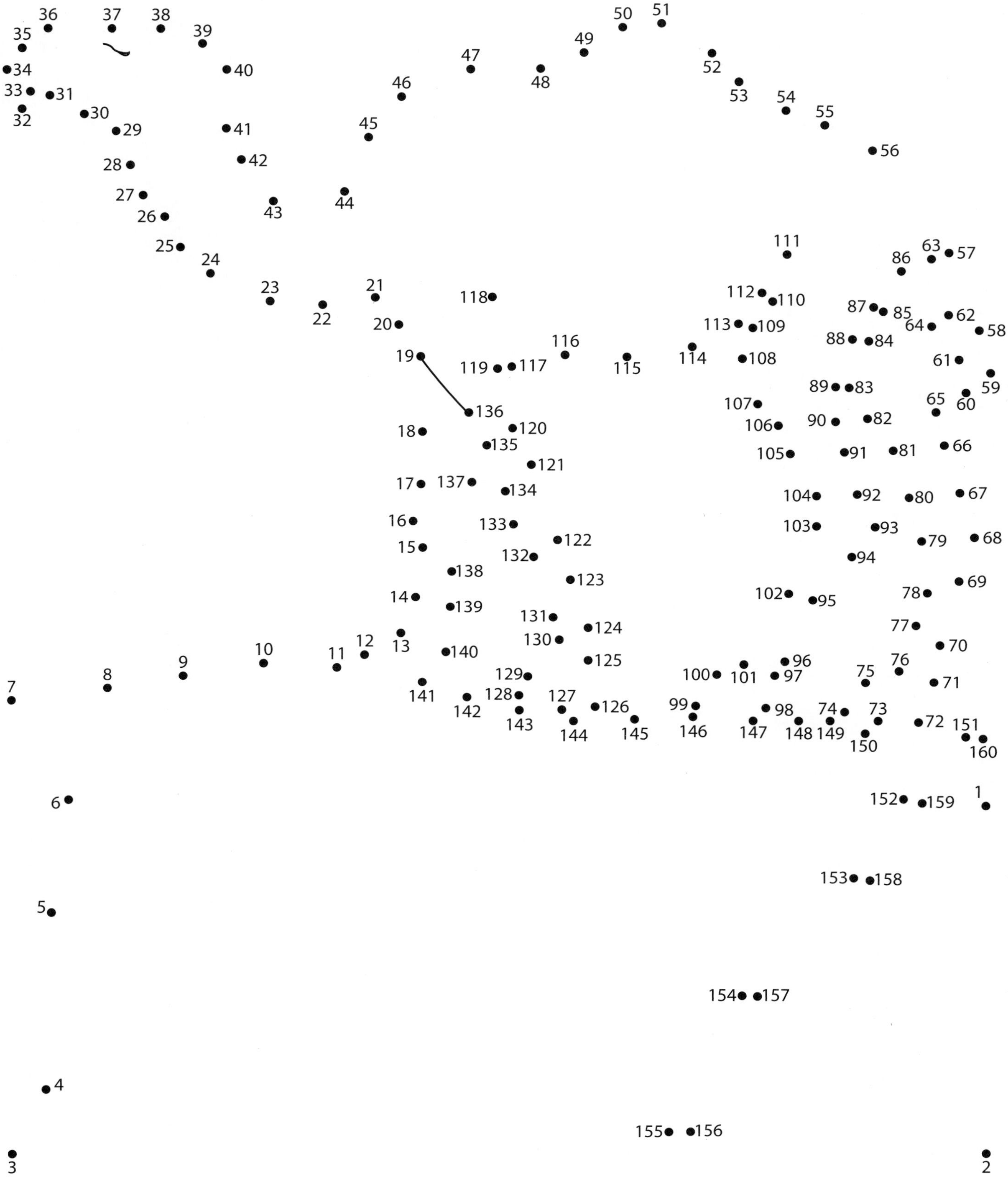

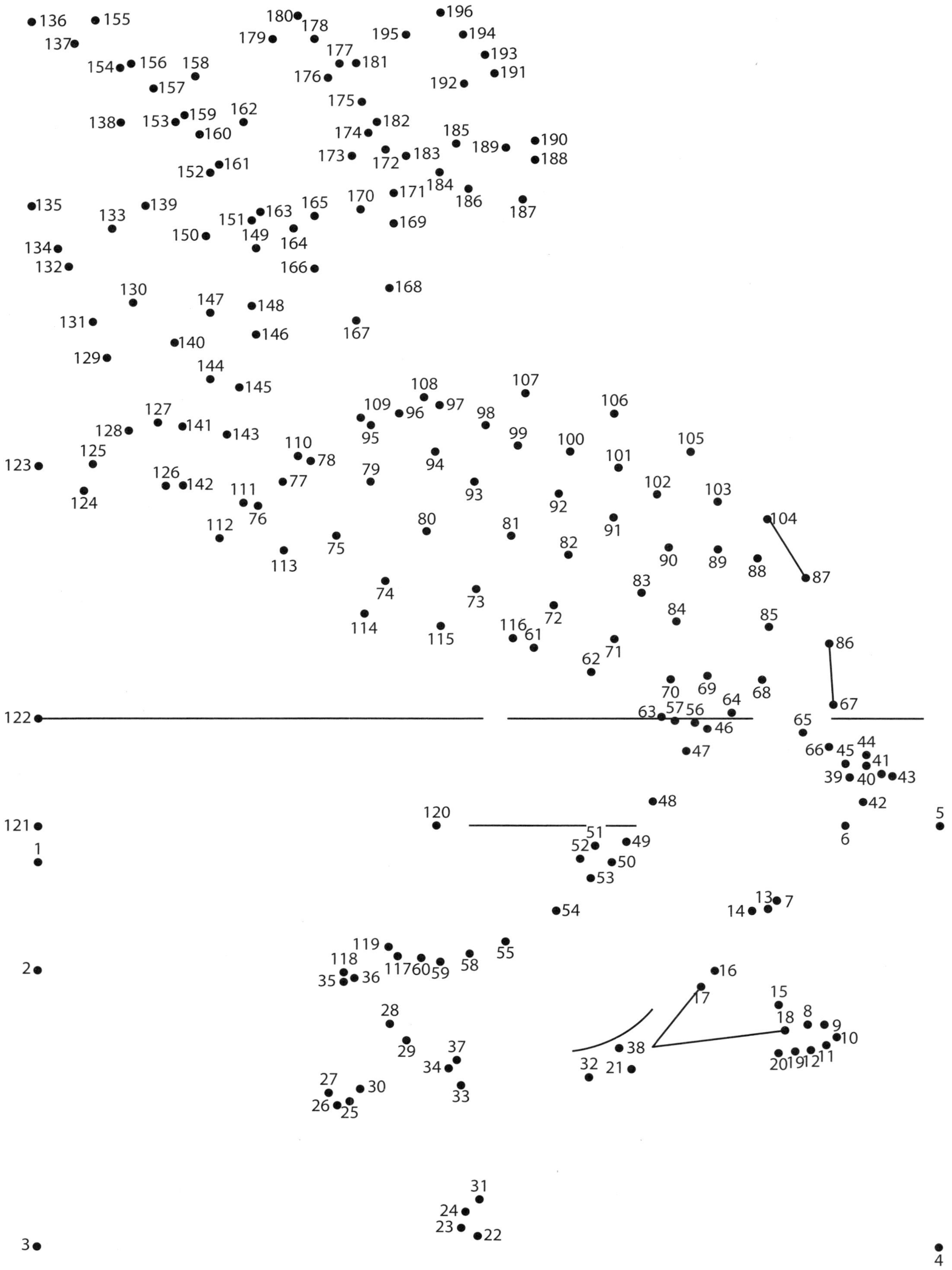

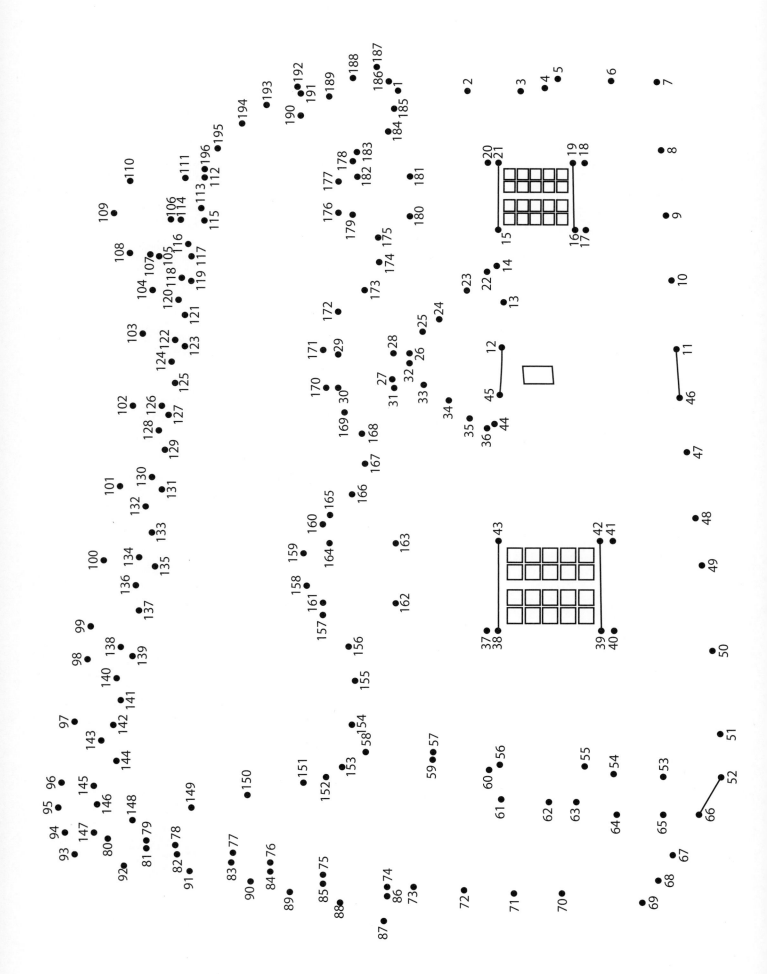

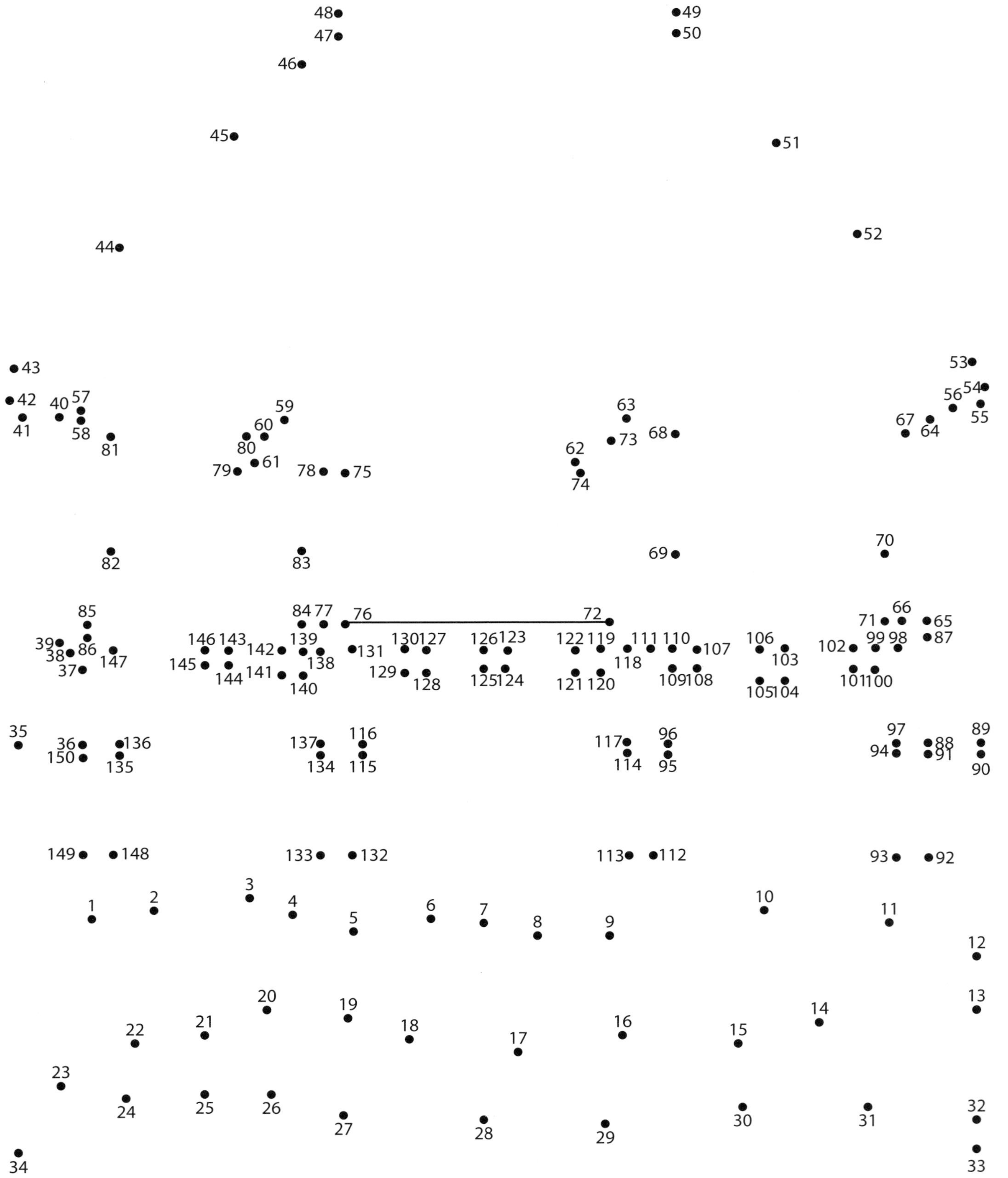

48 • 49

47 • 50

46 •

45 •   • 51

44 •   • 52

• 43   53 •
42 •   40 57   56 54
41 •   58   67   64 55
        81   59
               60
        80   63
79 • 61   78 • 75   62   73   68 •
                              74

82   83   69 •   70

85   84 77   76   72   66
   39 86 146 143 142 139   131 130 127 126 123 122 119 111 110 107   71 65
38   147   138   129   125 124 121 120 118   109 108   102 99 98 87
37   145 144 141   140   128   101 100
                                                              105 104

35   97 89
36 136   137 116   117 96   94 88
150 135   134 115   114 95   91
                                                                          90

149 • 148   133 • 132   113 • 112   93 • 92

            3
1   2   4   6   7   10
          5   8   9   11

                                                              12

         20   13
      21   19
22   18   17   16   15   14

23

24   25   26   27   28   29   30   31   32

34   33

42

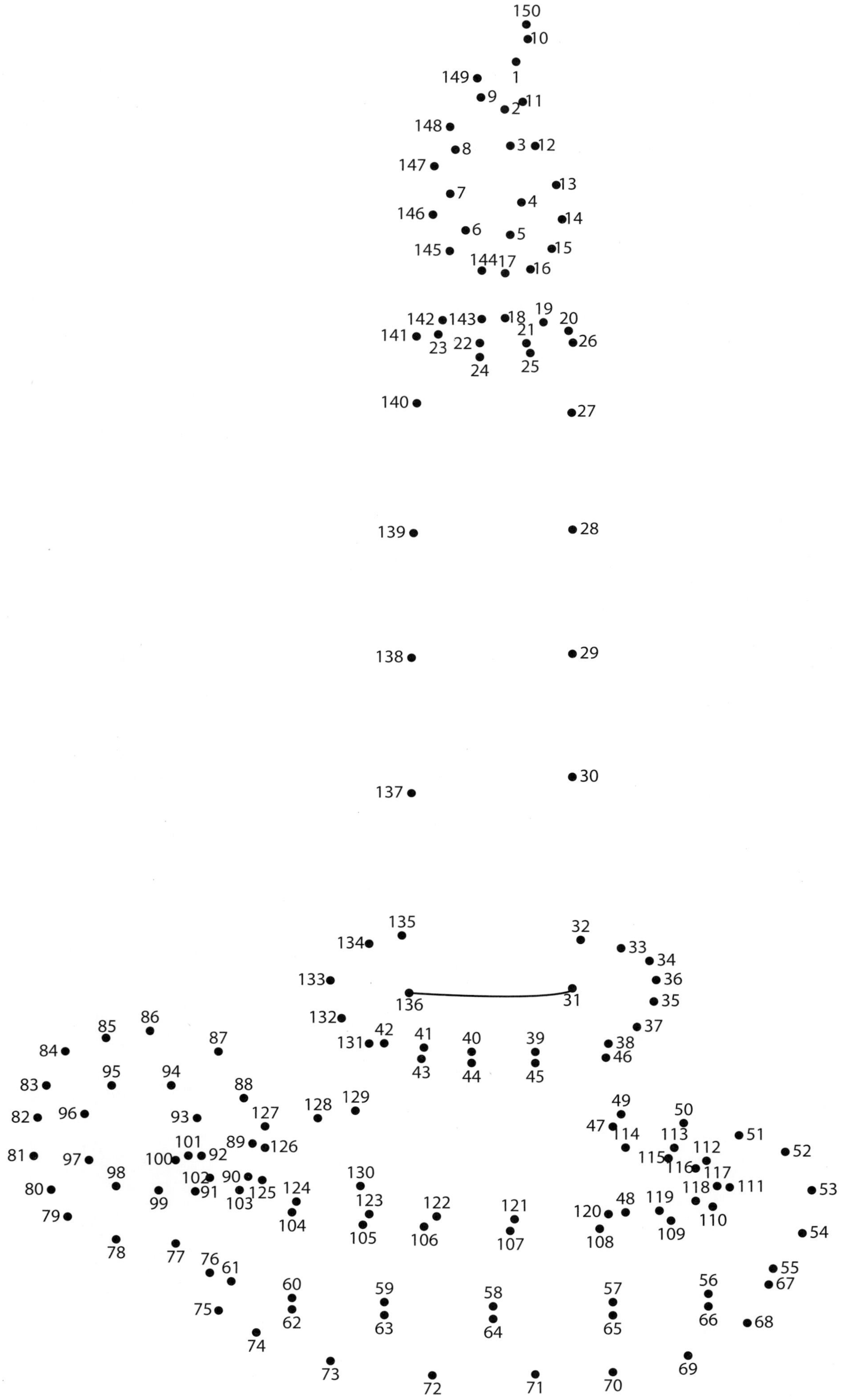

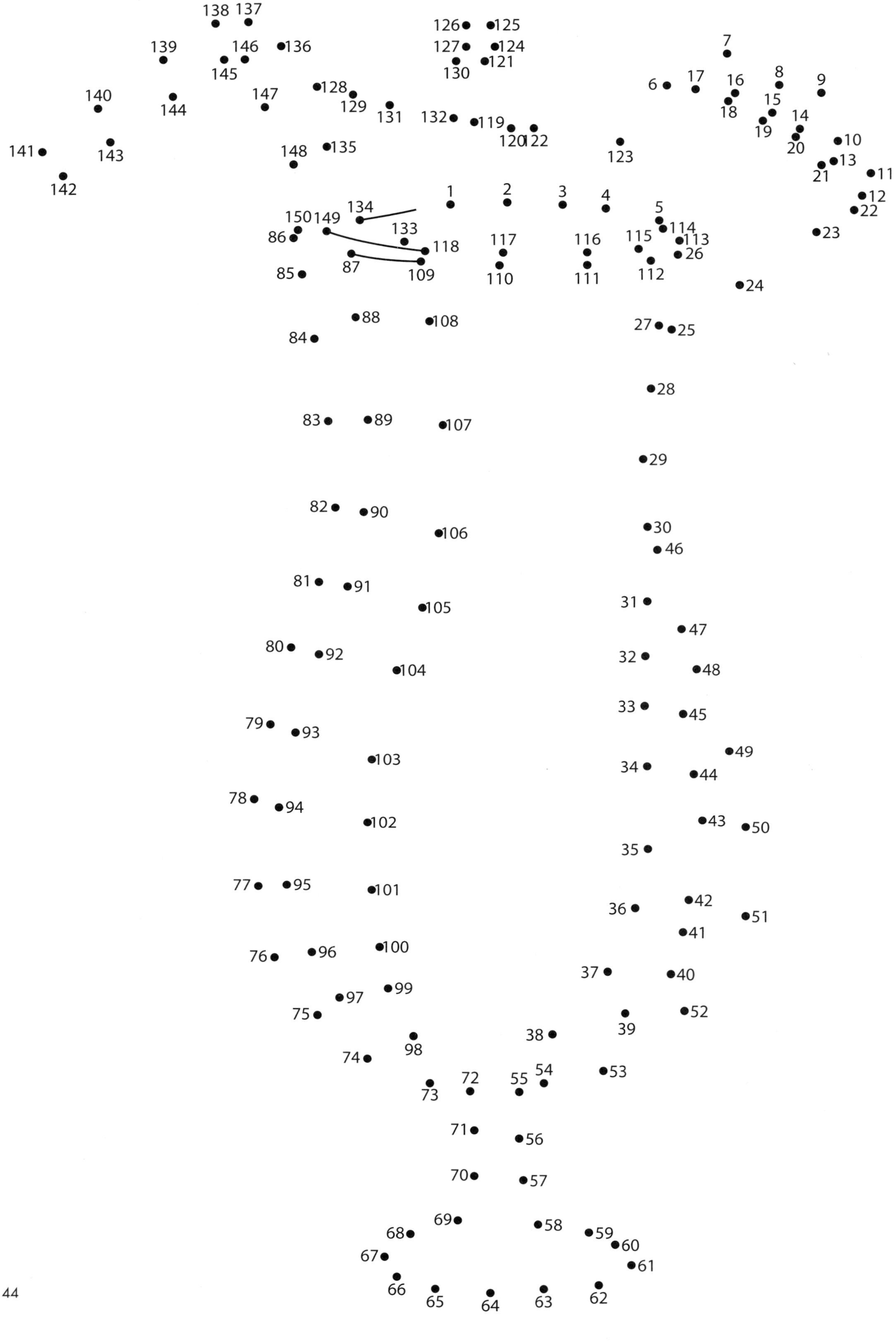

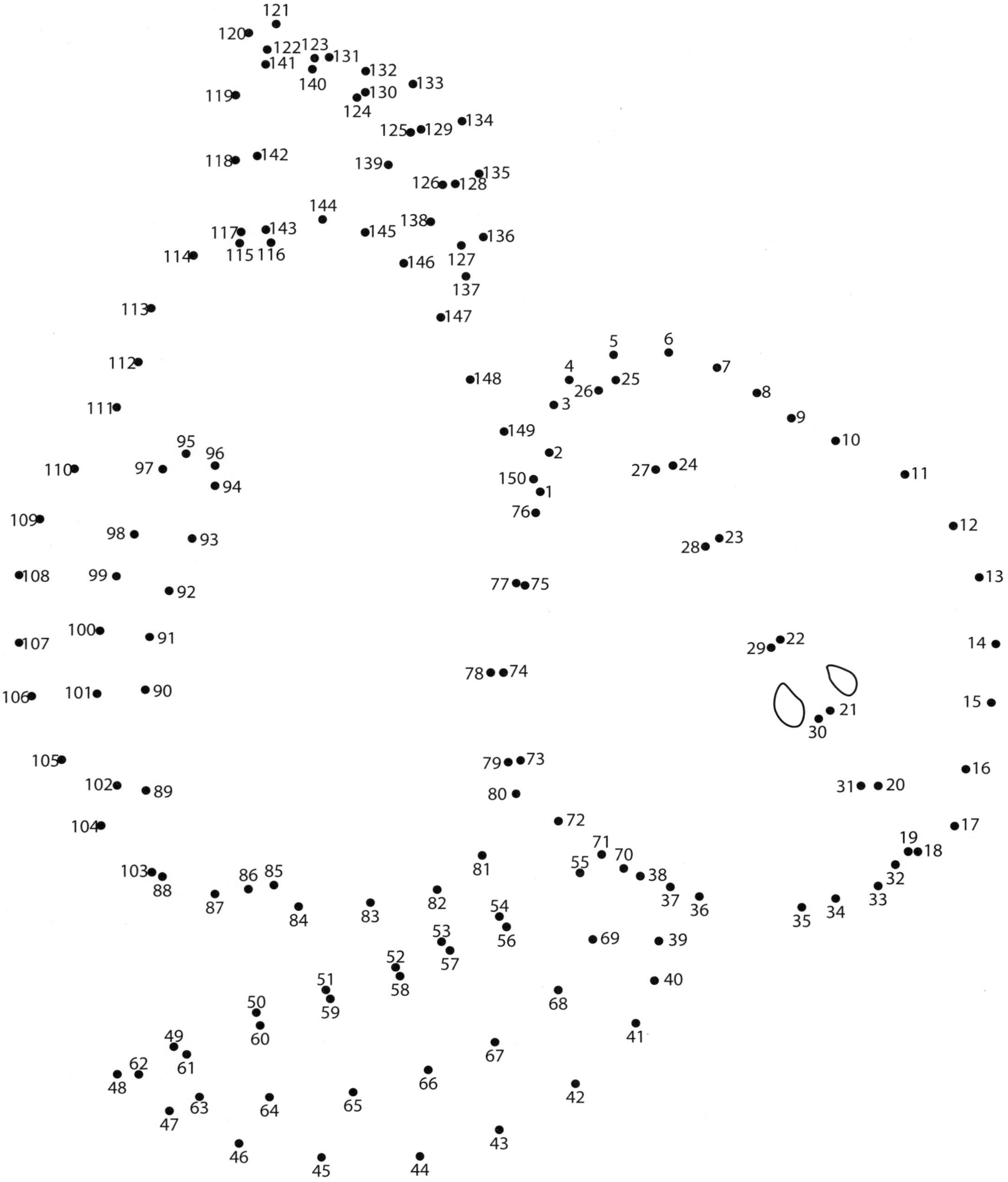

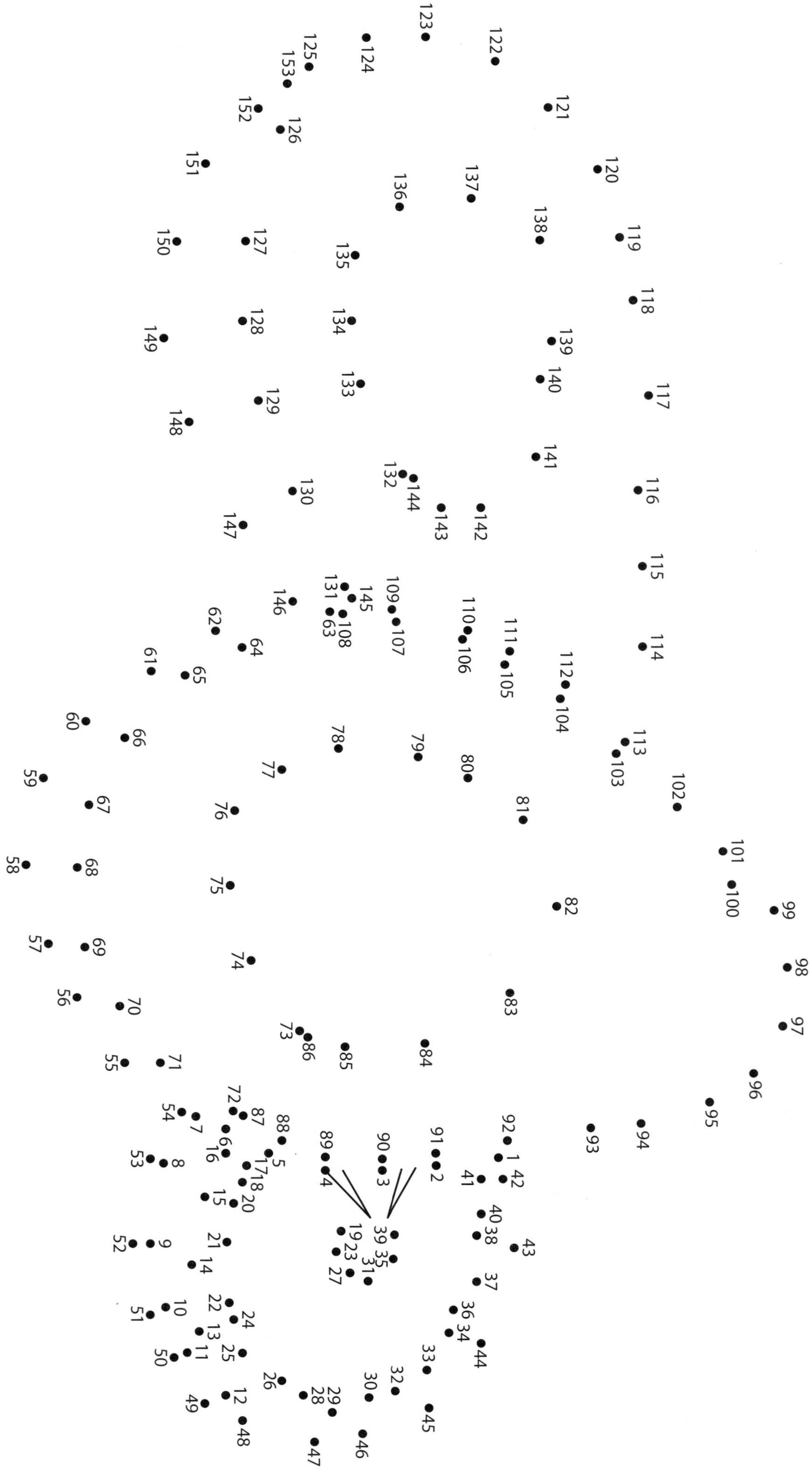

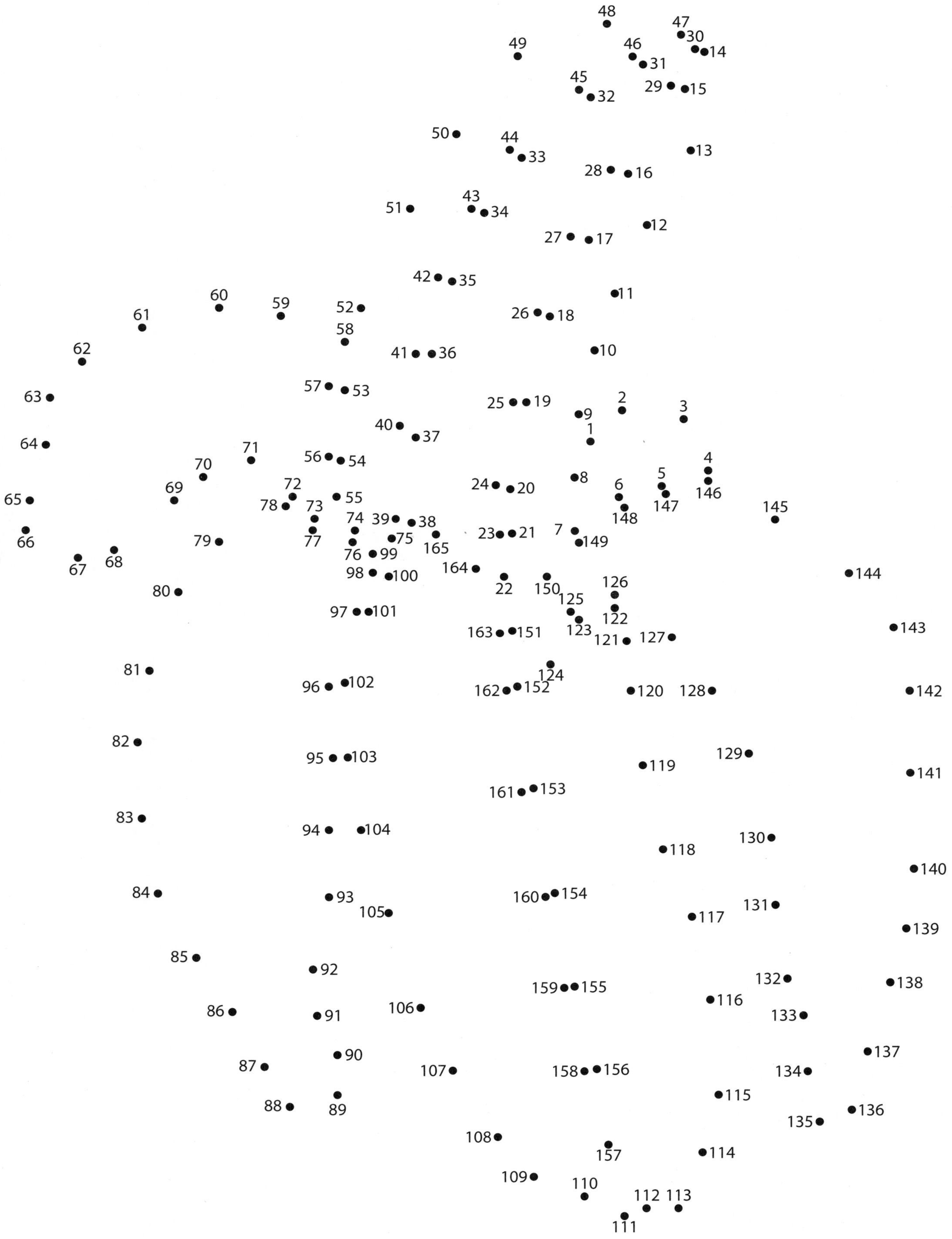

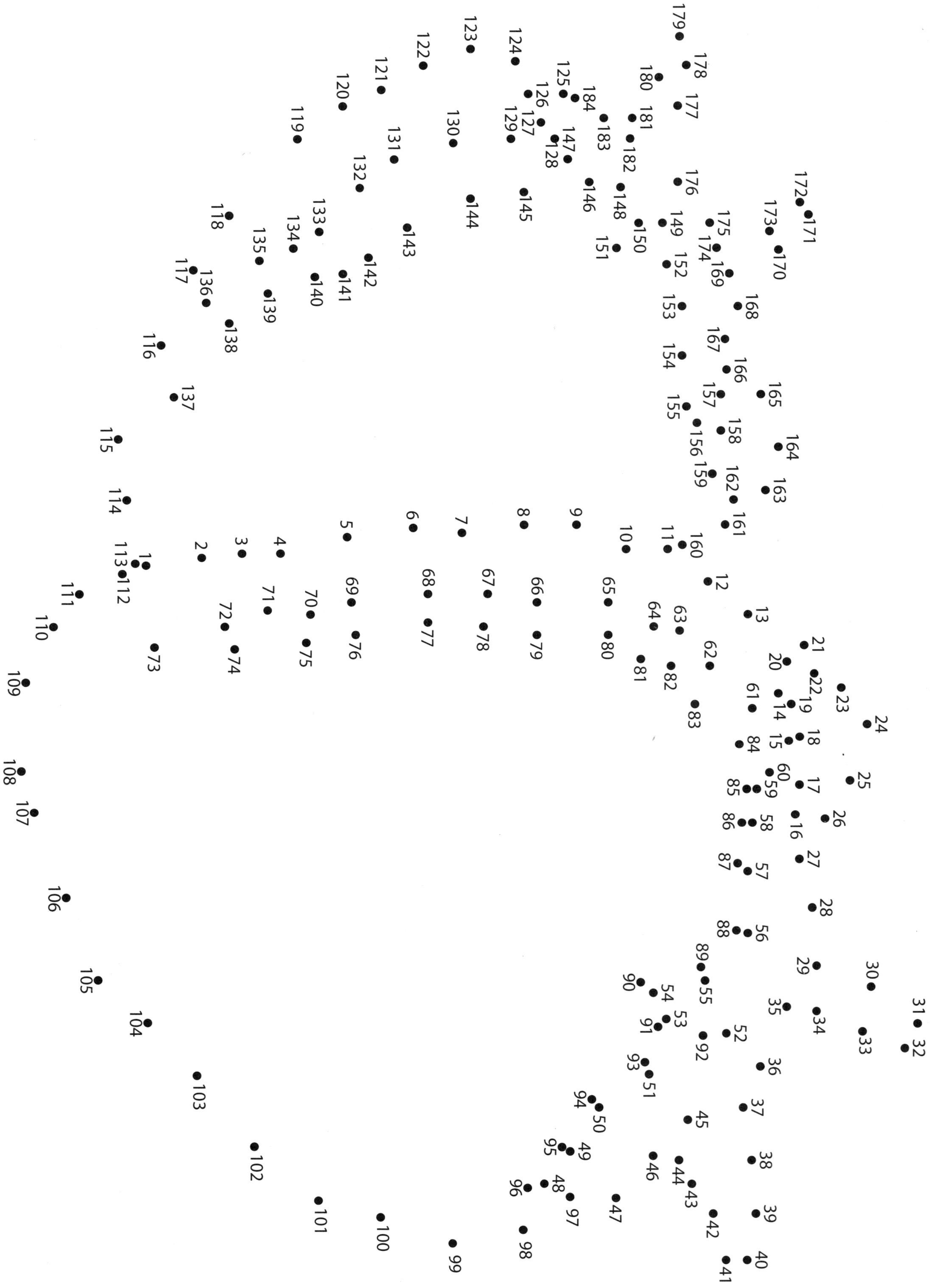

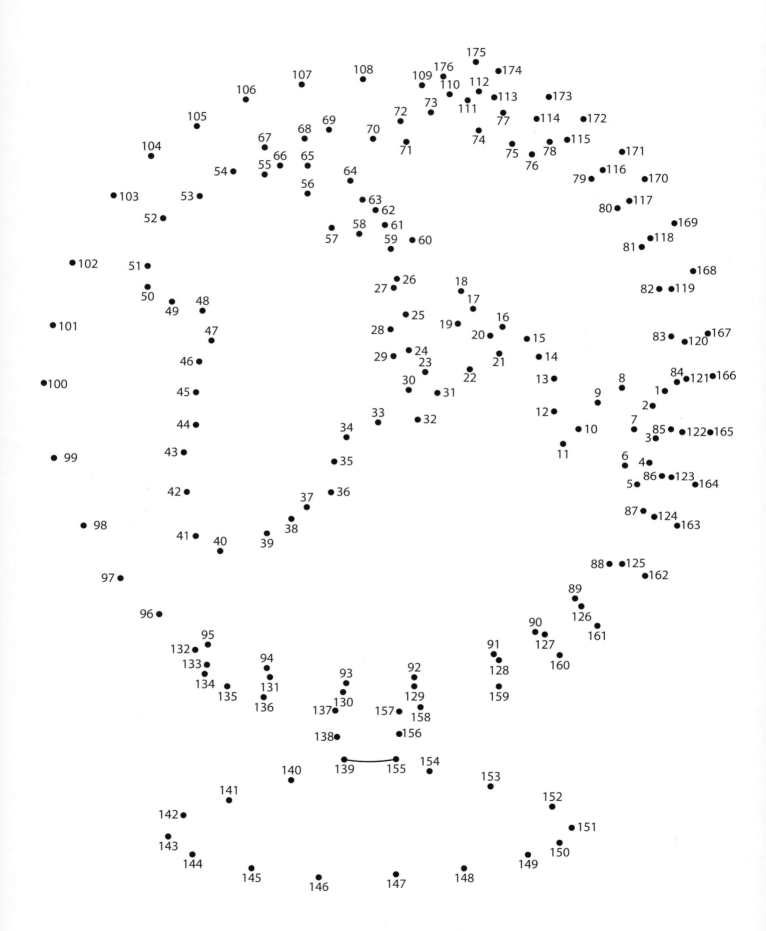

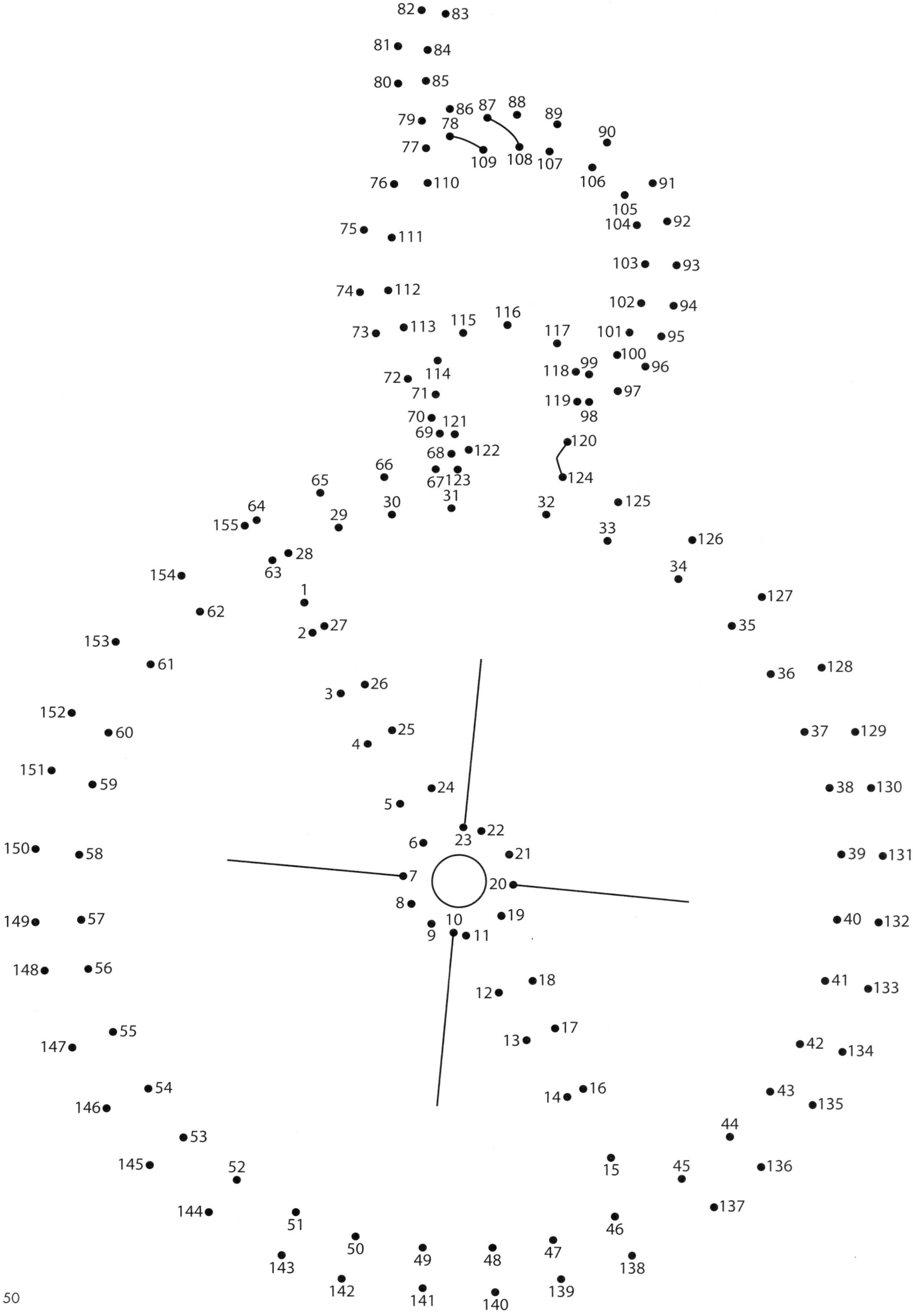

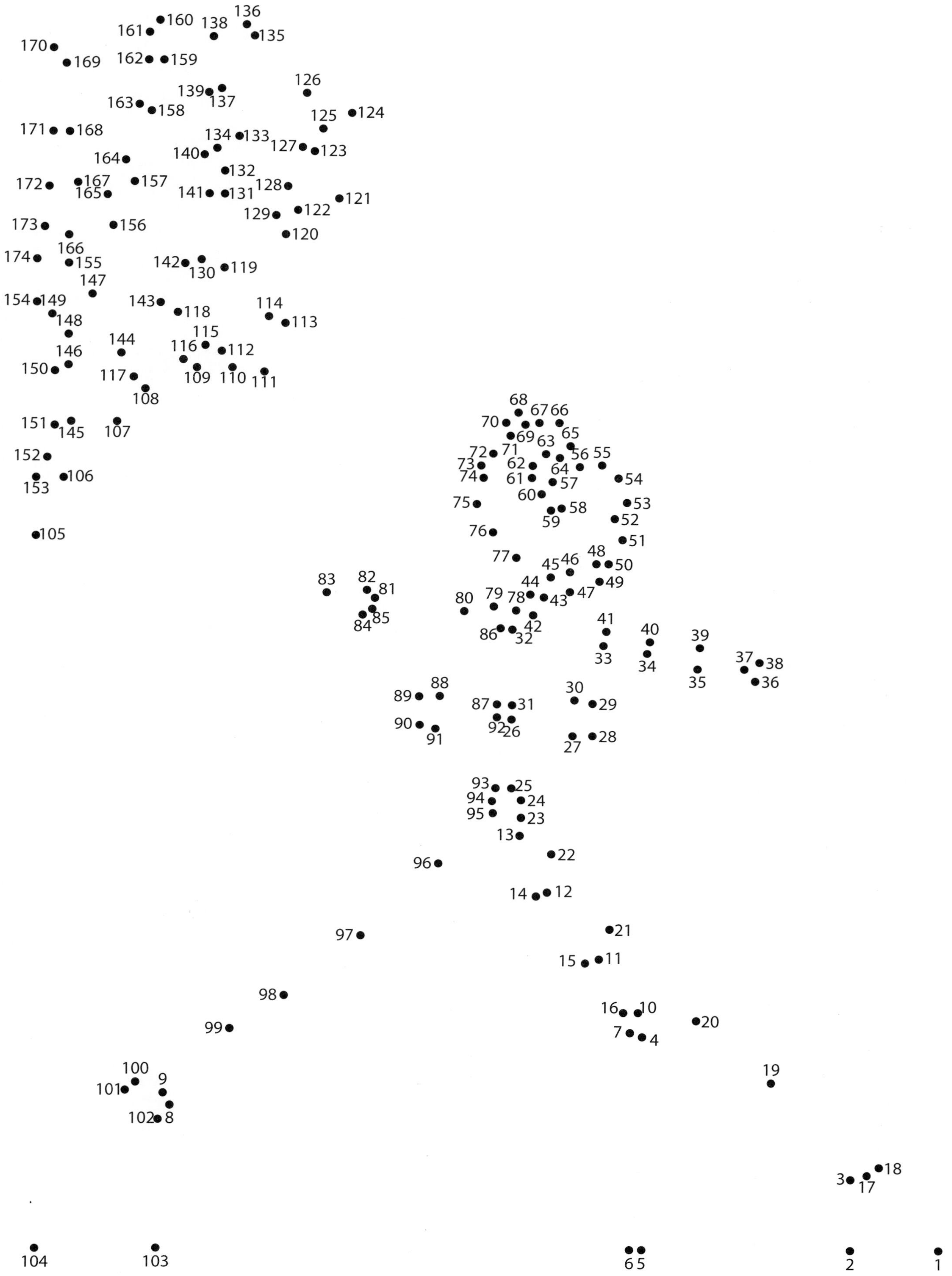

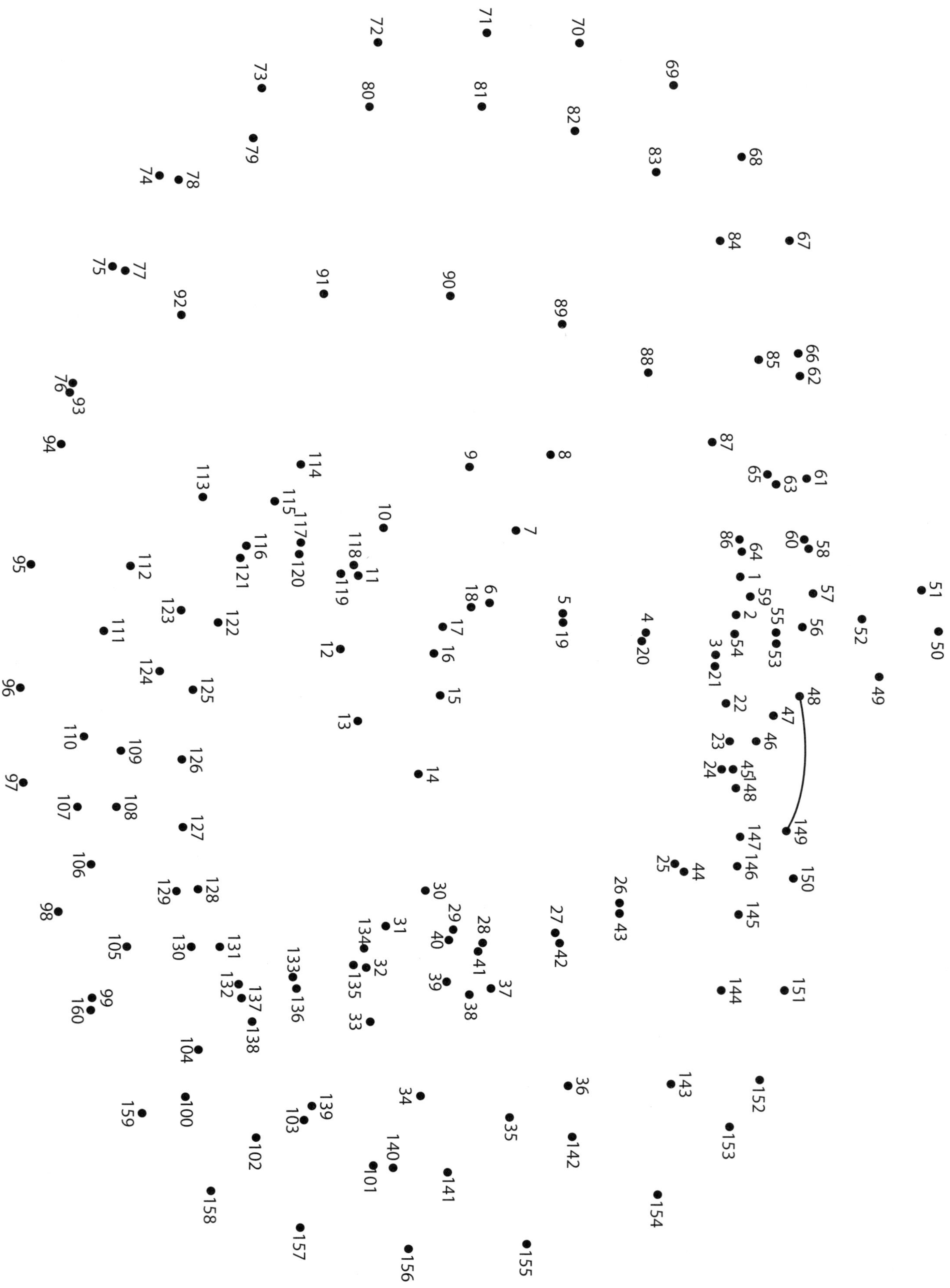

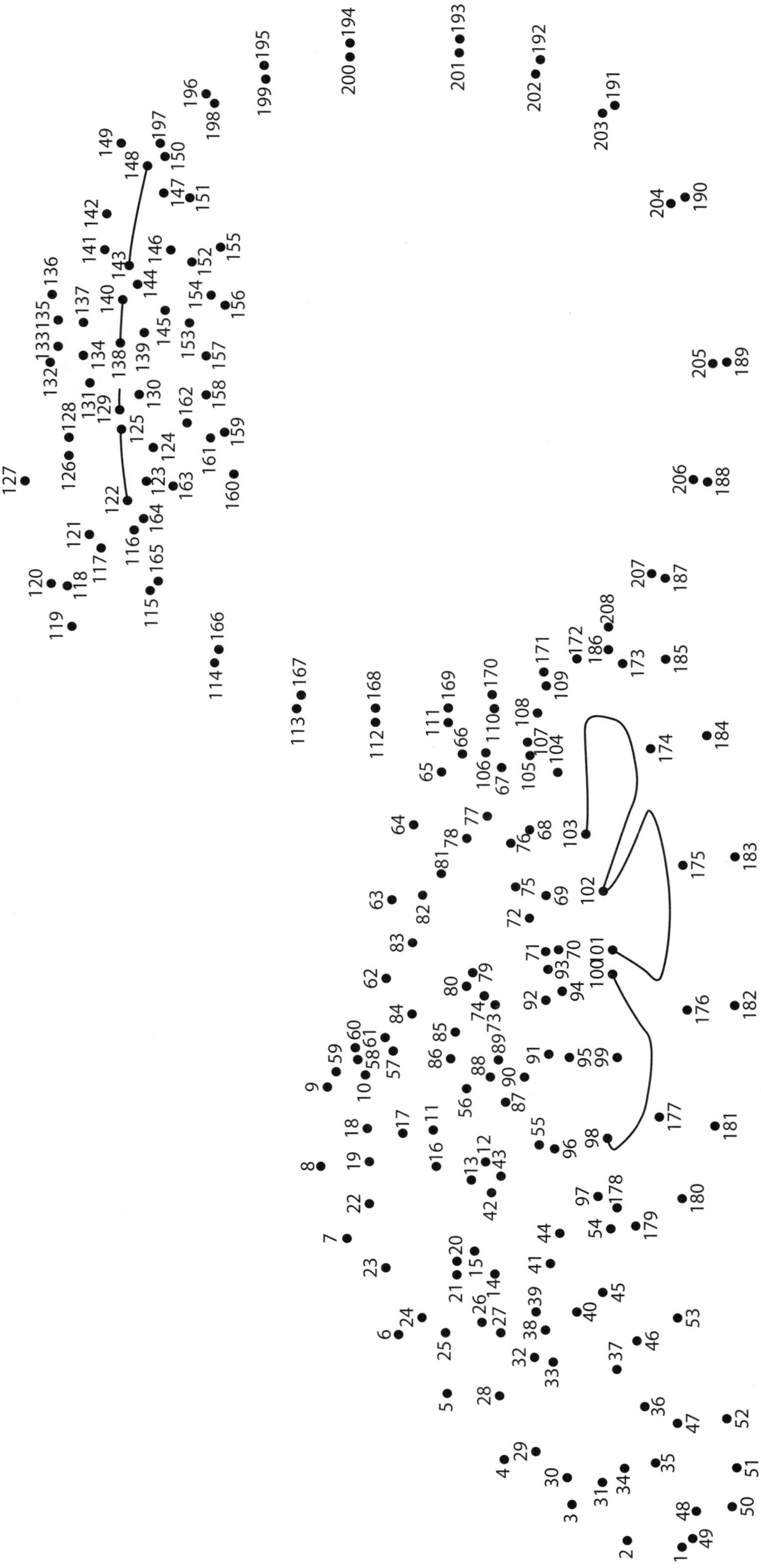

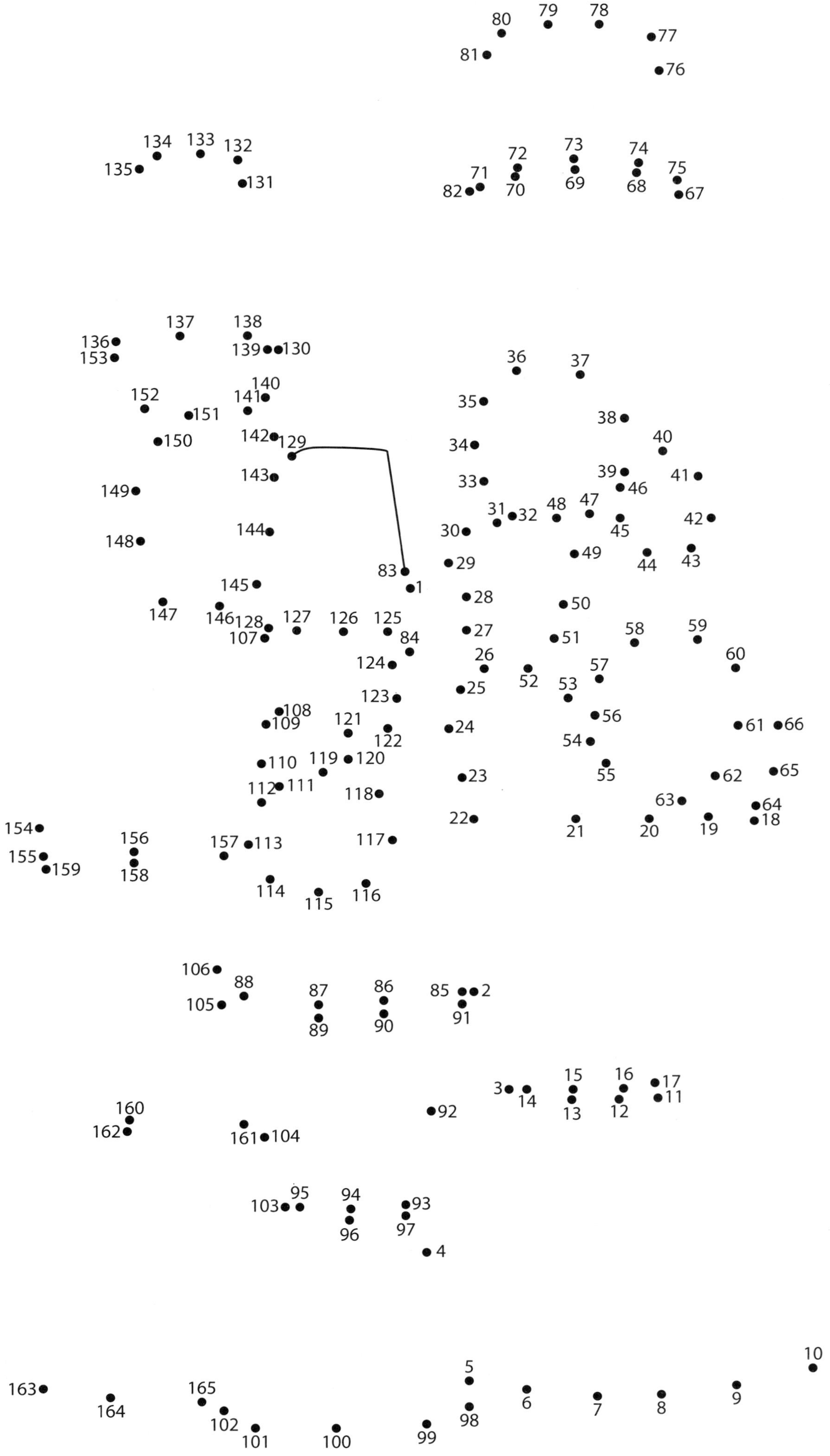

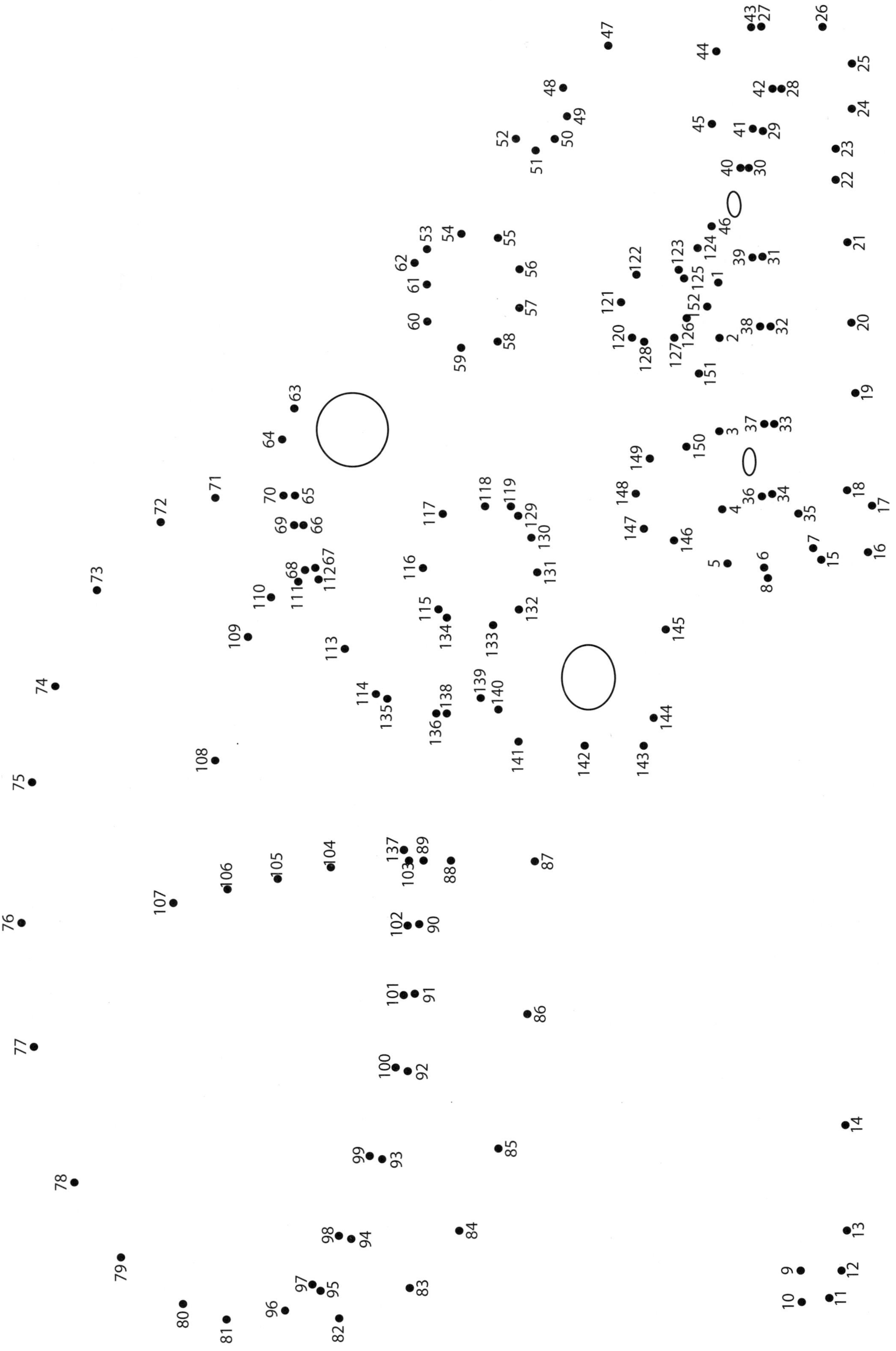

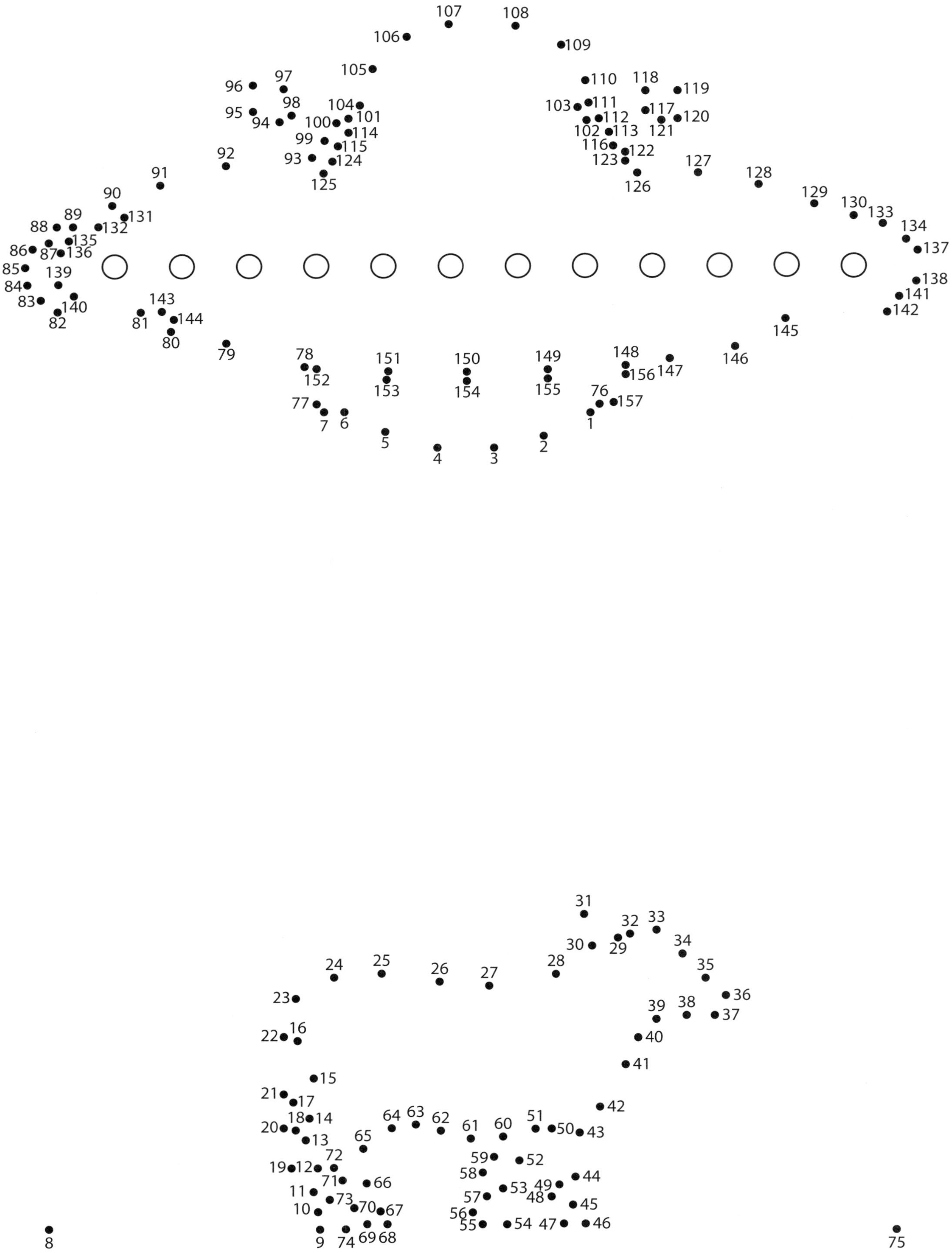

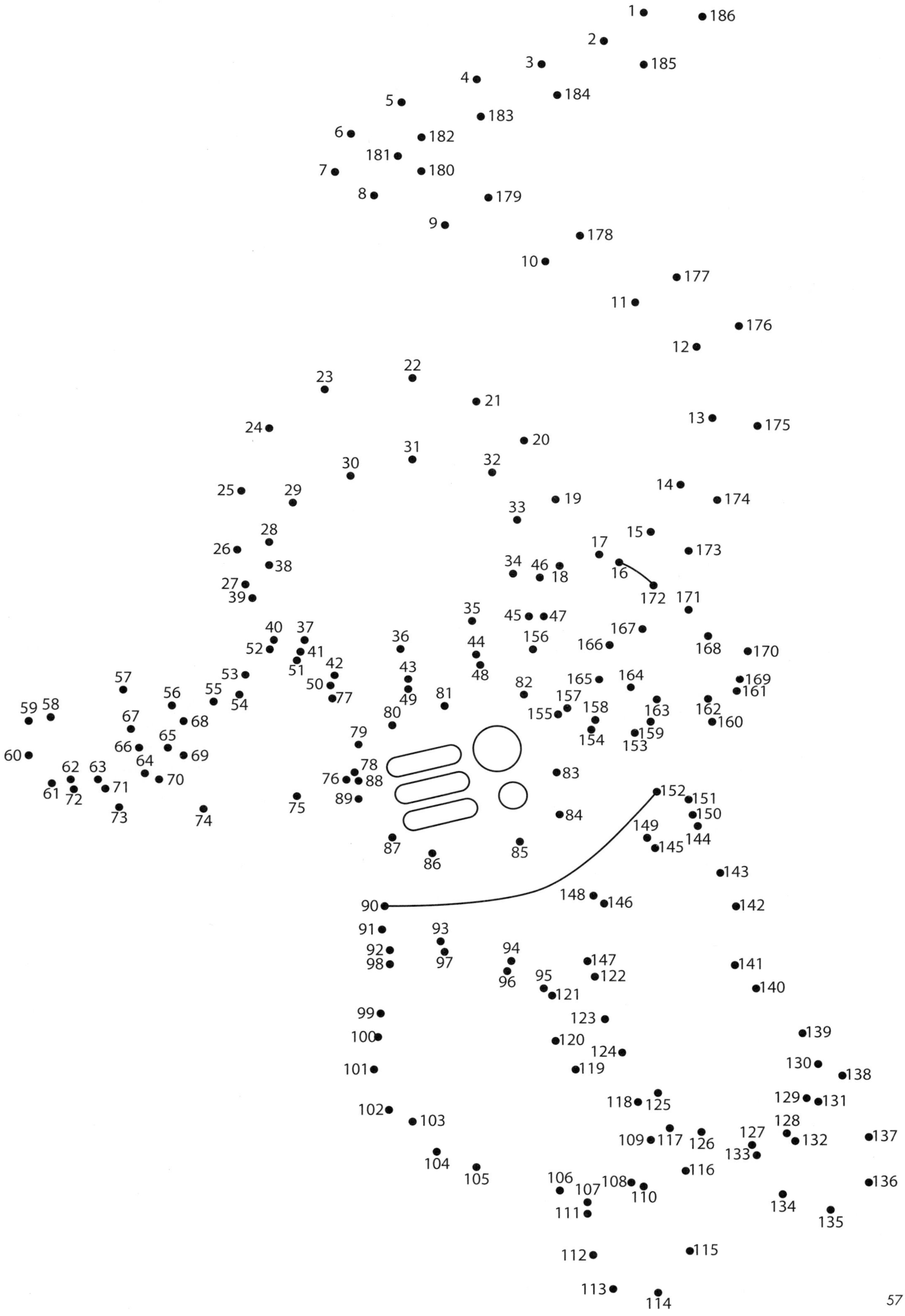

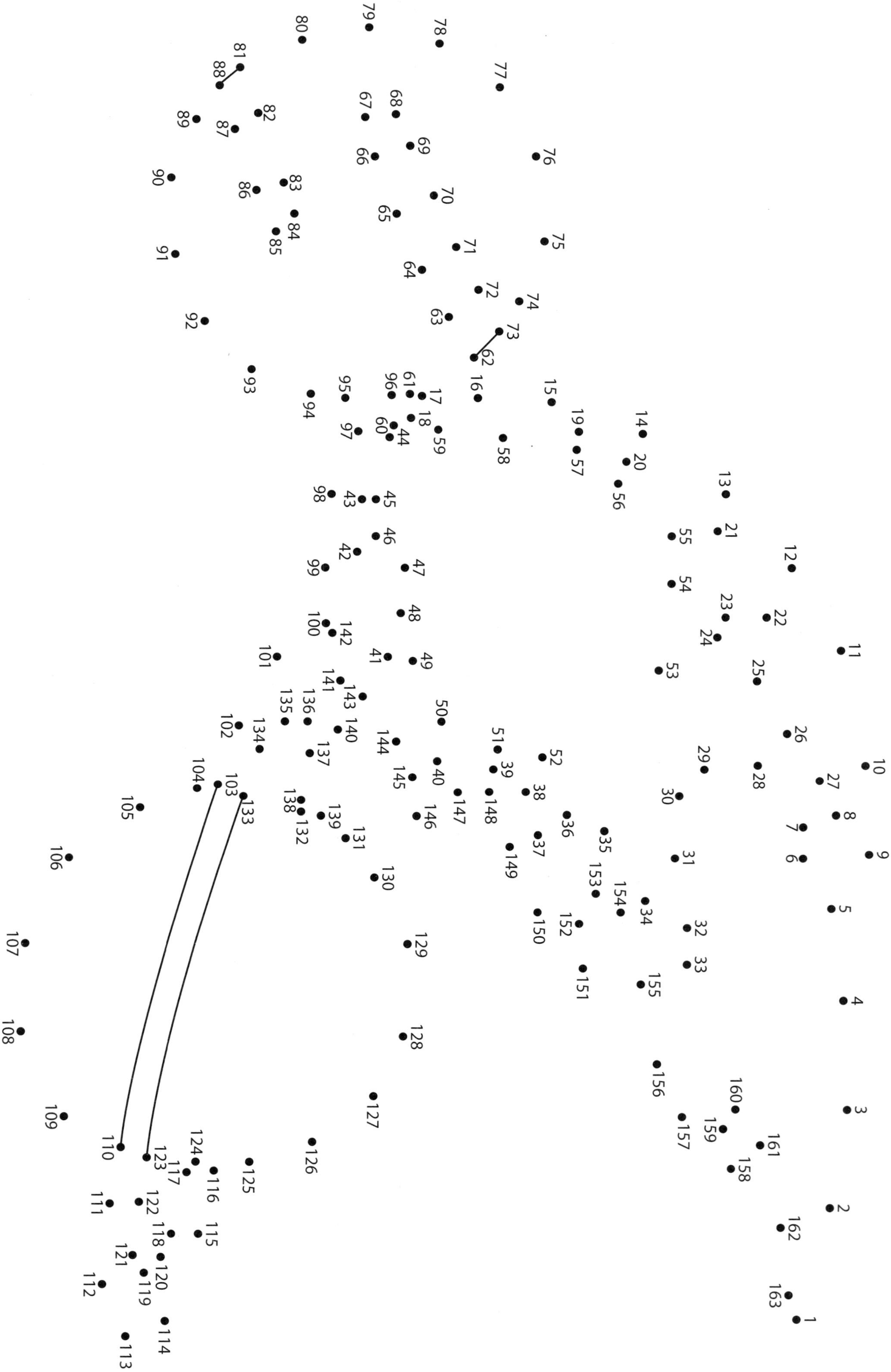

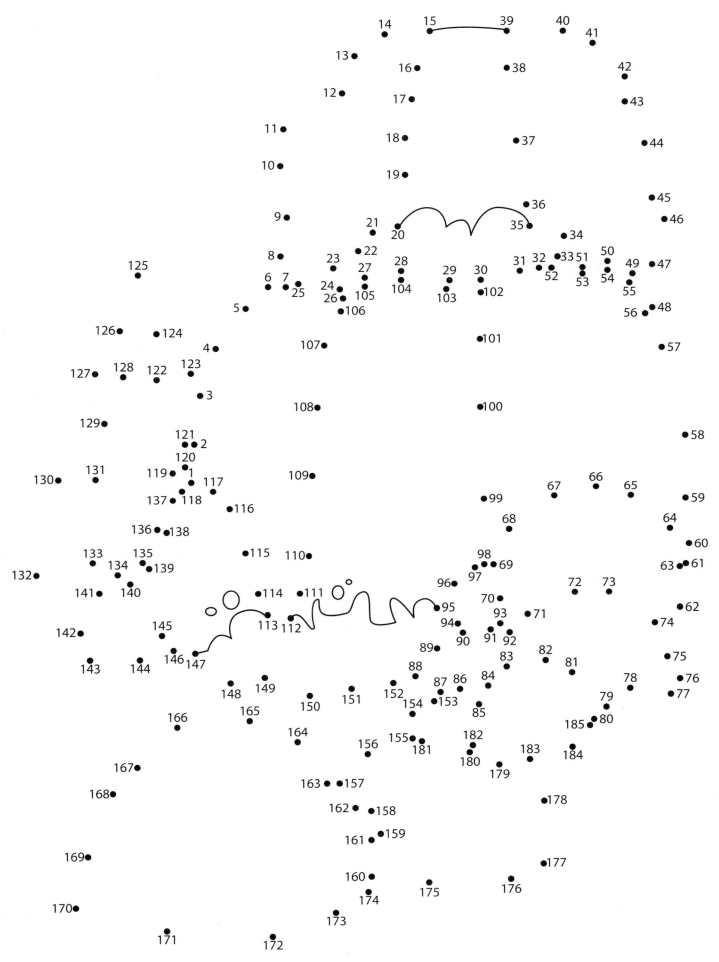

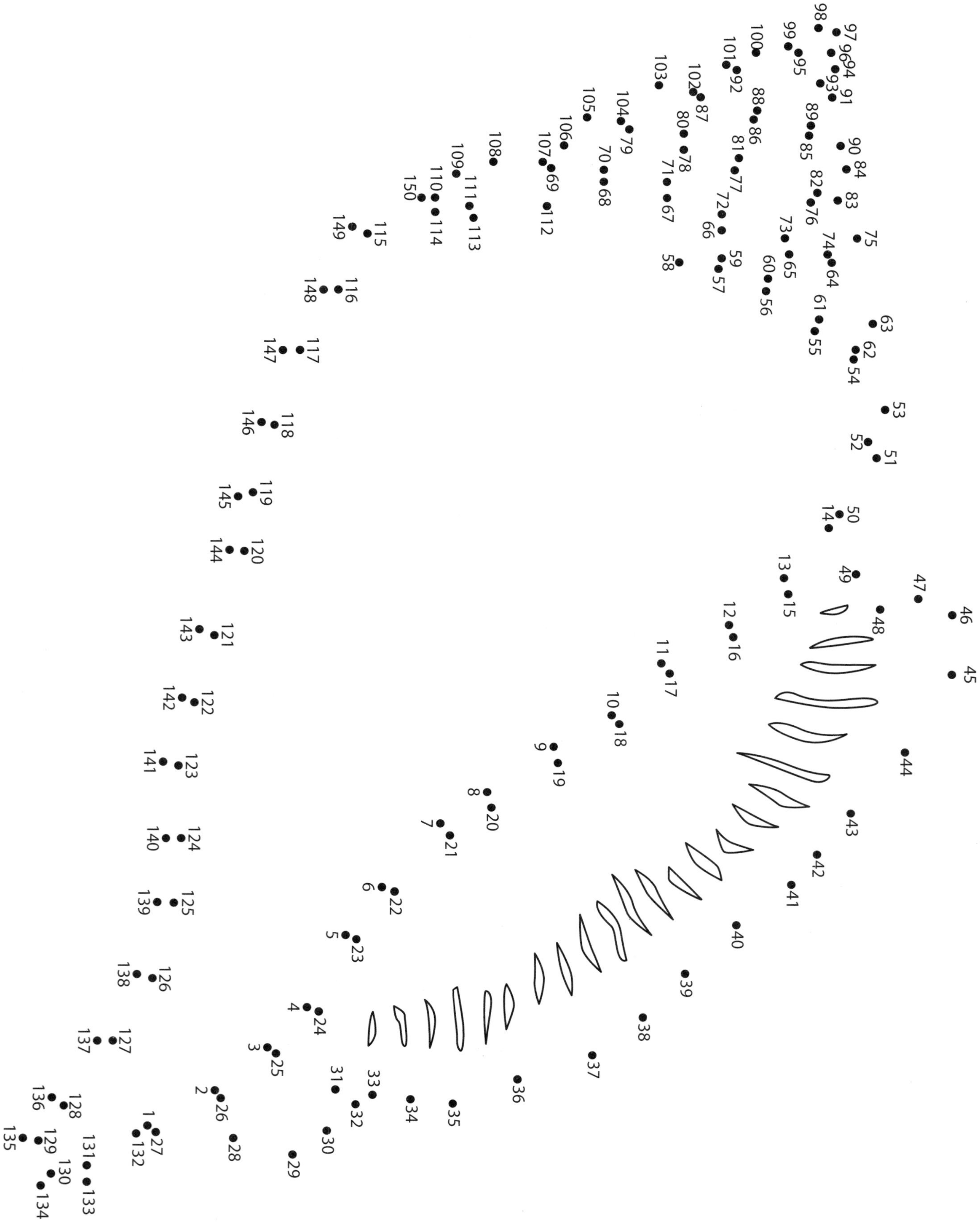

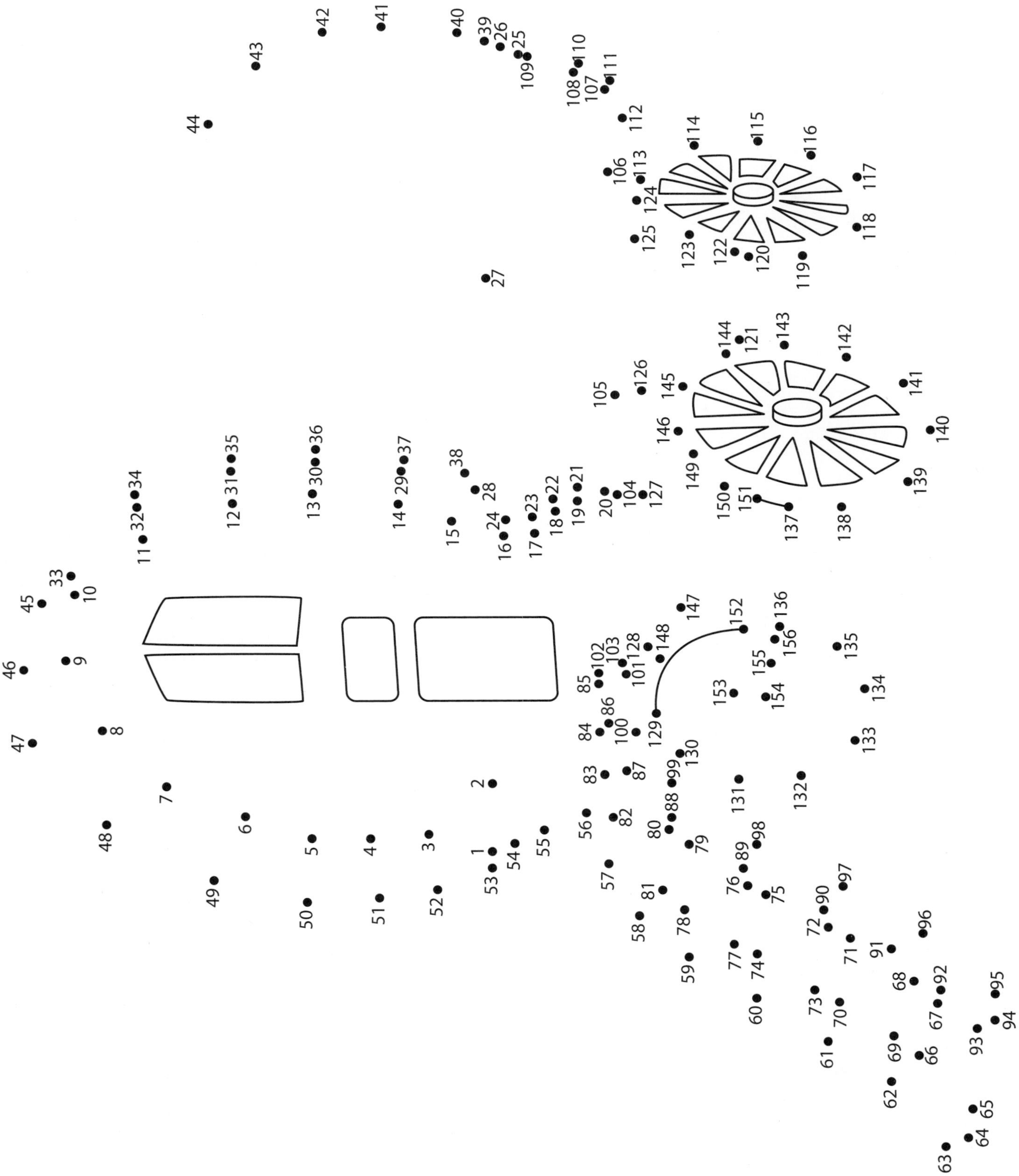

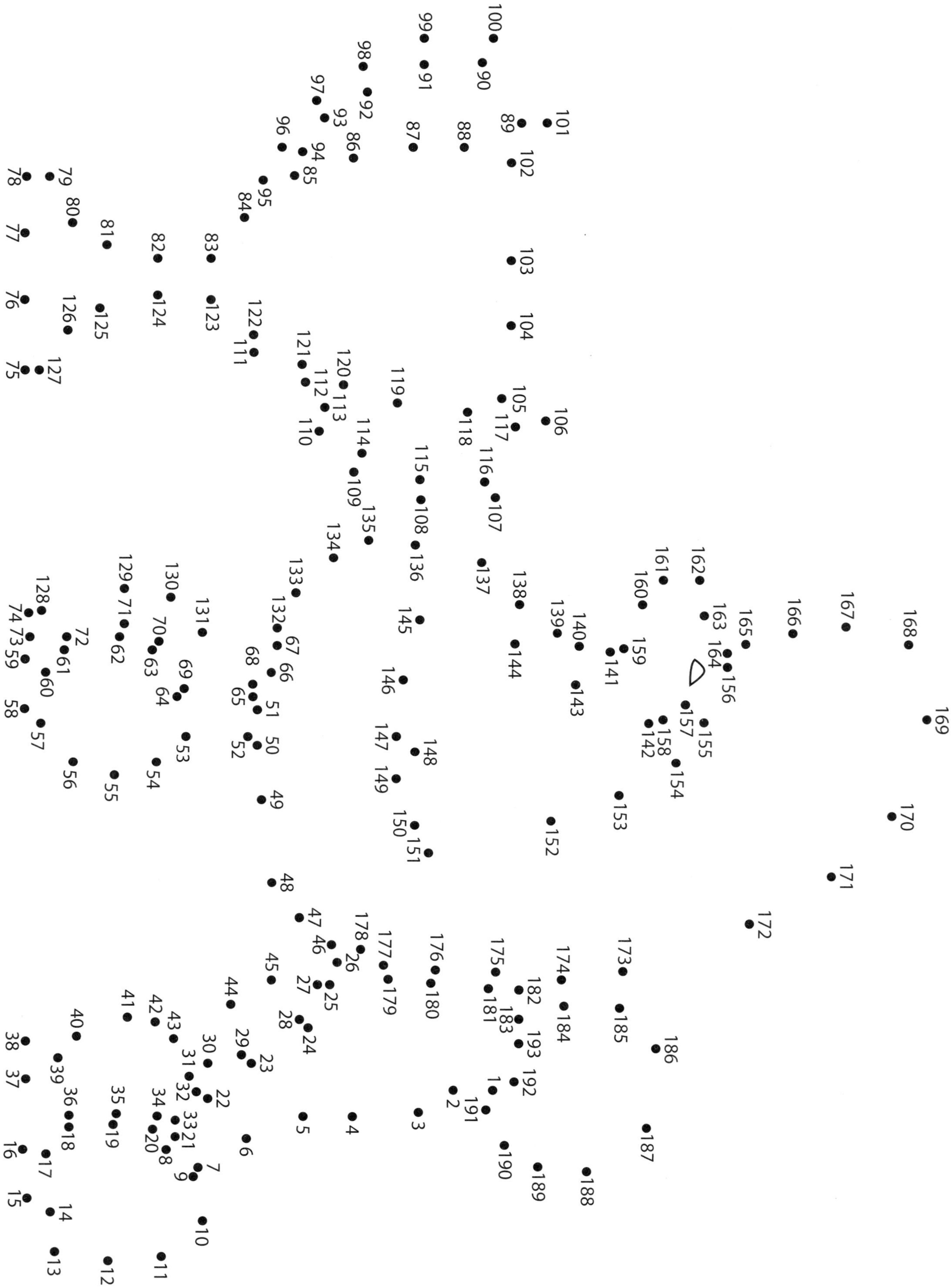

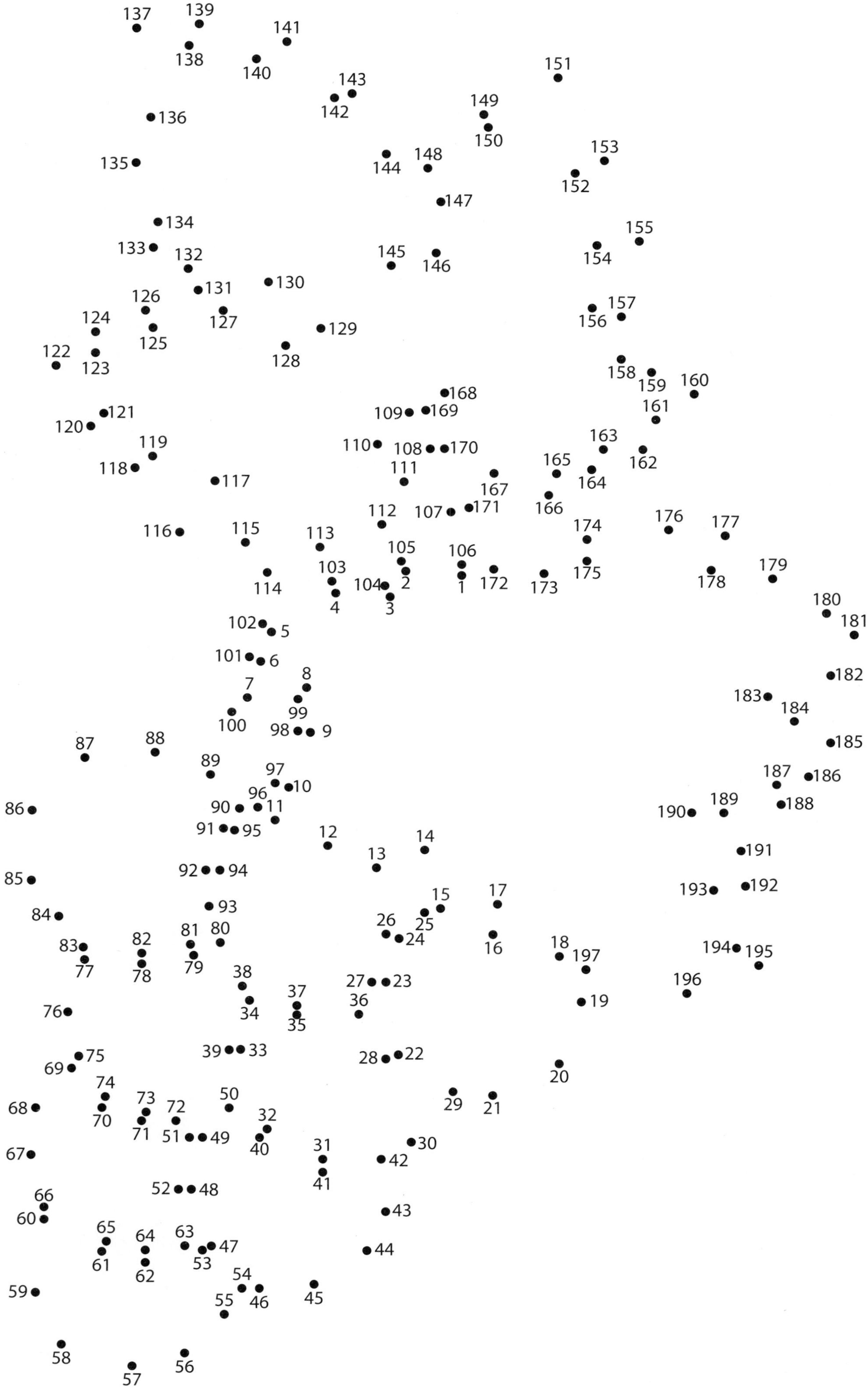

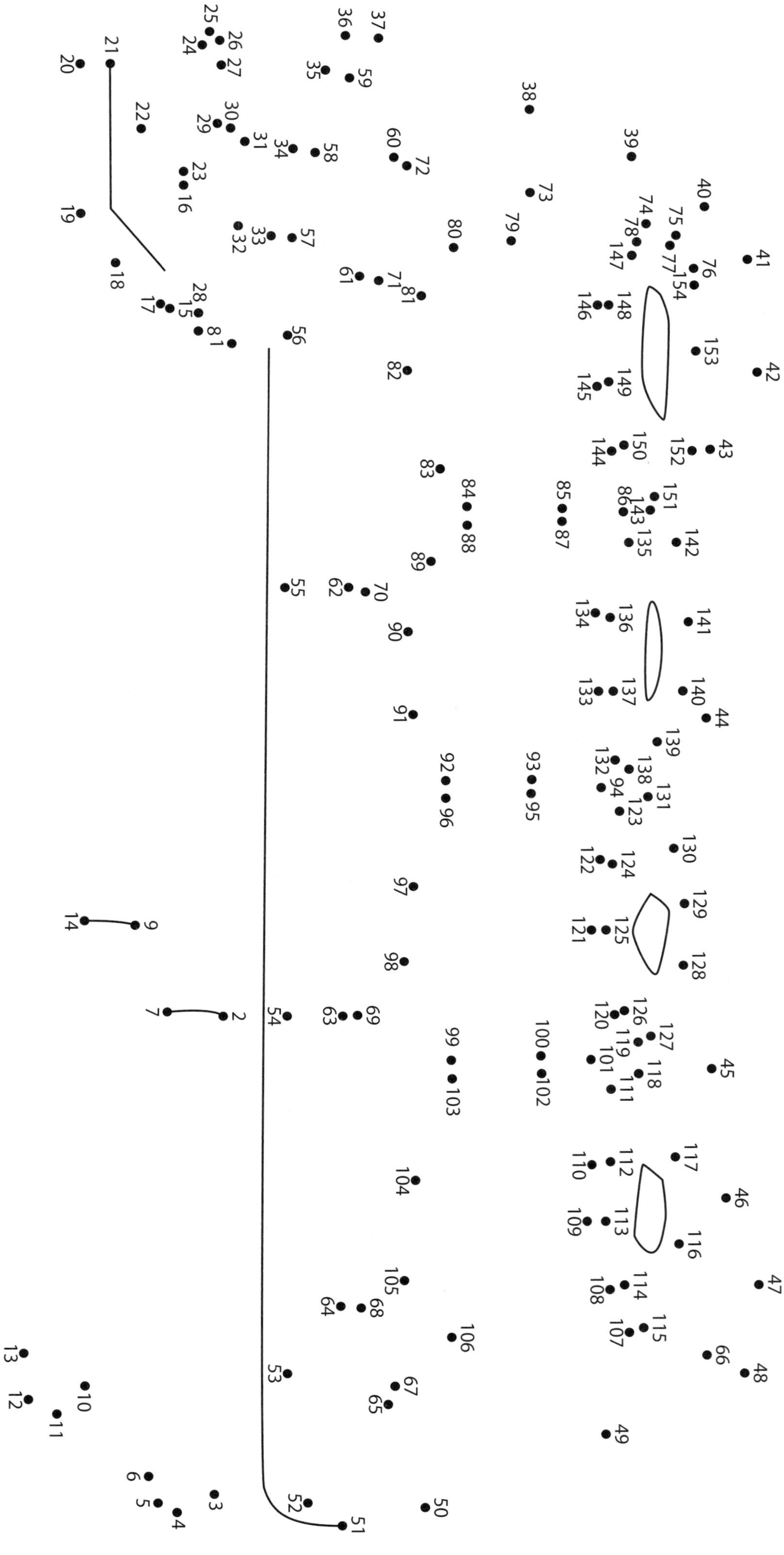

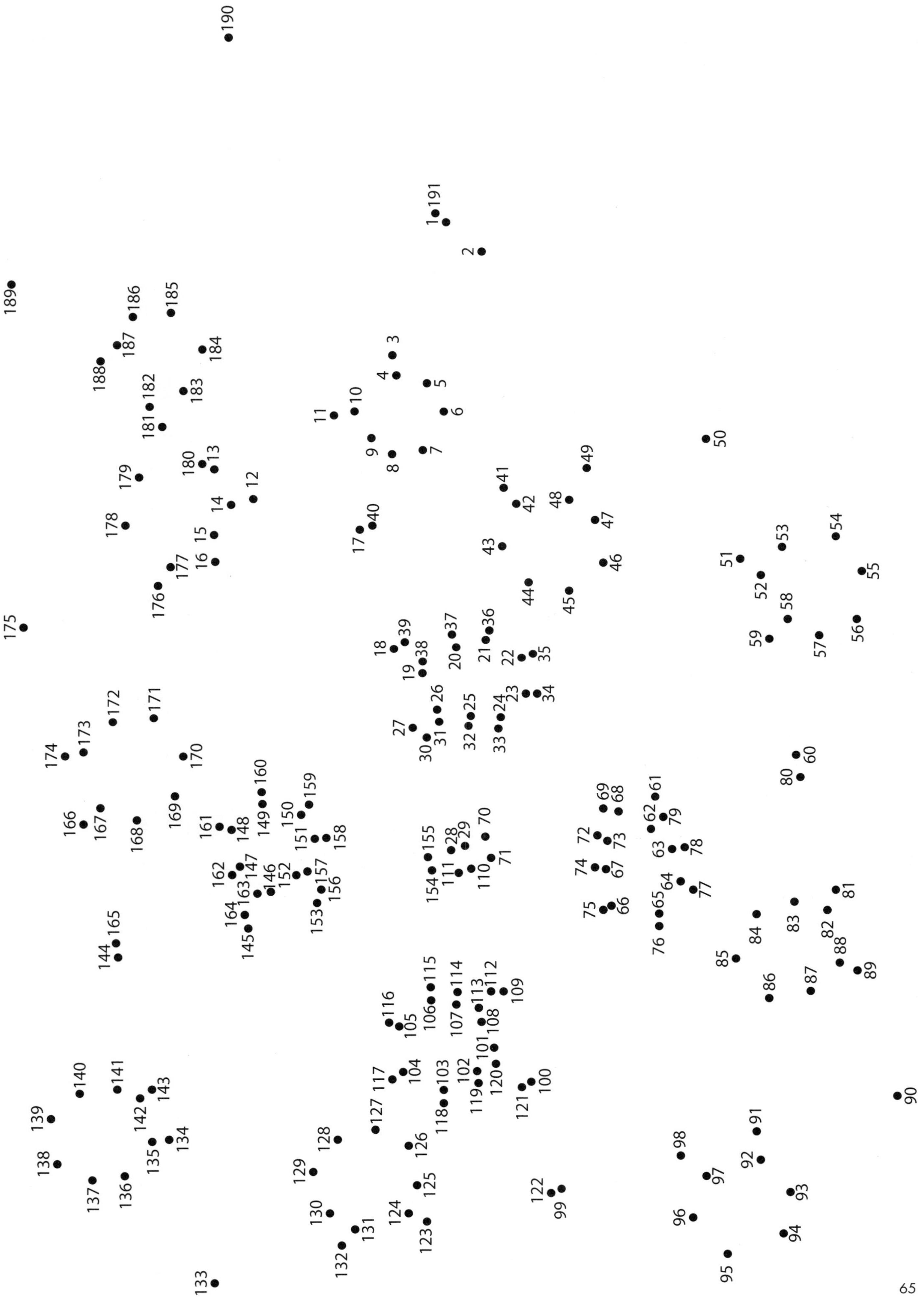

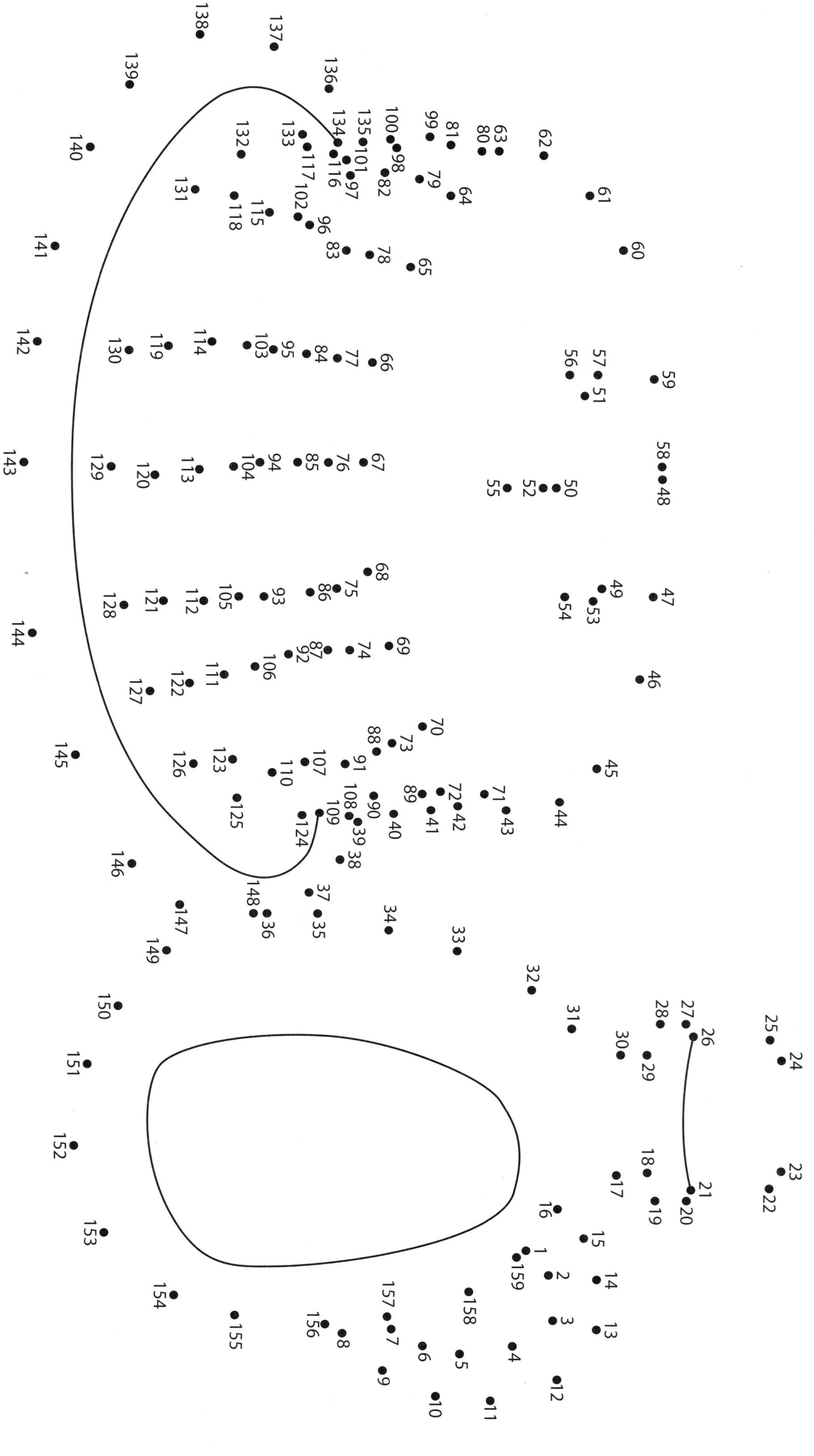

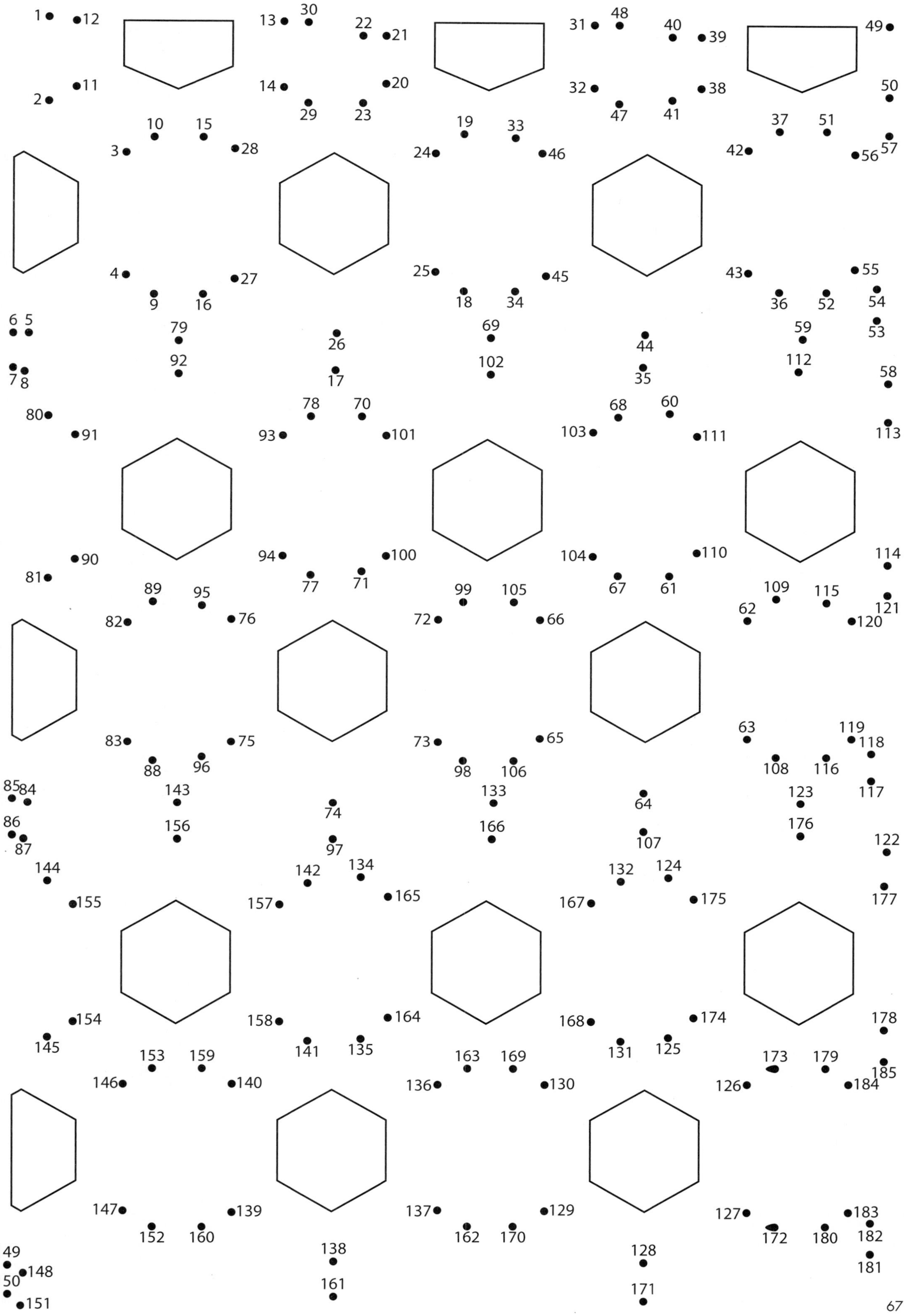

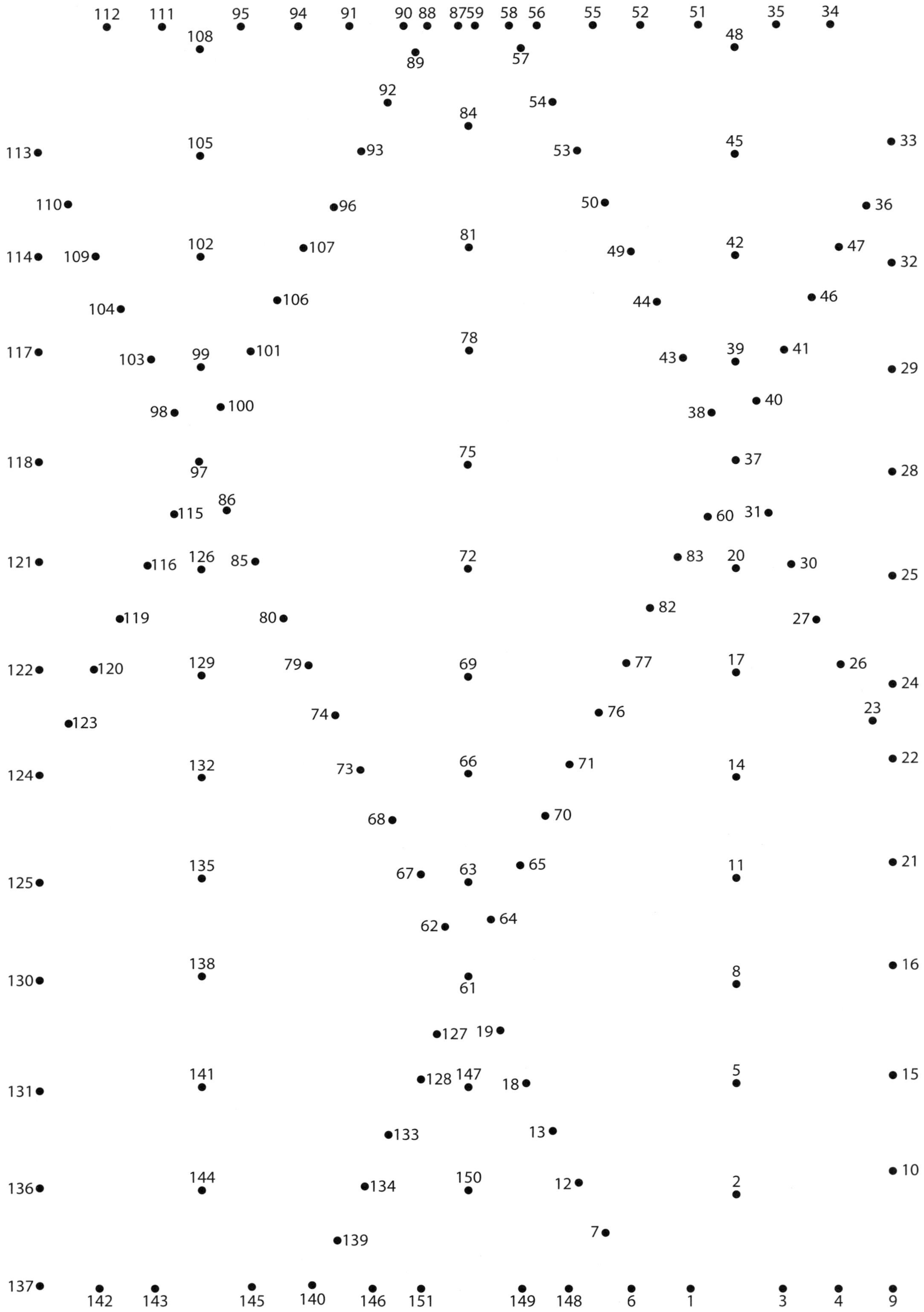

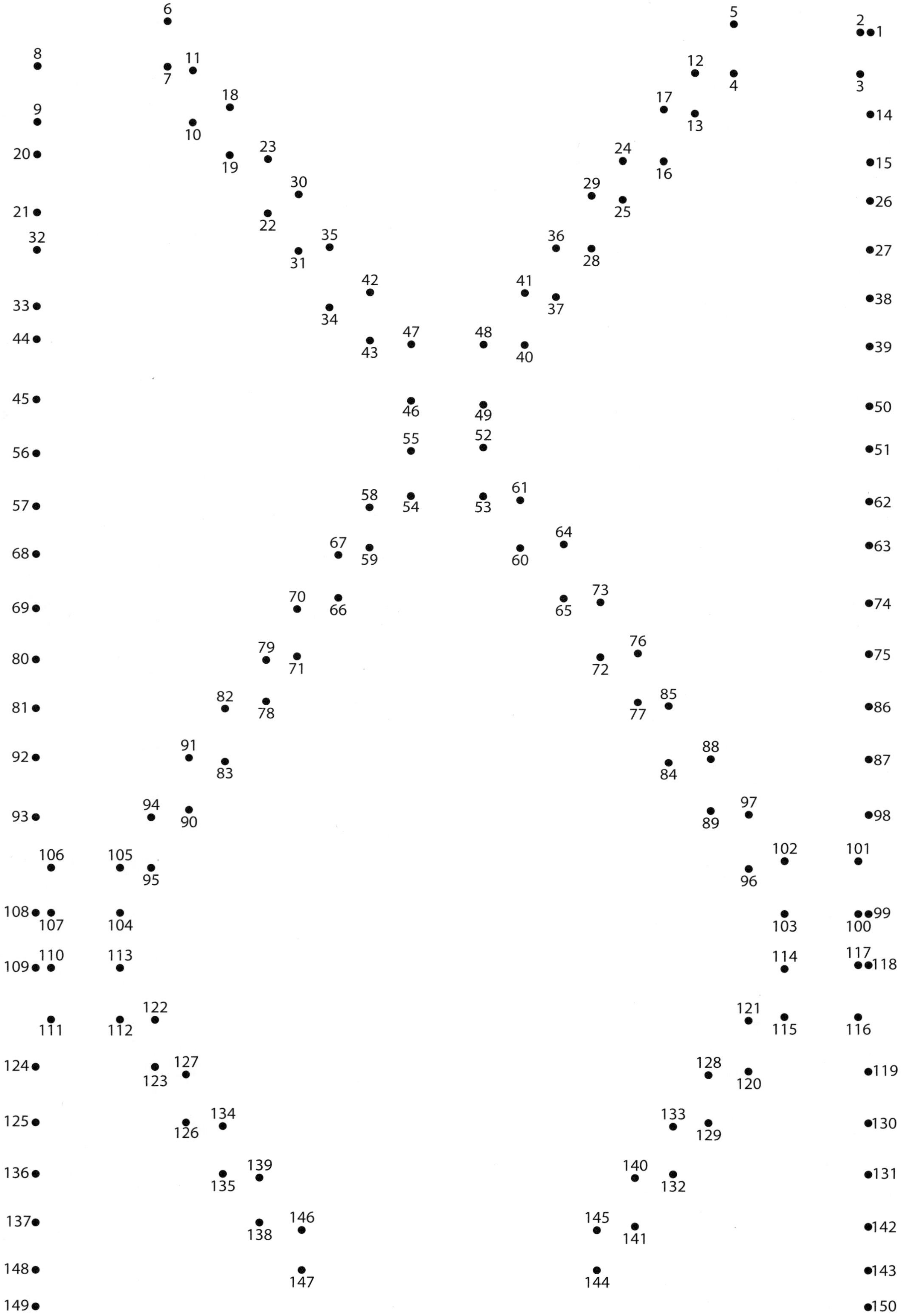

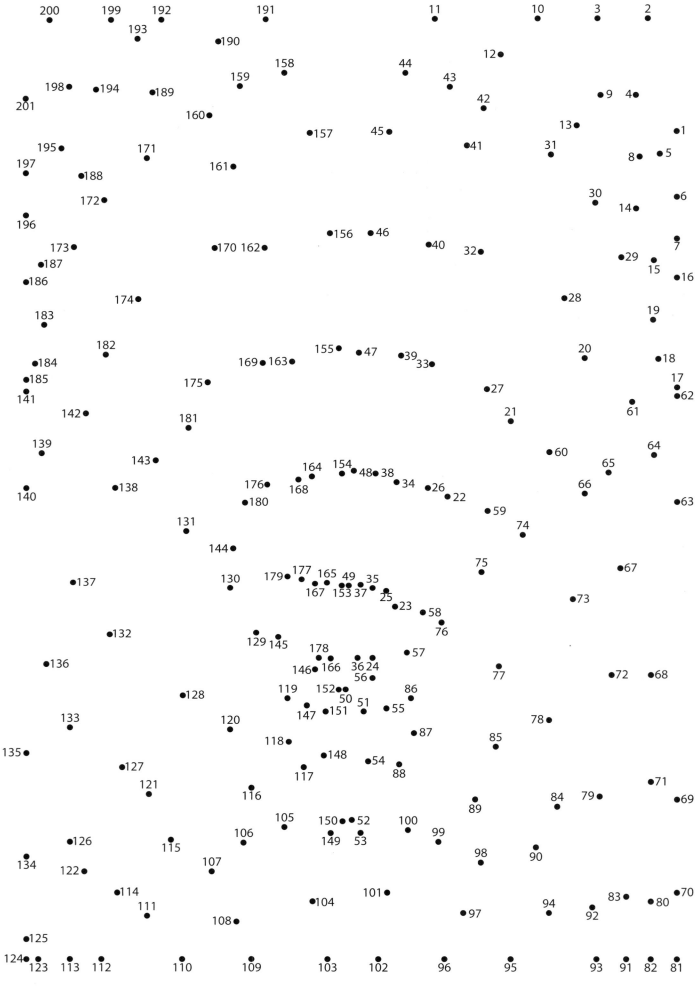

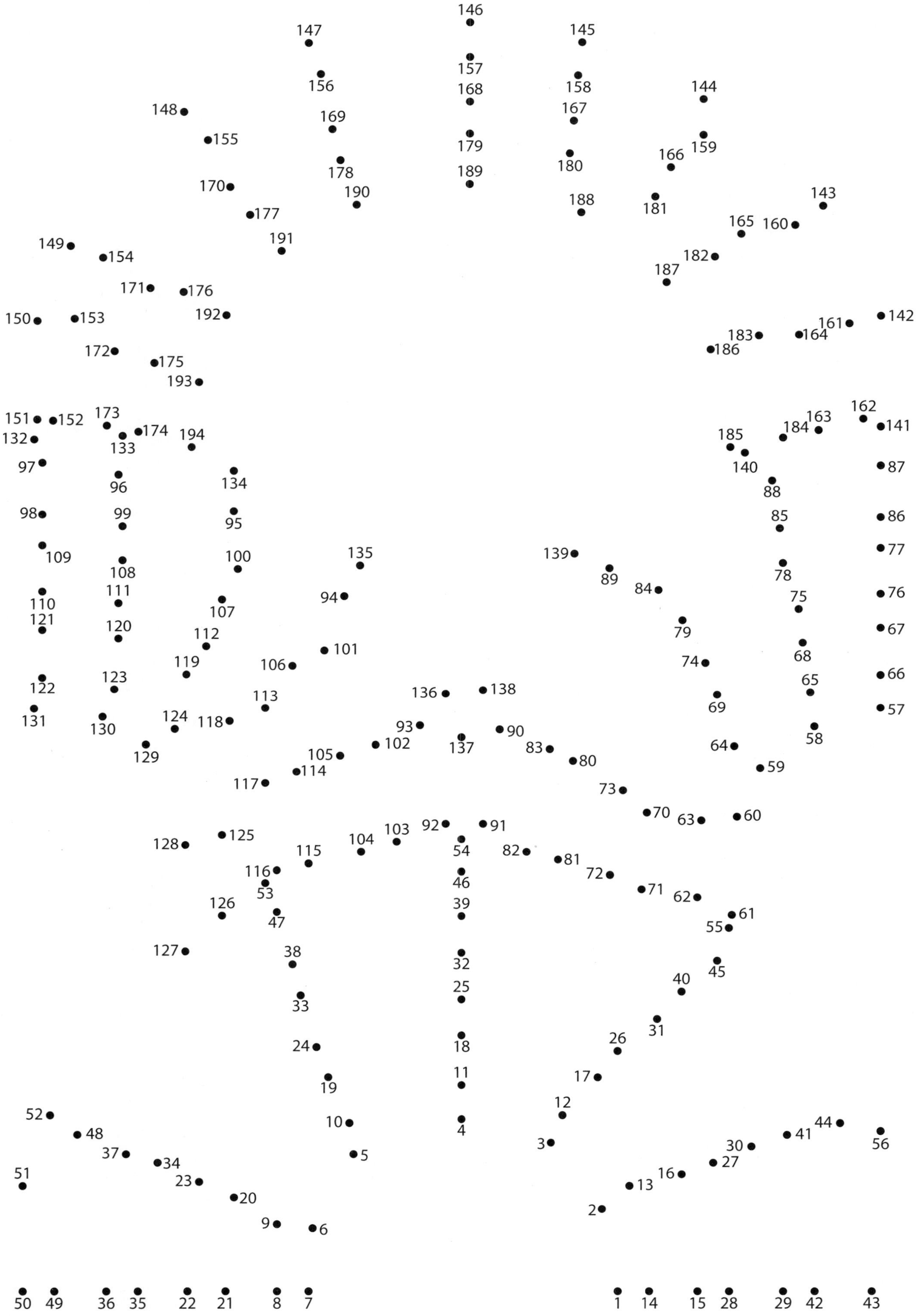

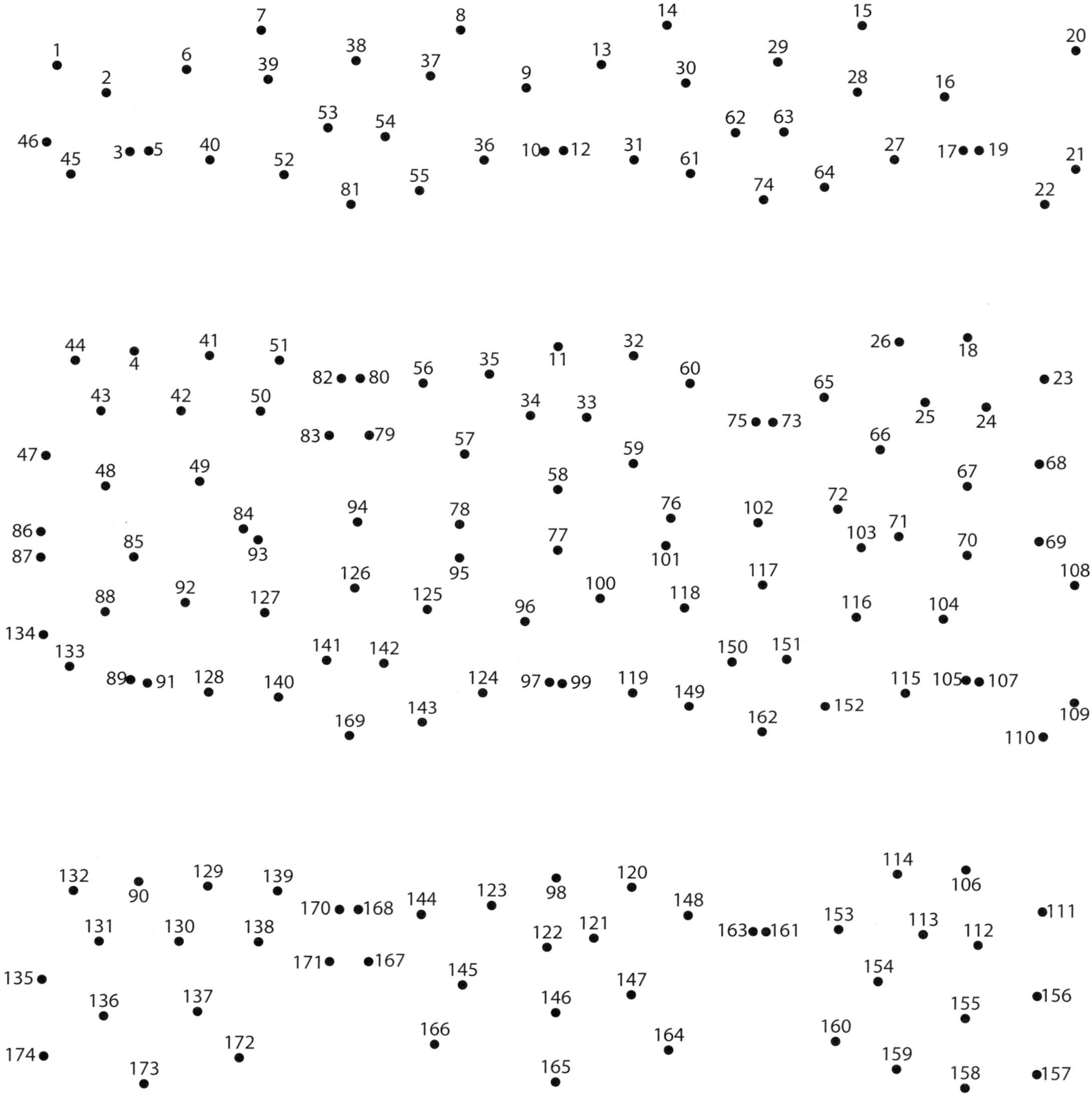

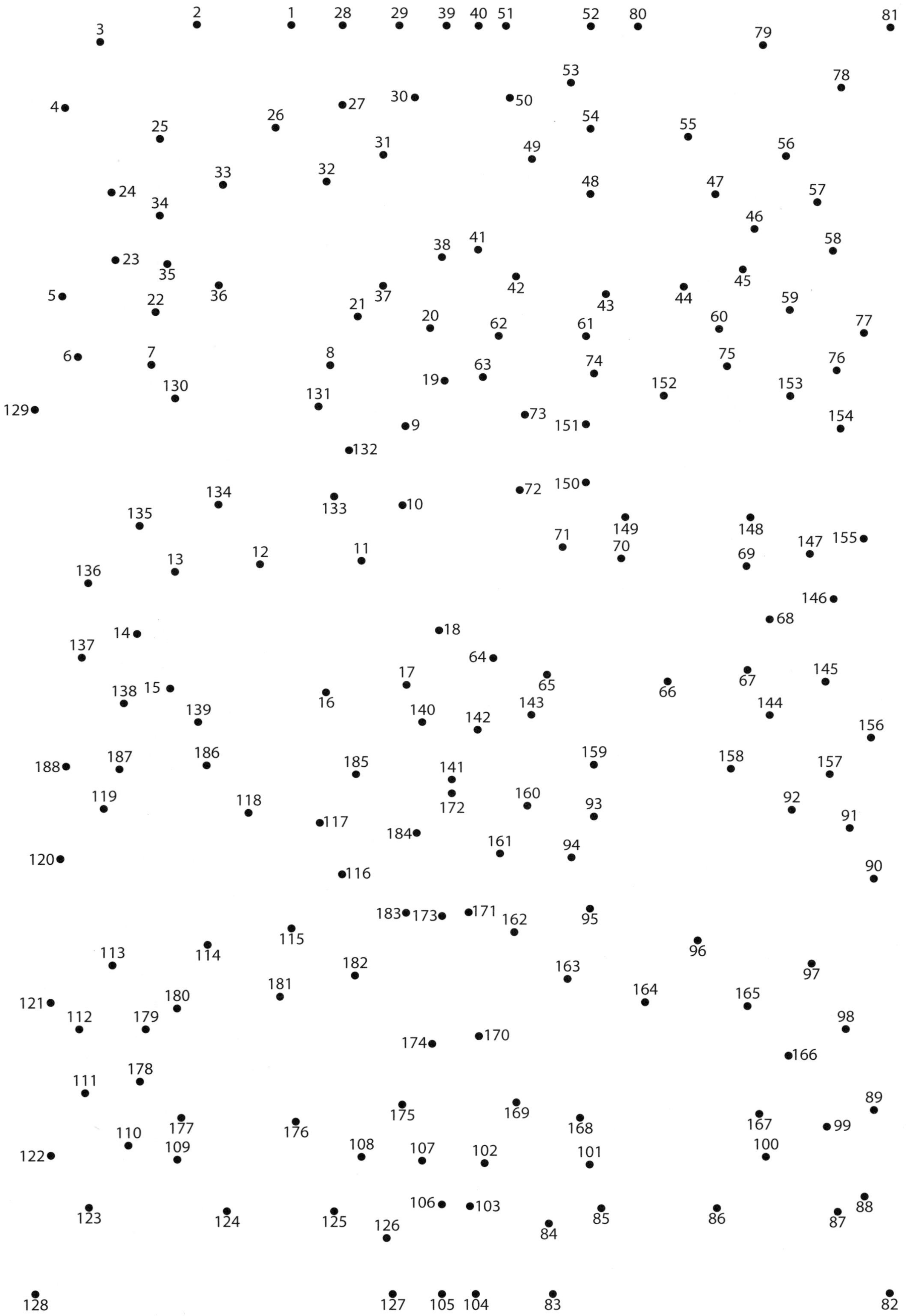

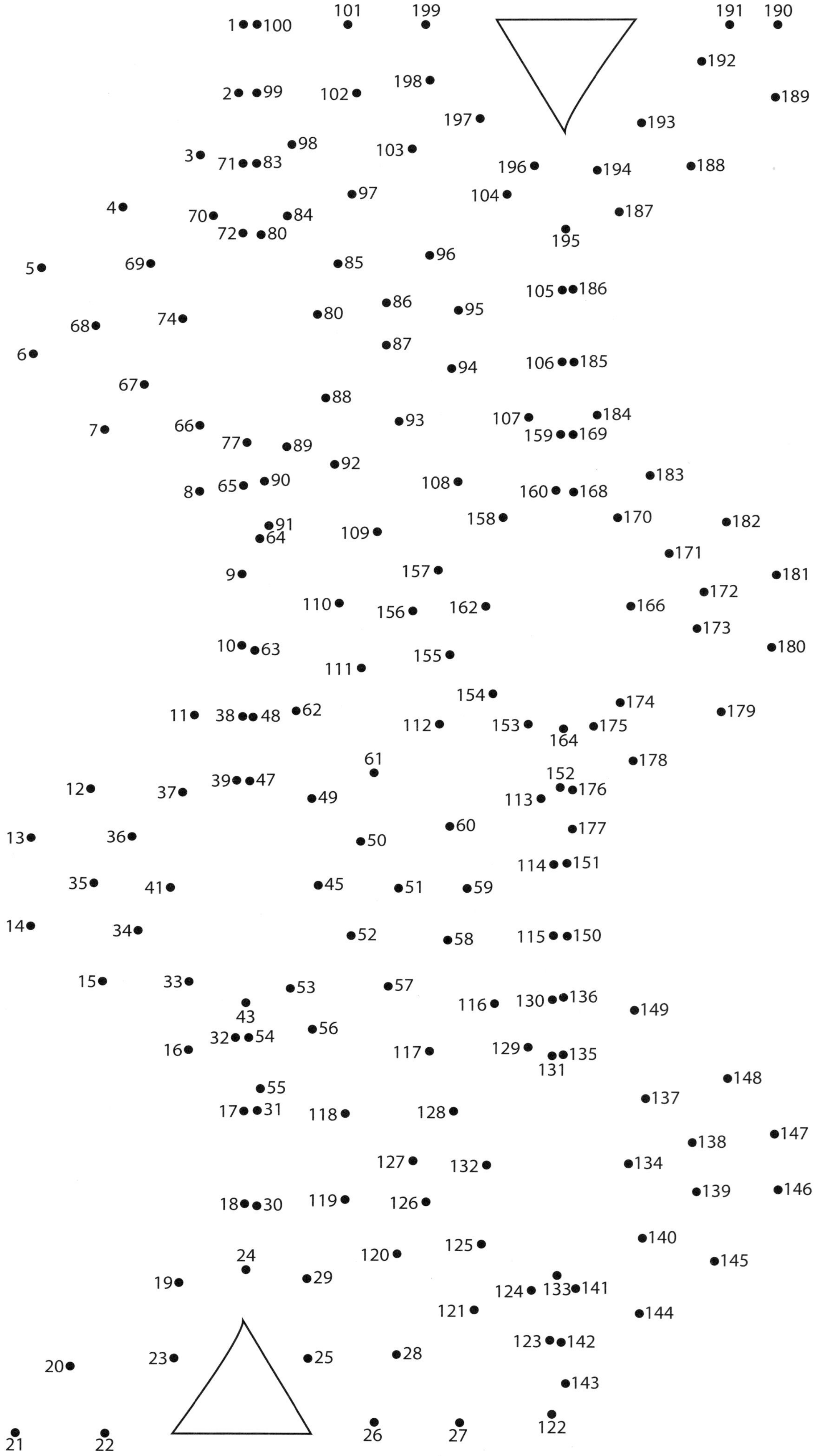

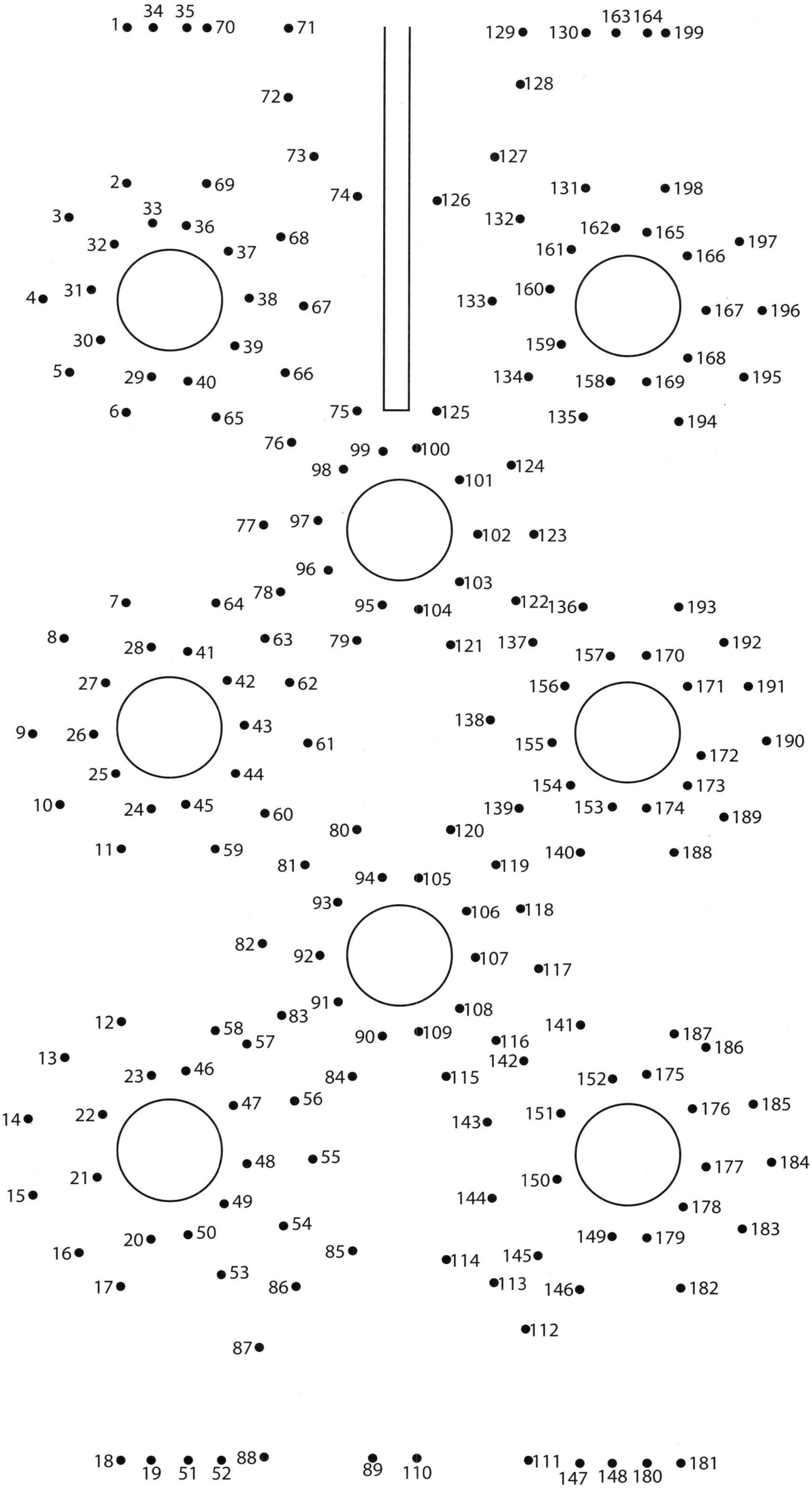

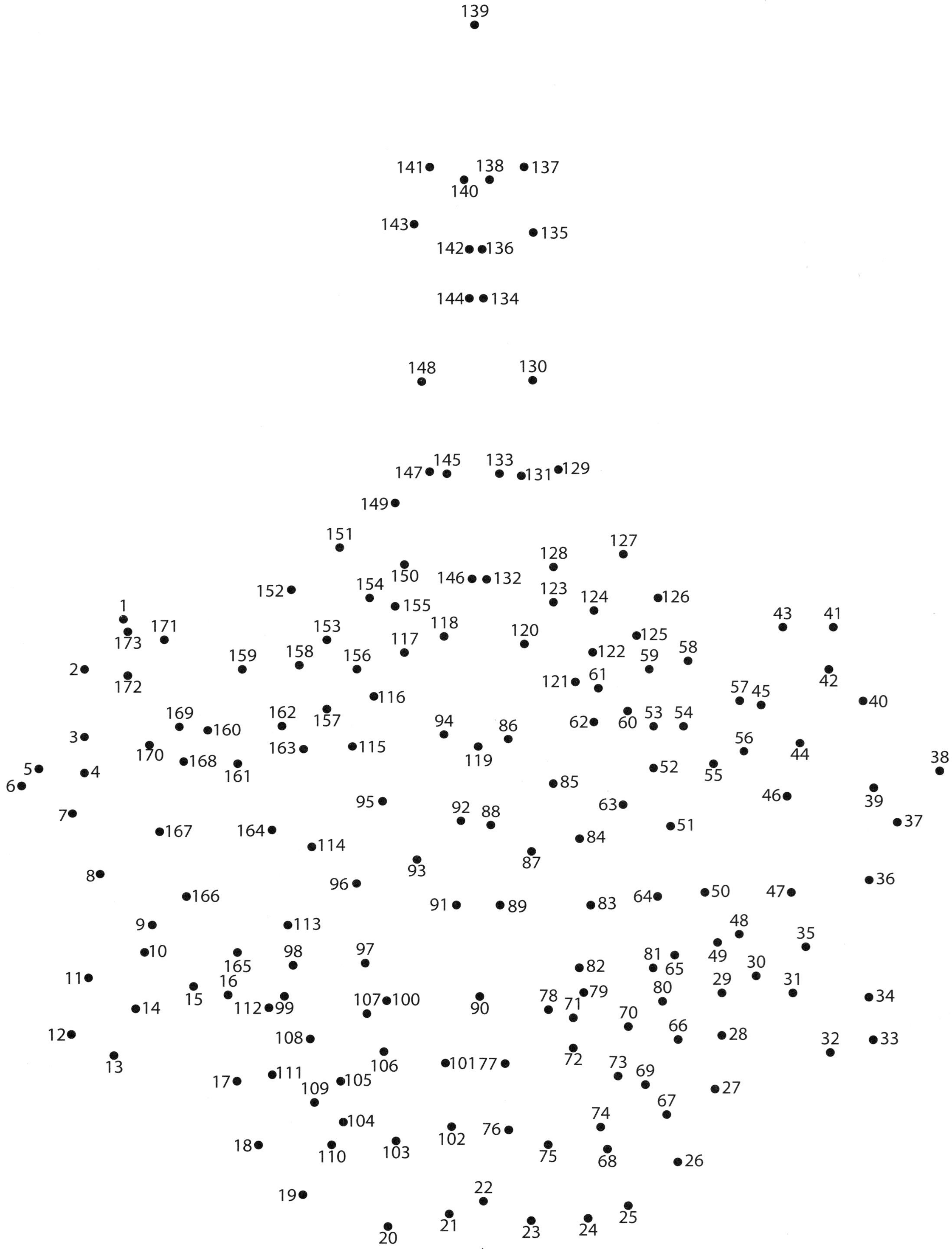

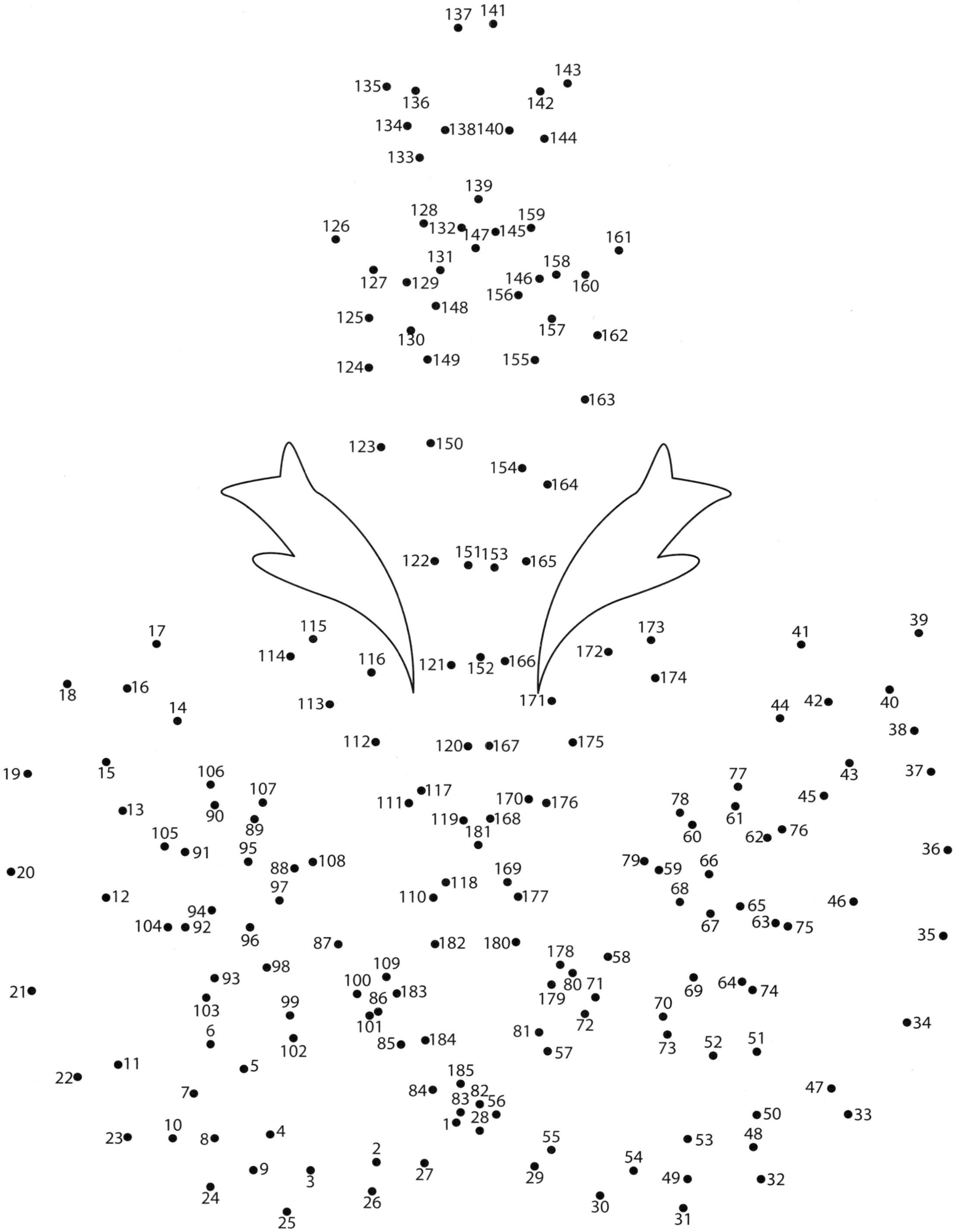

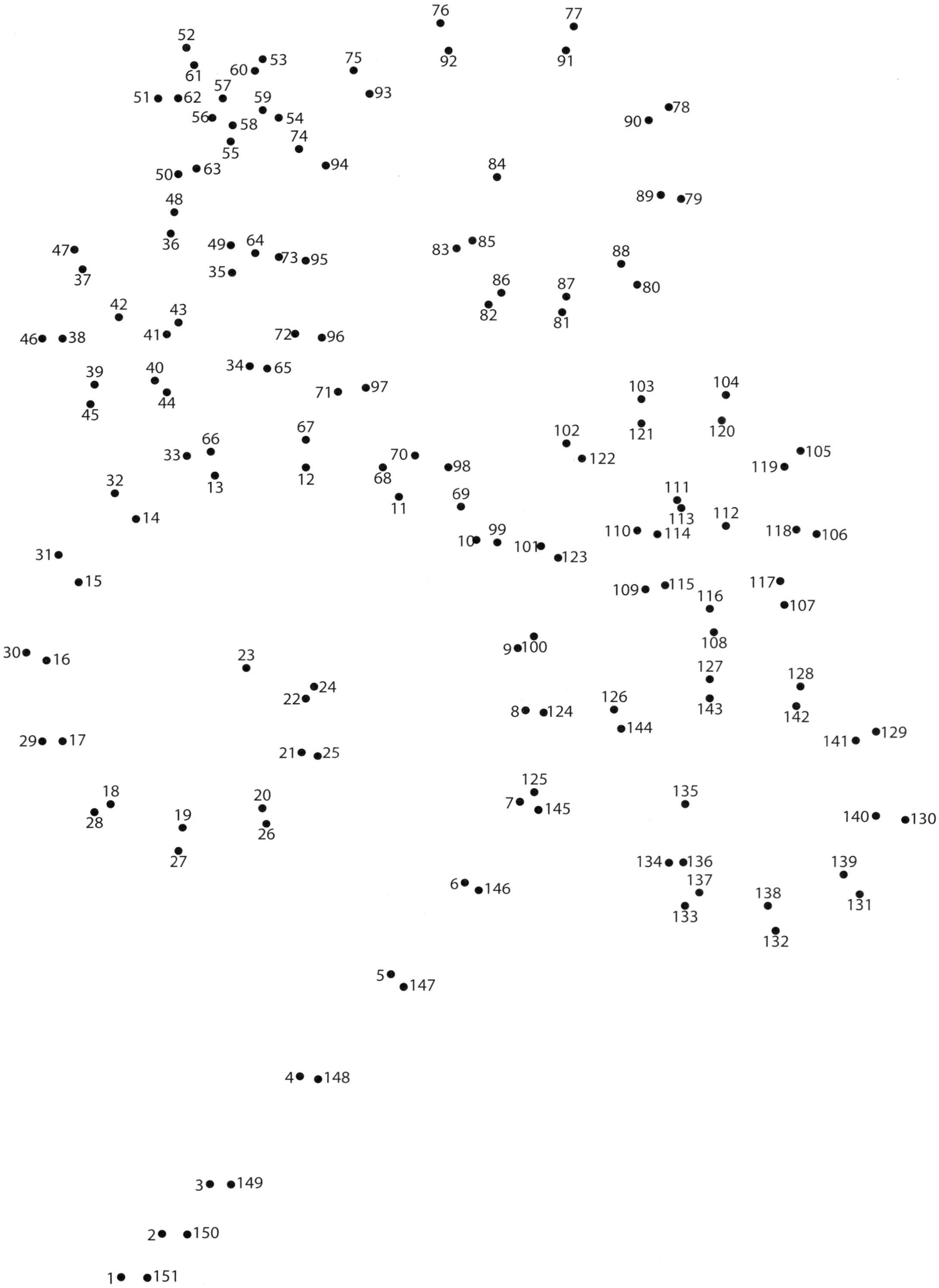

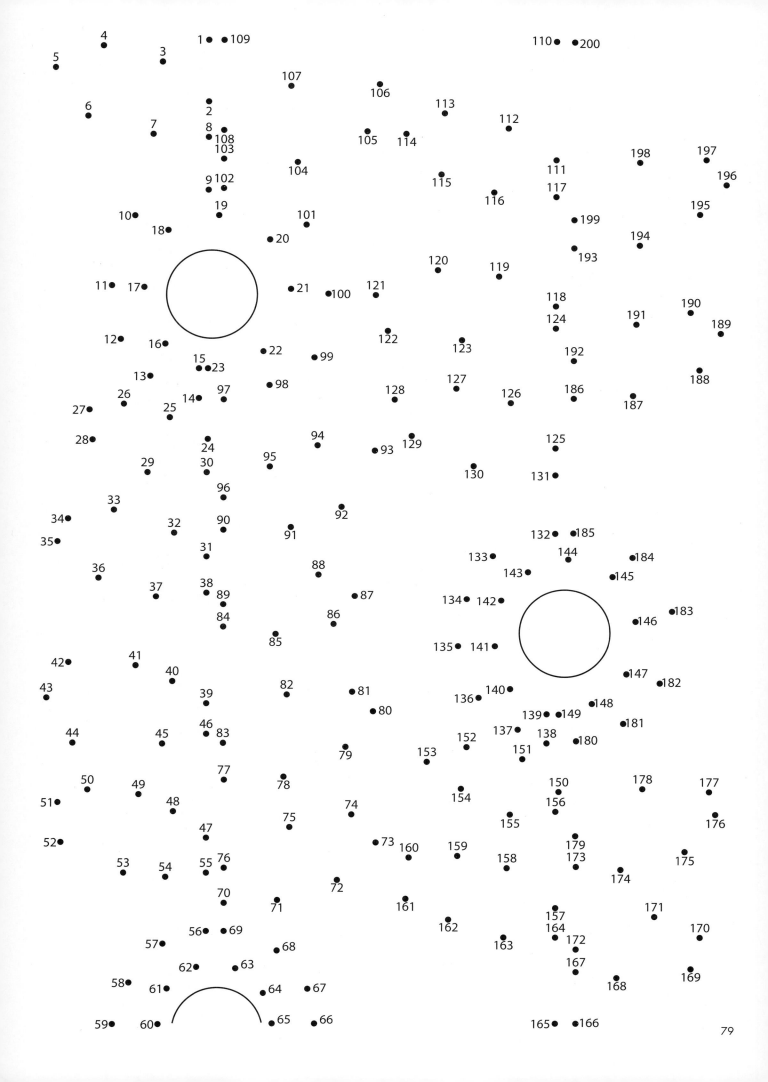

79

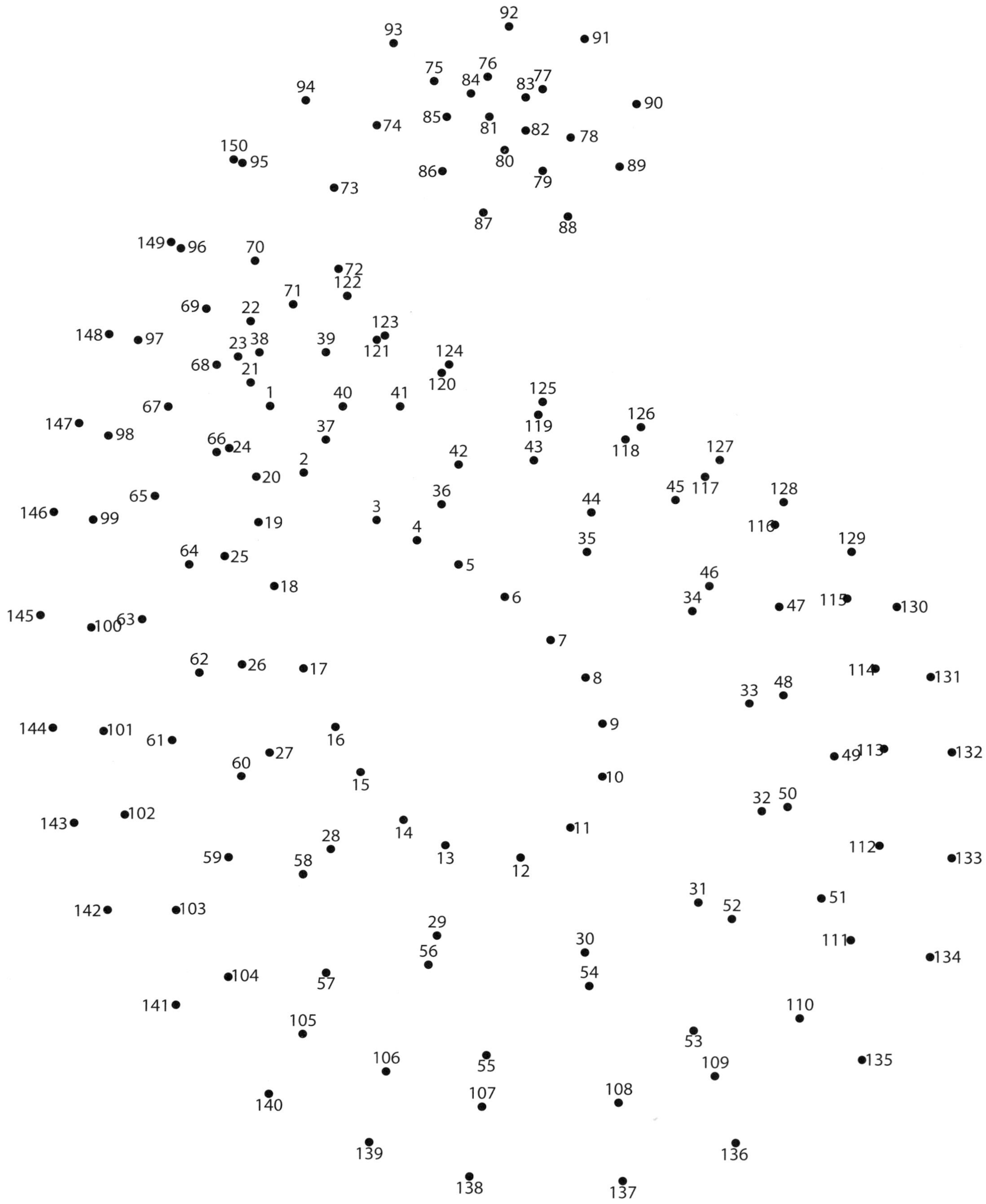

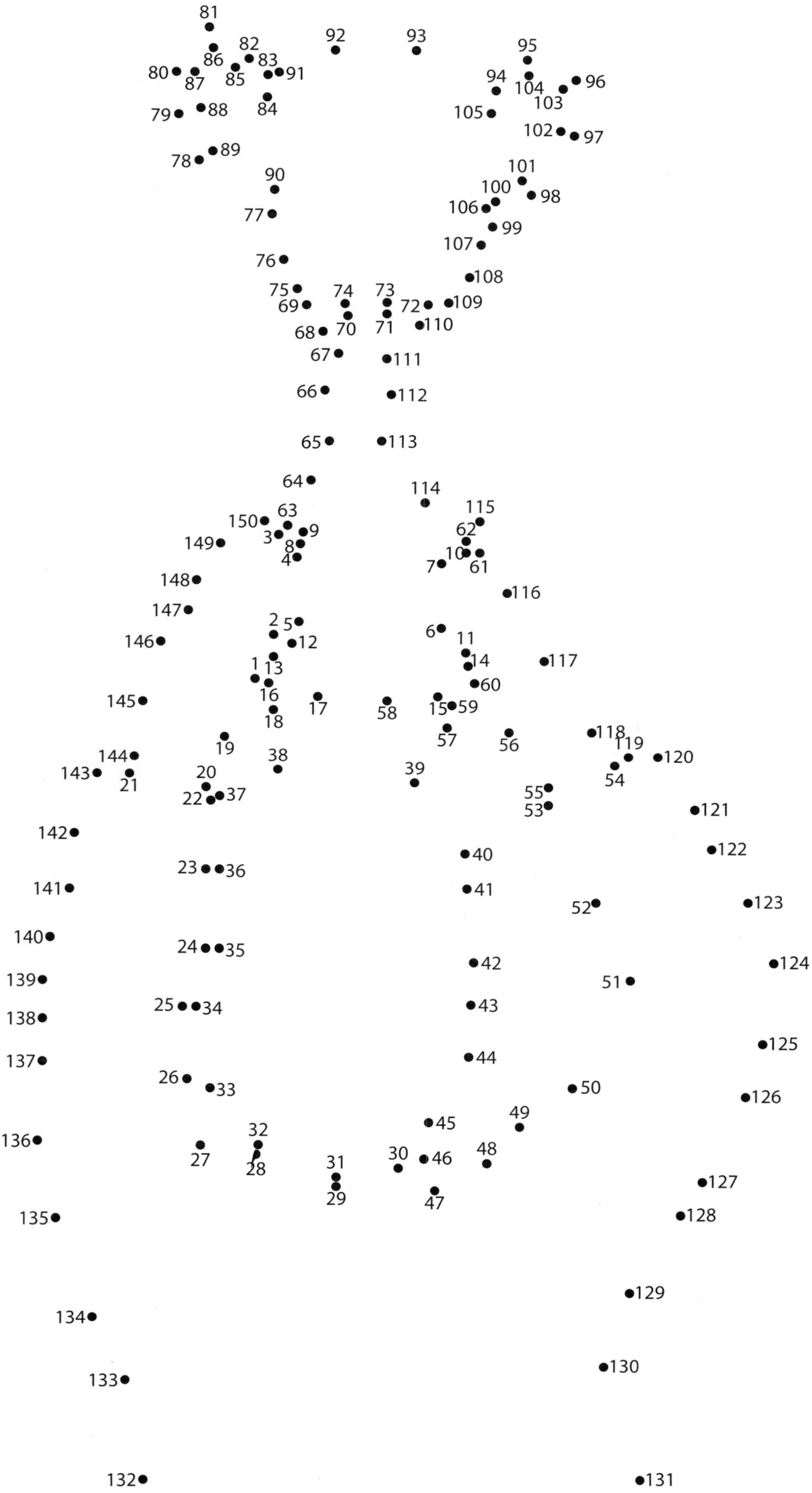

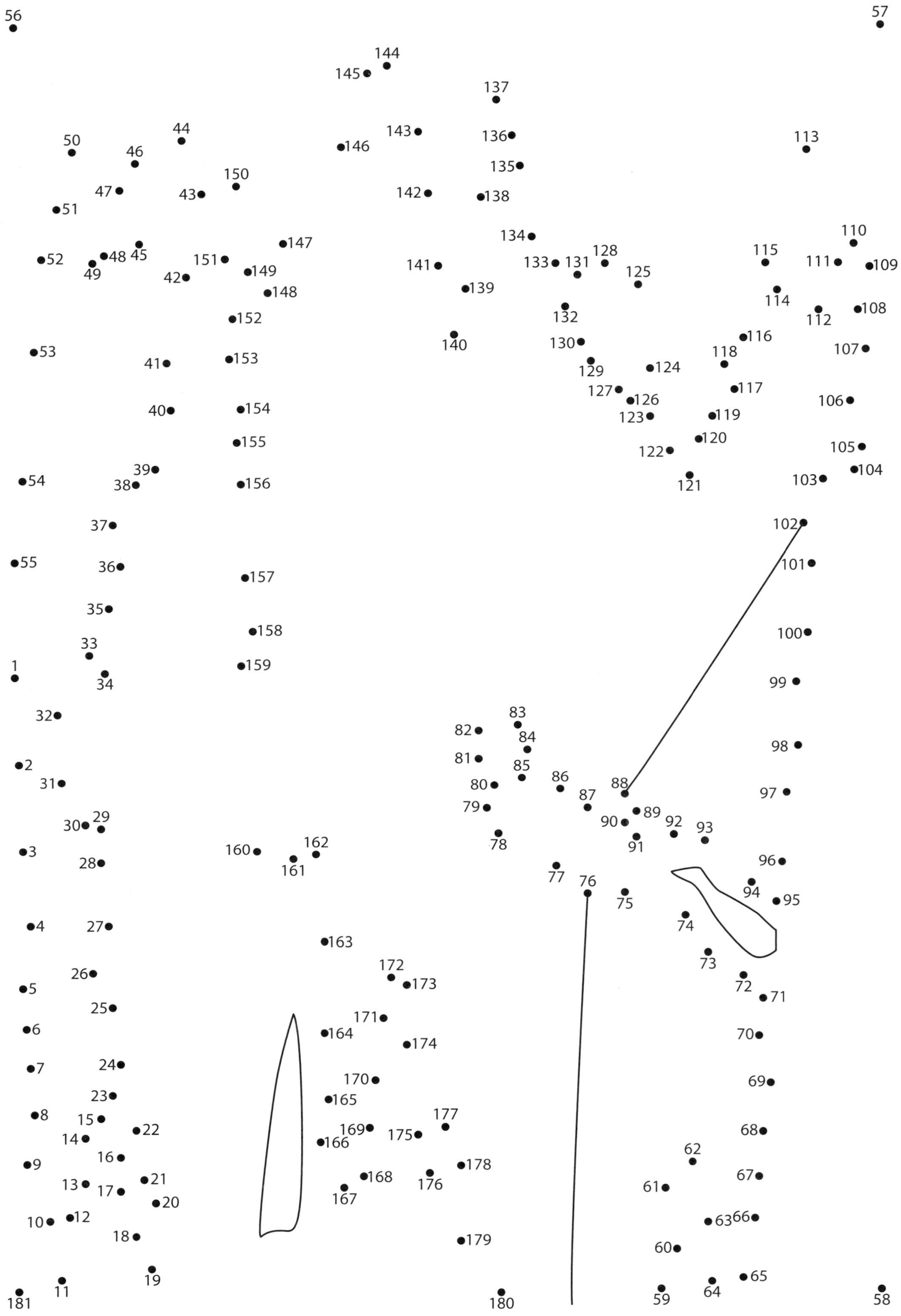

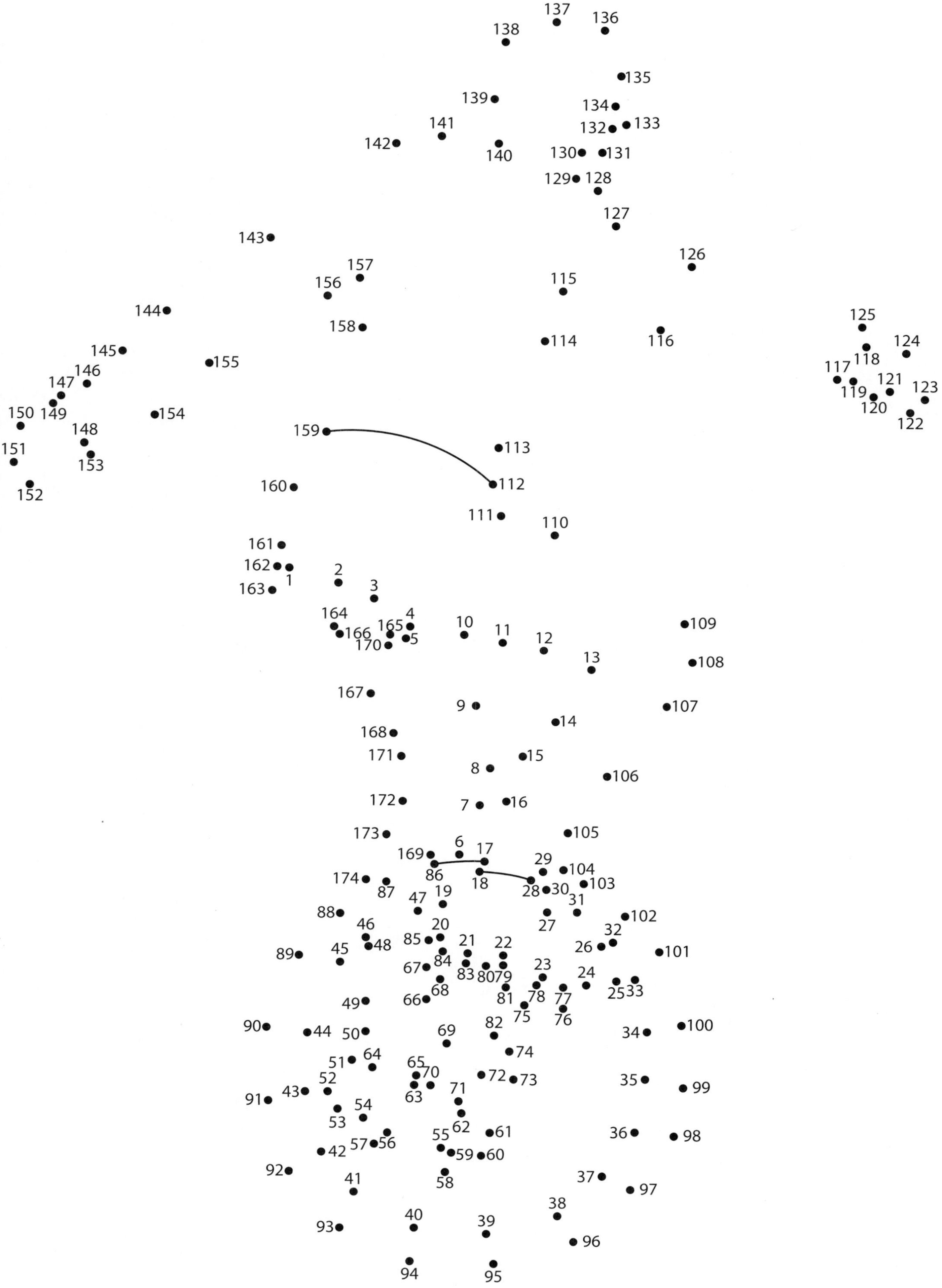

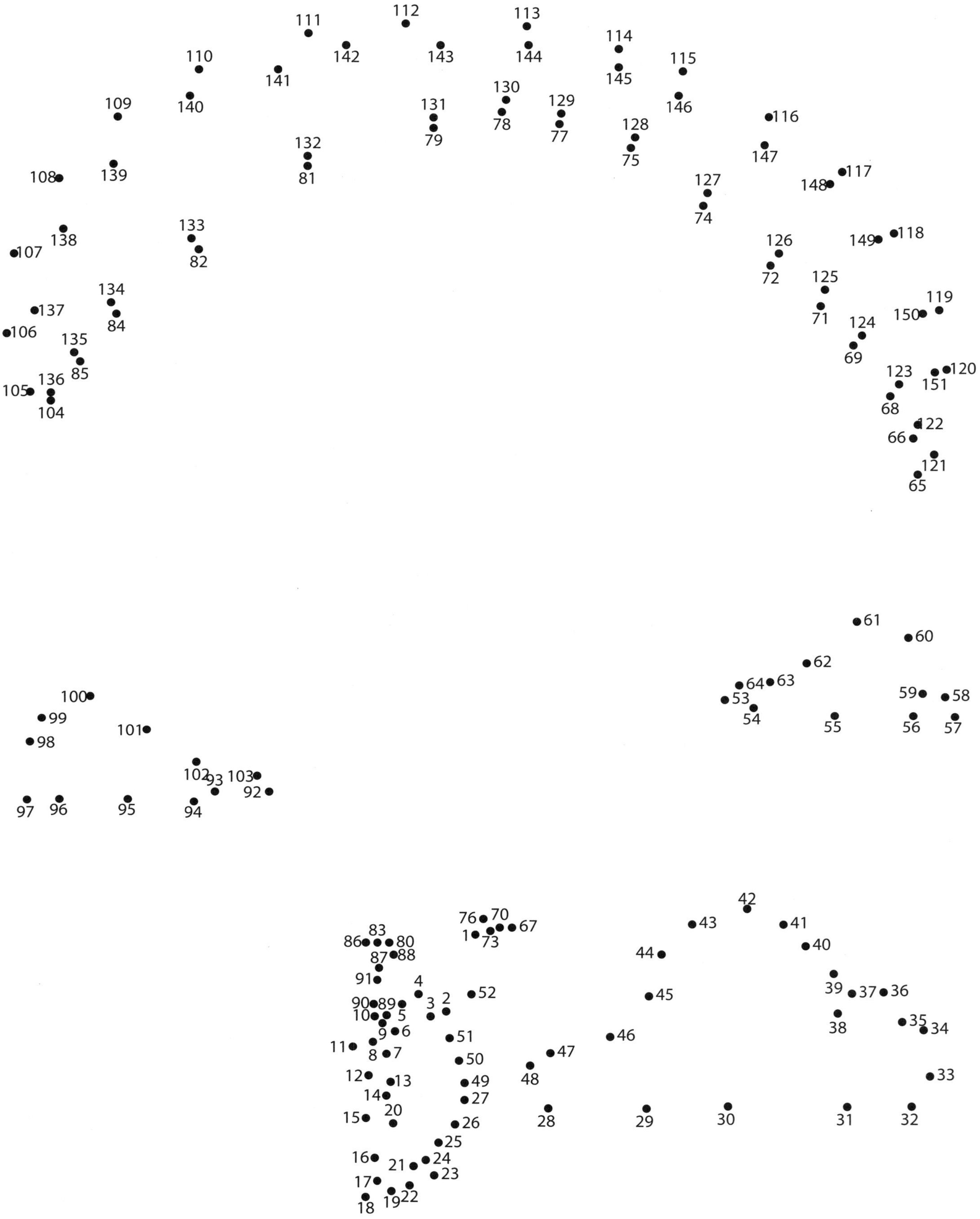

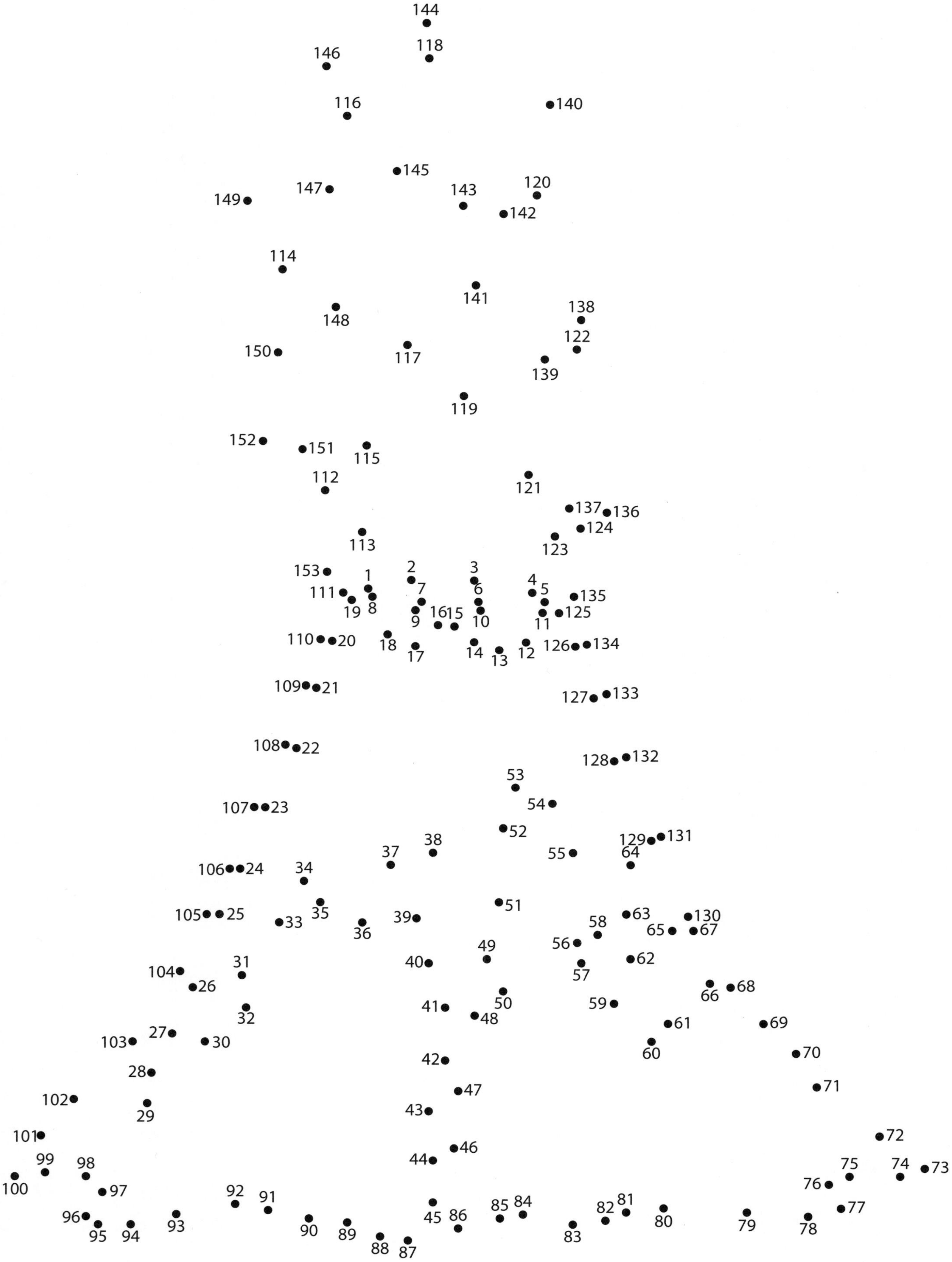
144
146
118
116
140
145
147
149
143
120
142
114
141
148
138
122
150
117
139
119
152
151
115
112
121
137
136
124
113
123
153
1
2
3
4
5
6
7
8
9
10
11
111
19
16
15
135
125
110
20
18
17
14
13
12
126
134
109
21
127
133
108
22
128
132
53
107
23
54
52
38
37
129
131
55
64
106
24
34
35
51
105
25
33
36
39
63
130
58
65
67
49
56
40
104
31
26
62
57
66
68
32
41
50
48
59
61
69
103
27
30
60
70
42
28
47
71
102
29
43
101
72
46
44
99
98
100
97
75
74
73
76
96
95
94
93
92
91
90
89
88
87
45
86
85
84
83
82
81
80
79
78
77

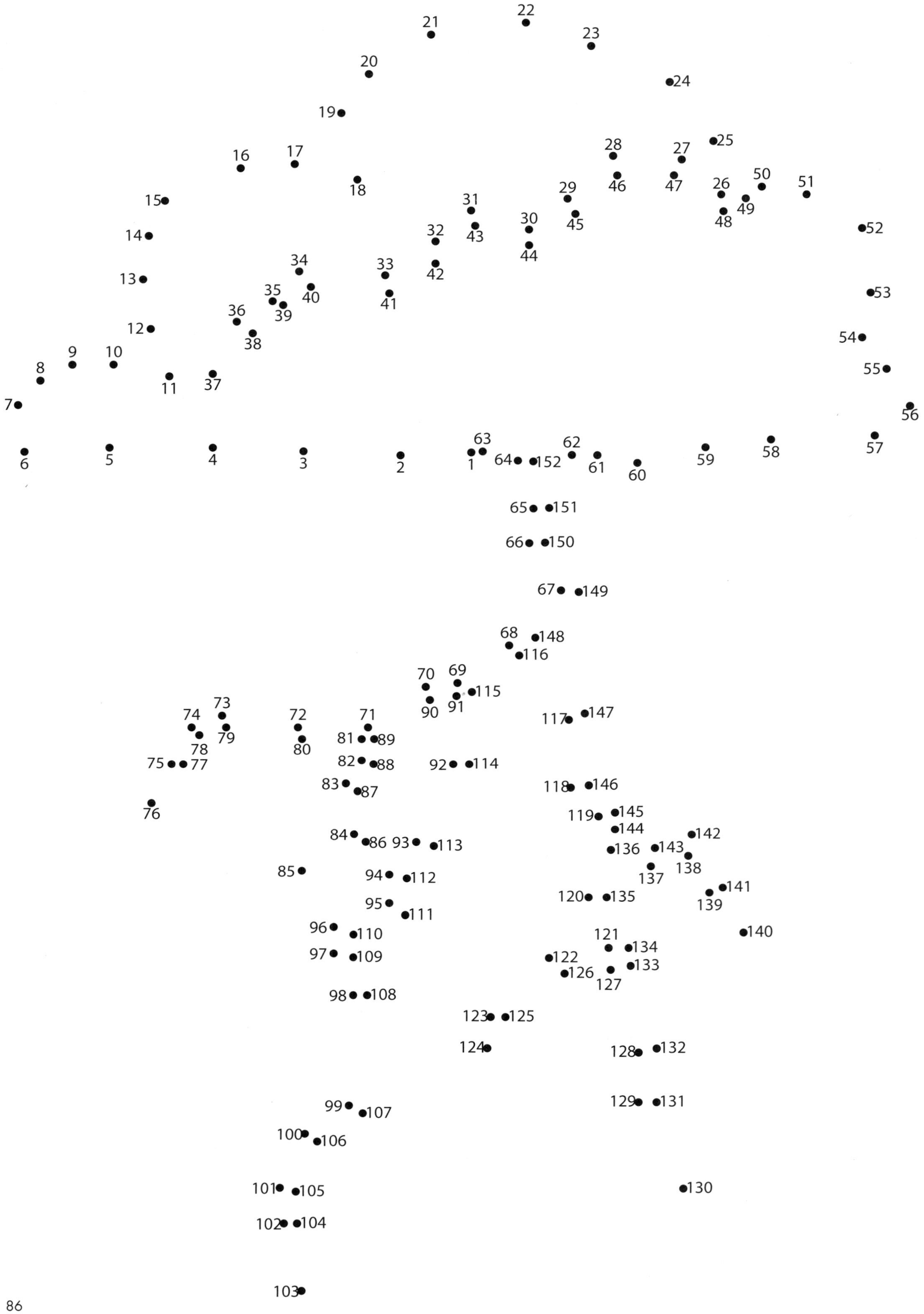

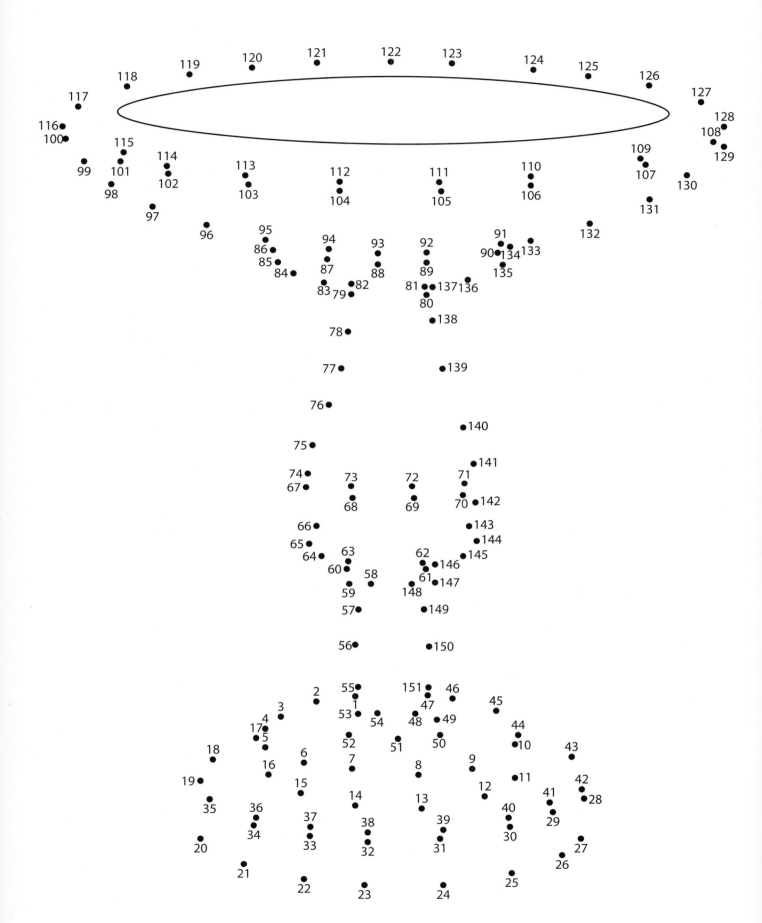

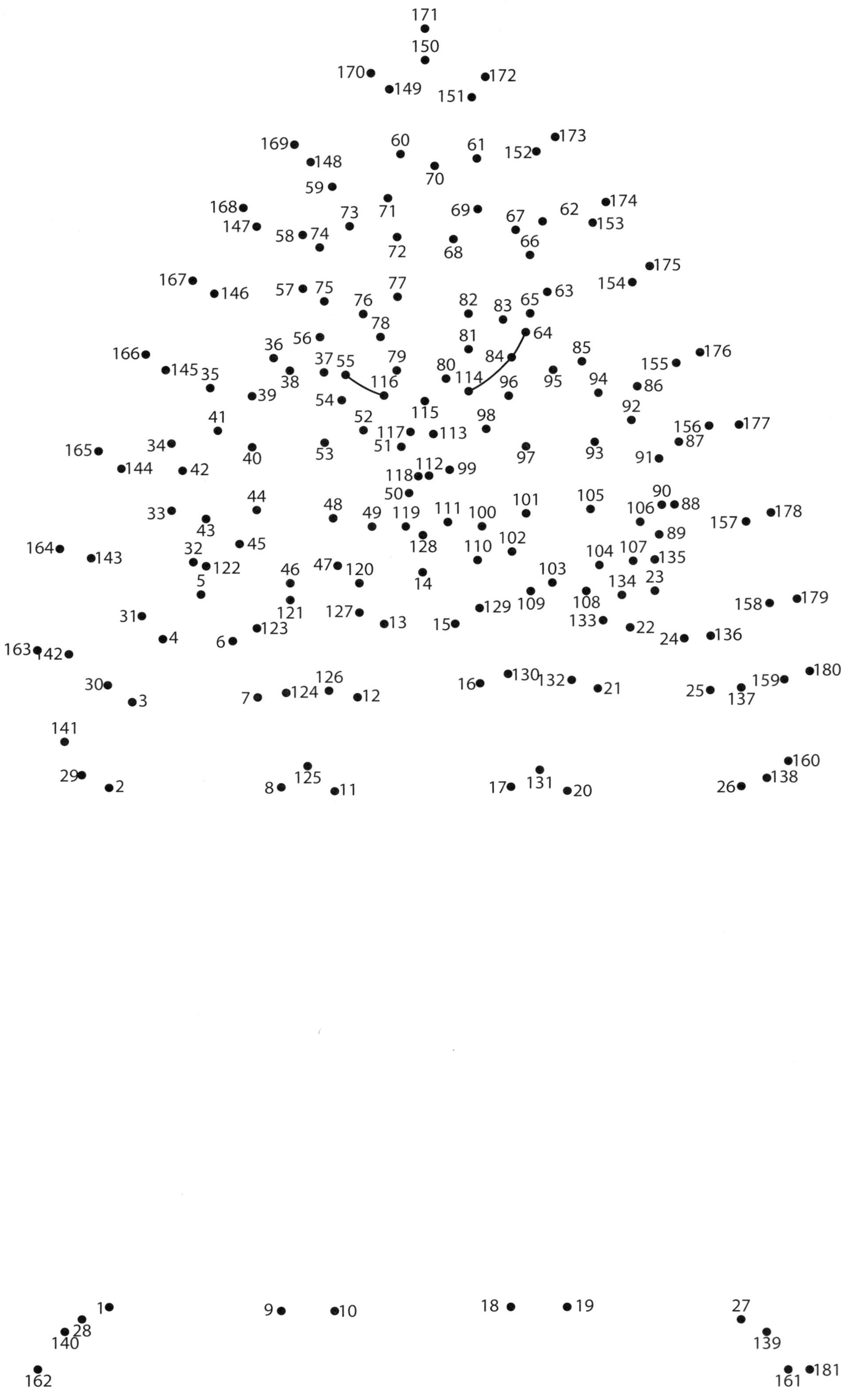

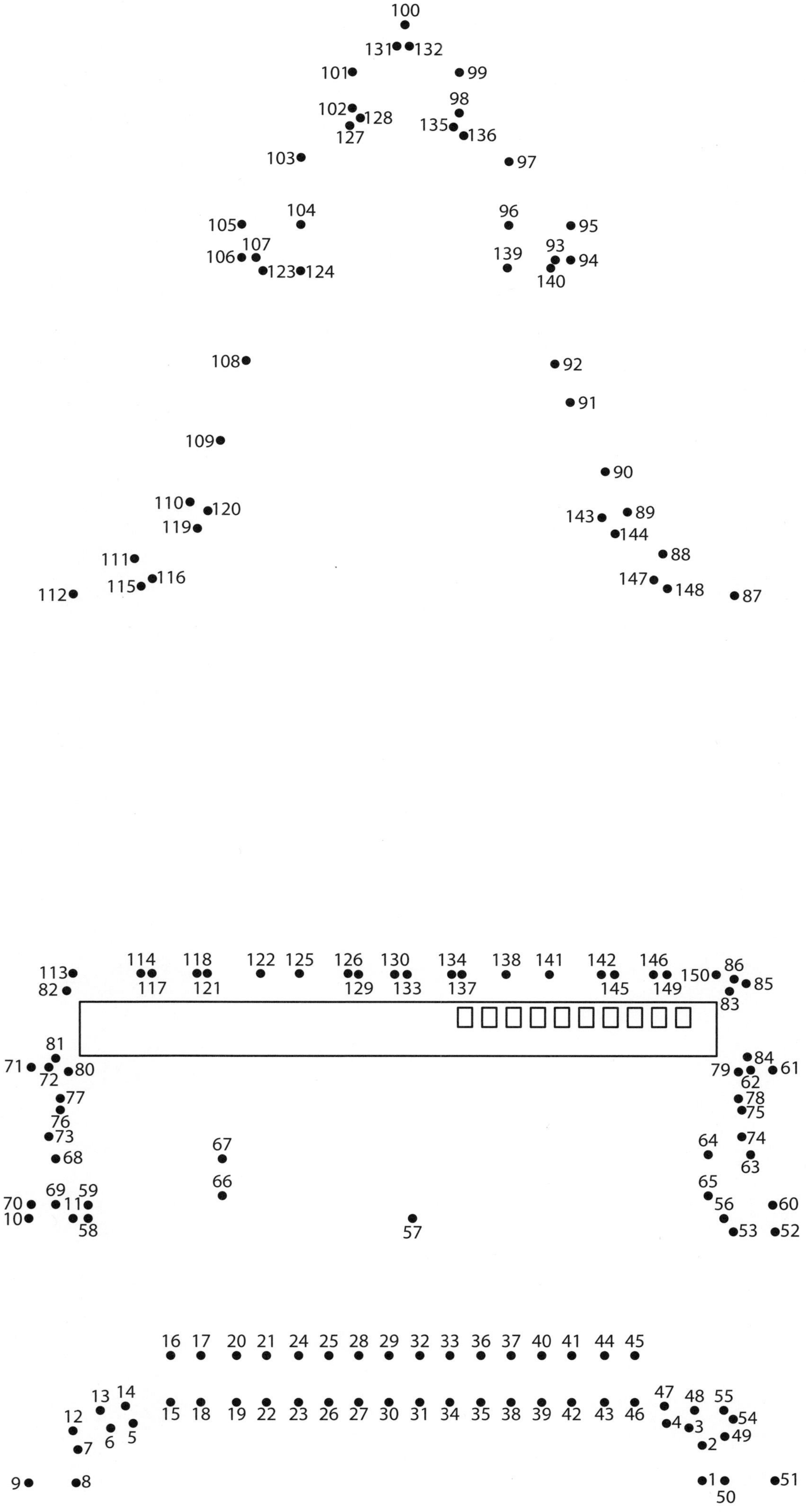

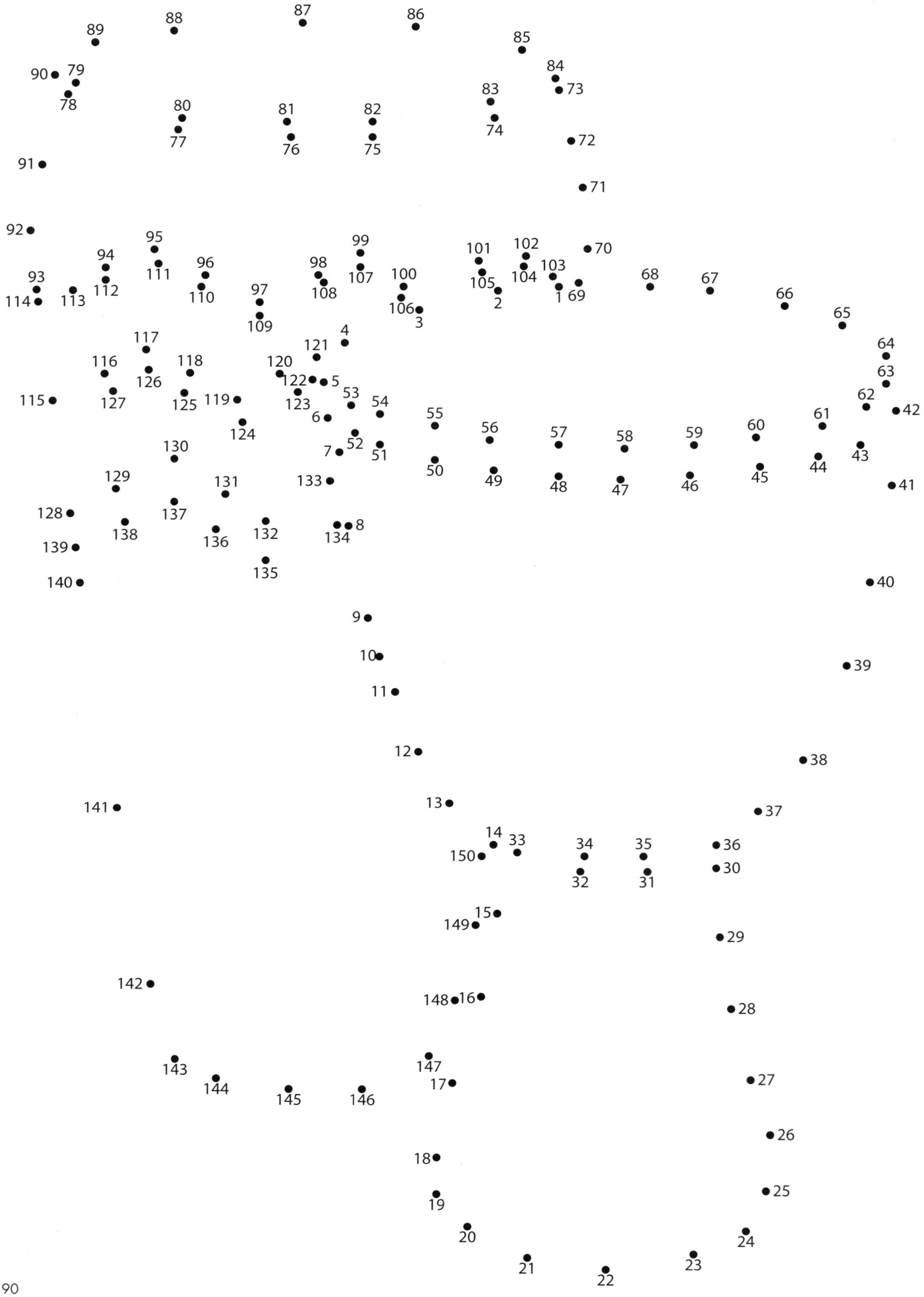

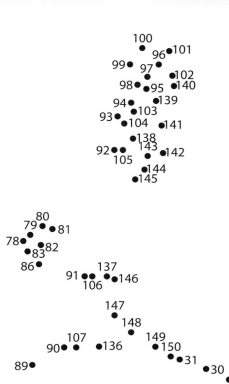
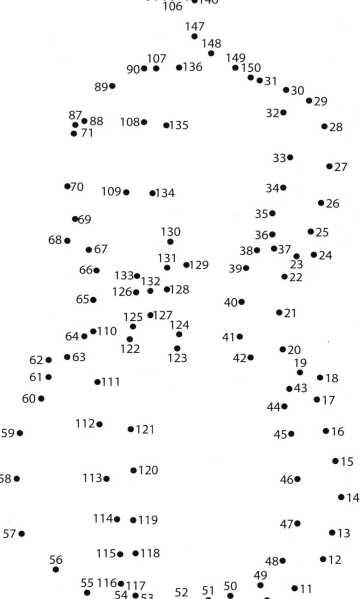
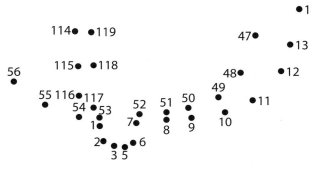

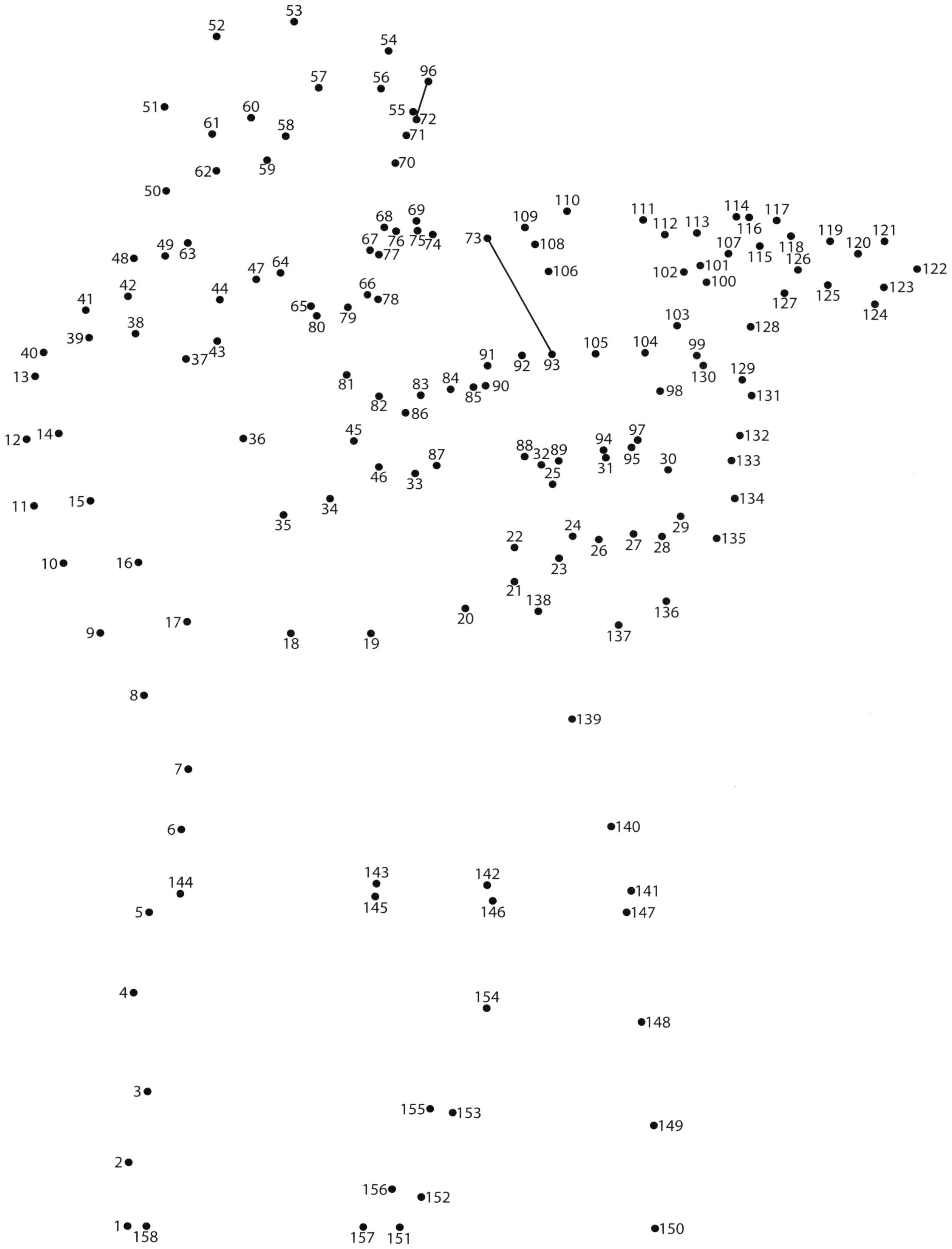

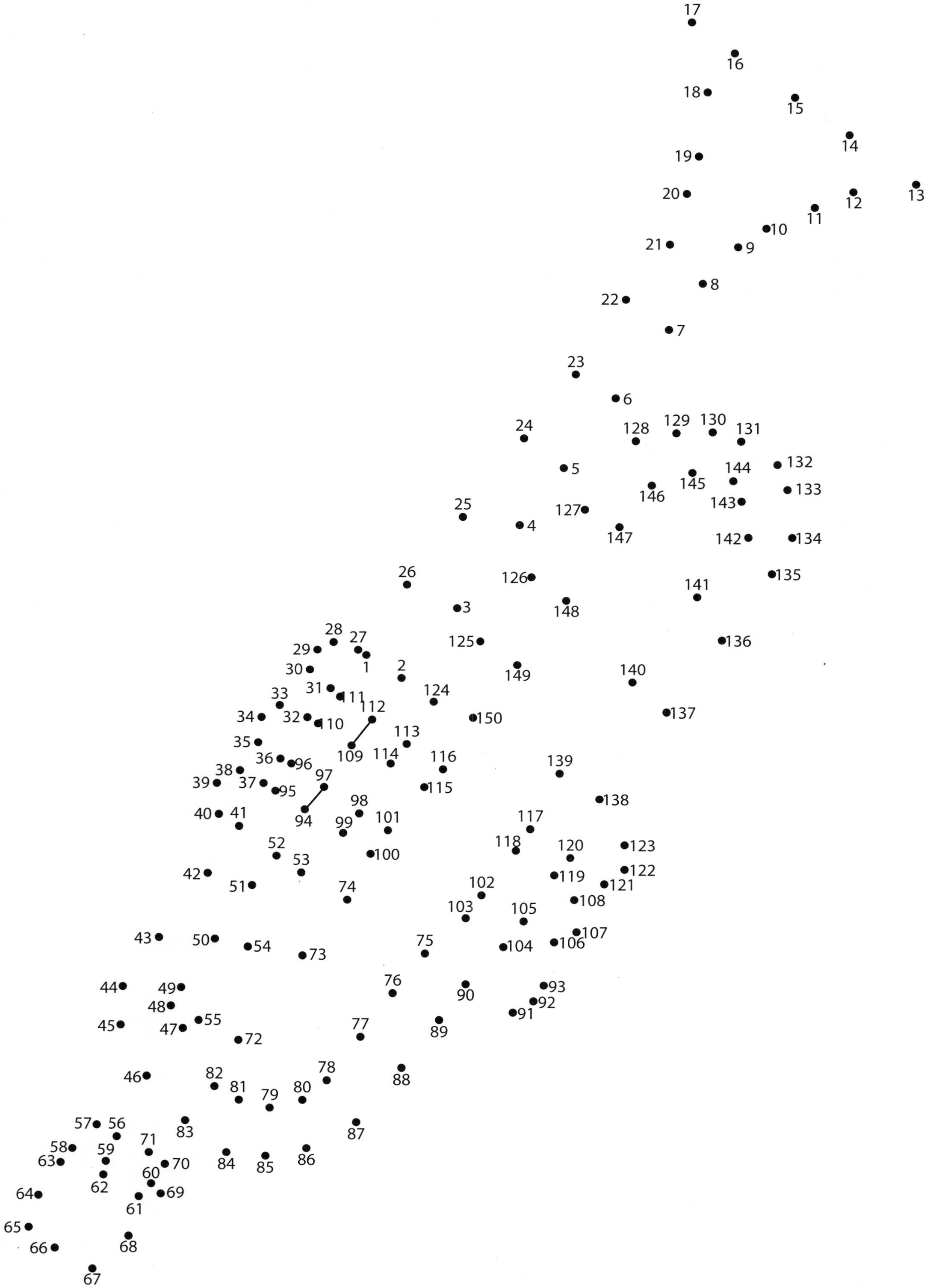

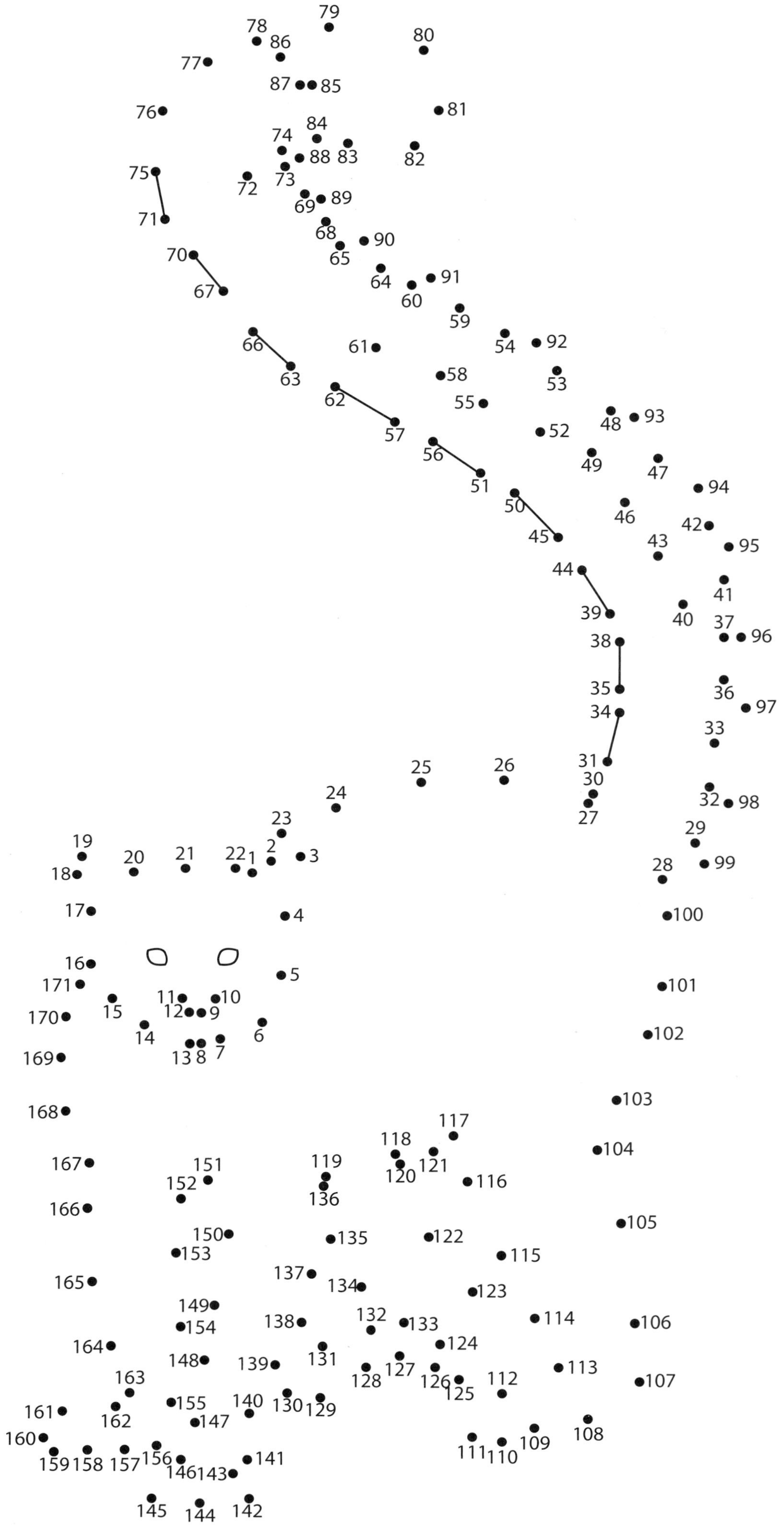

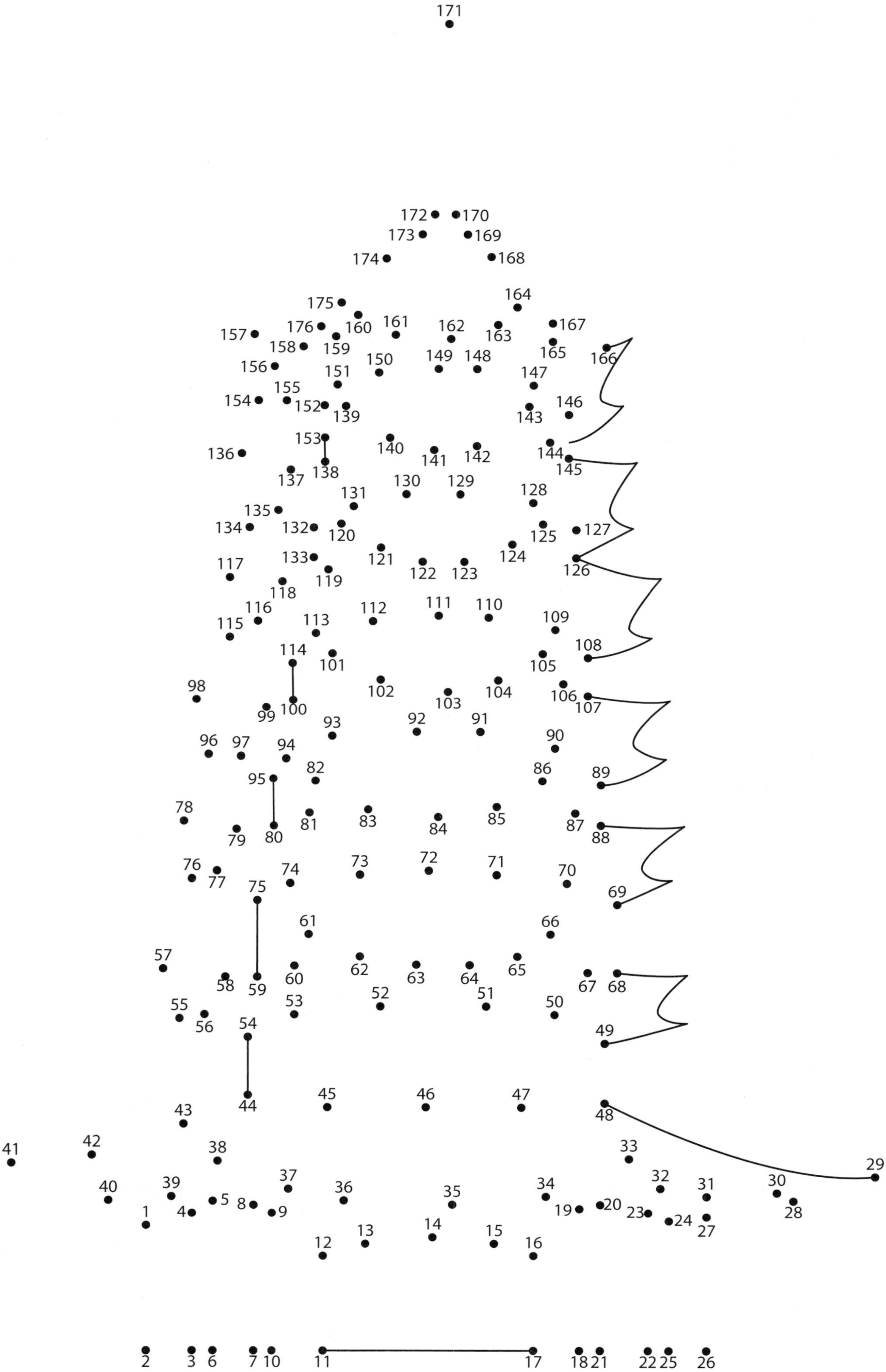

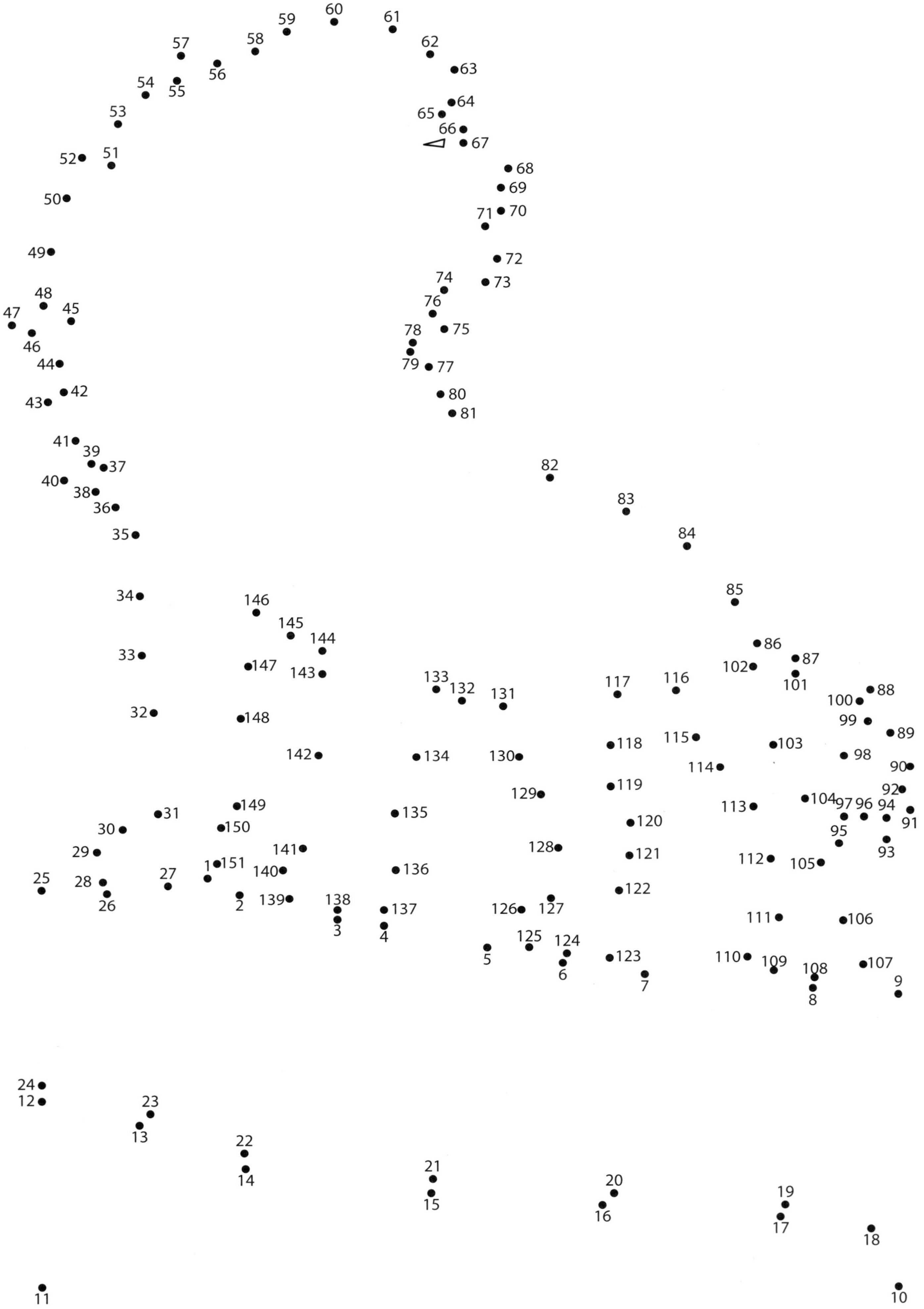

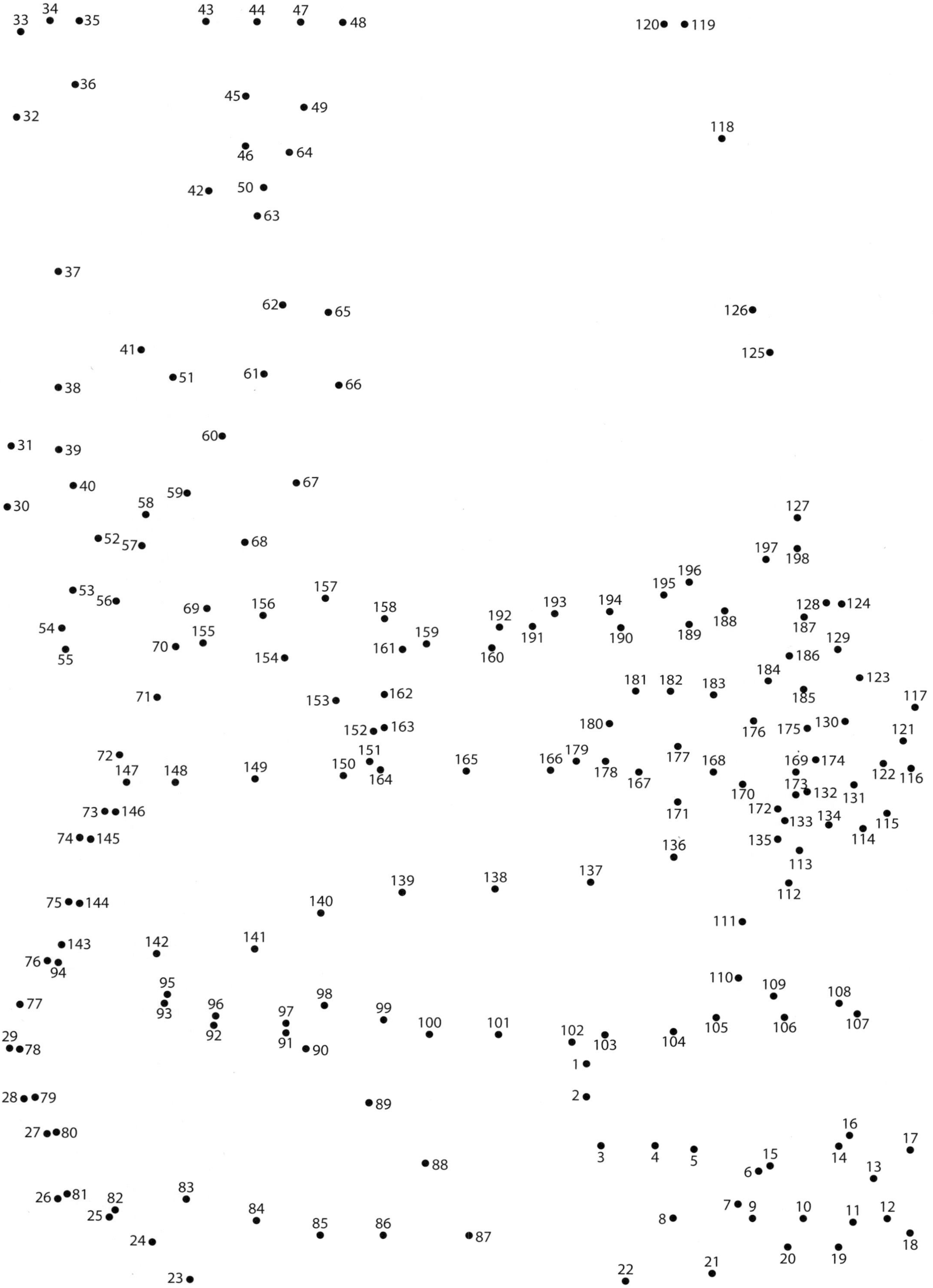

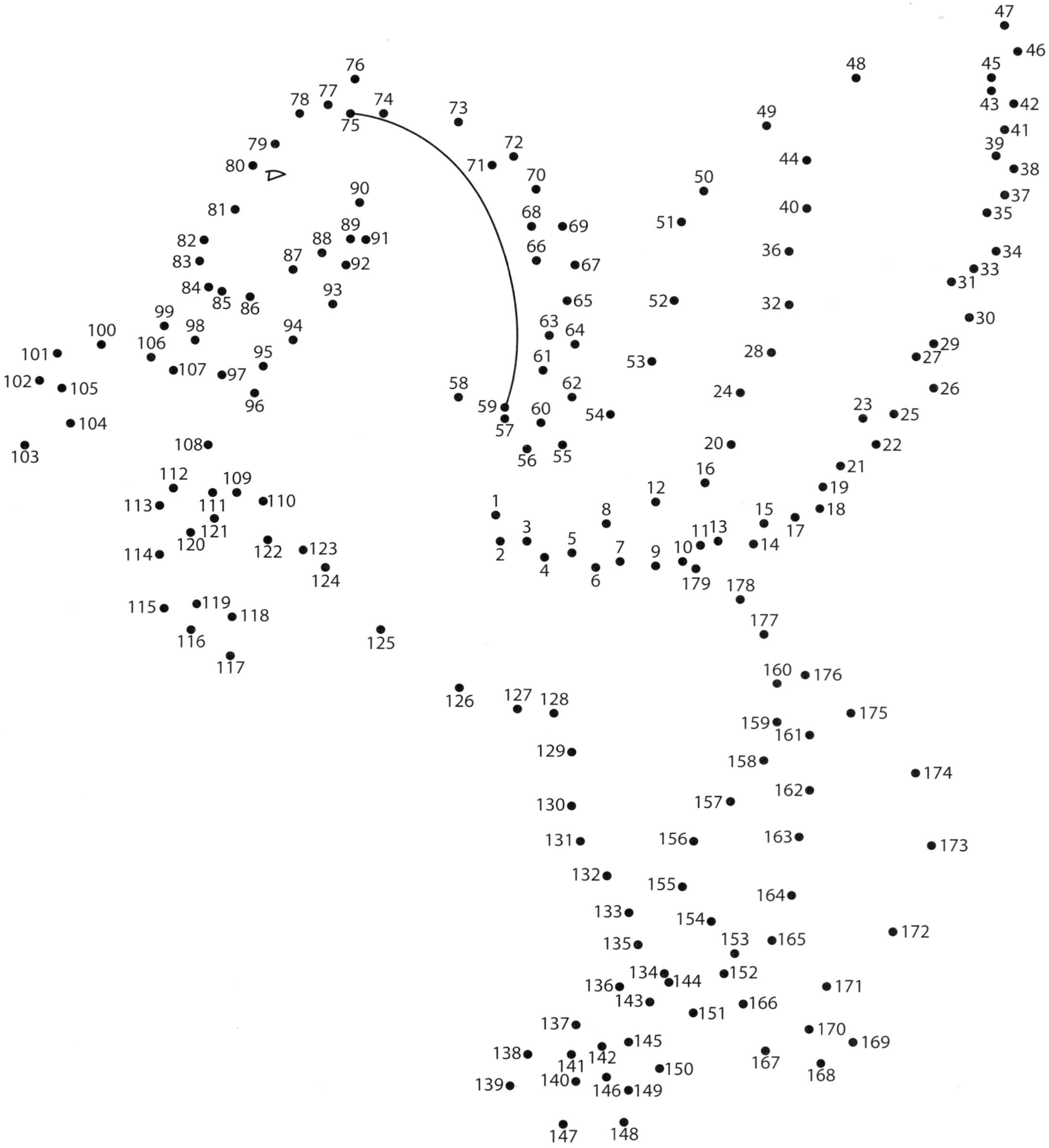

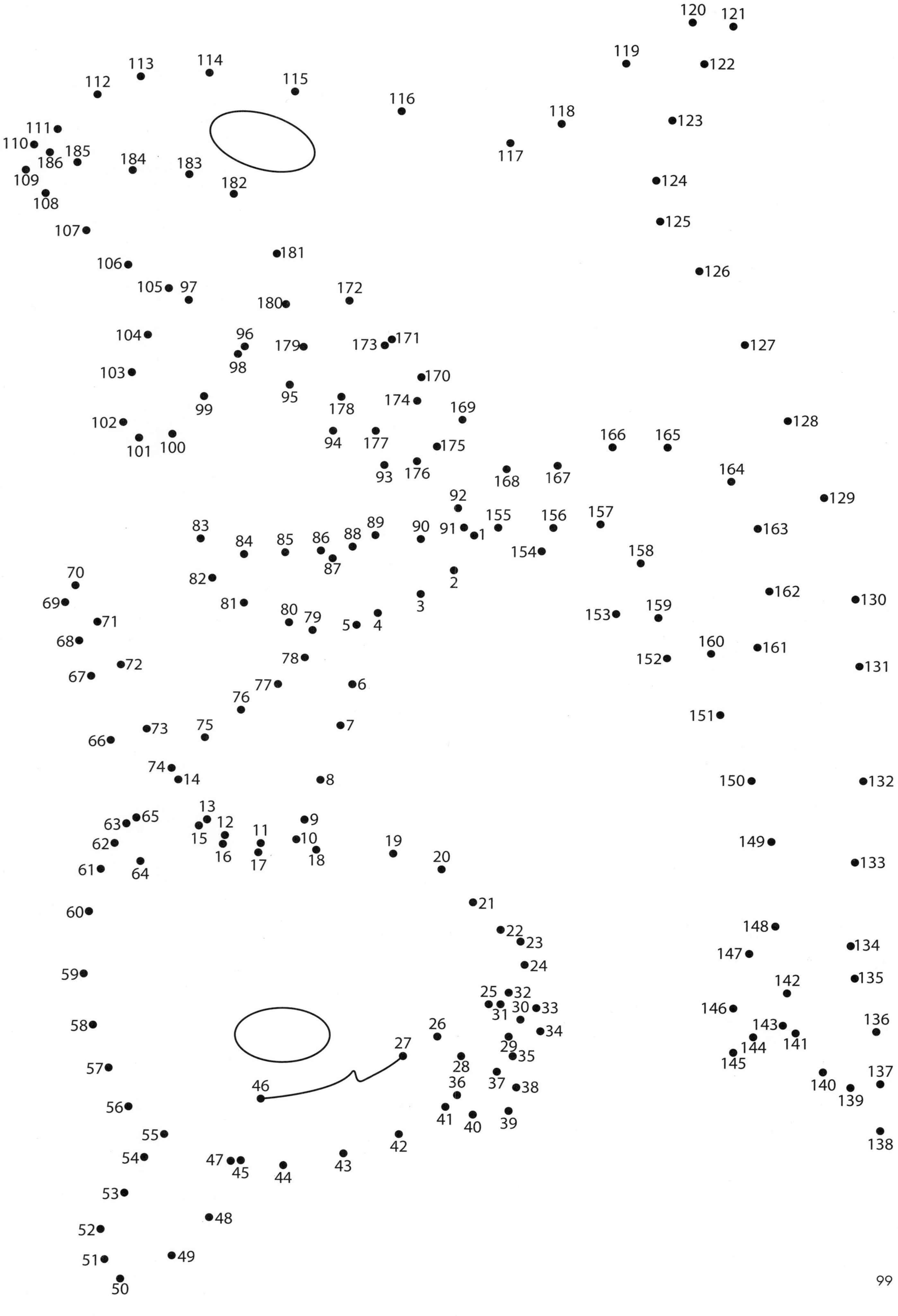

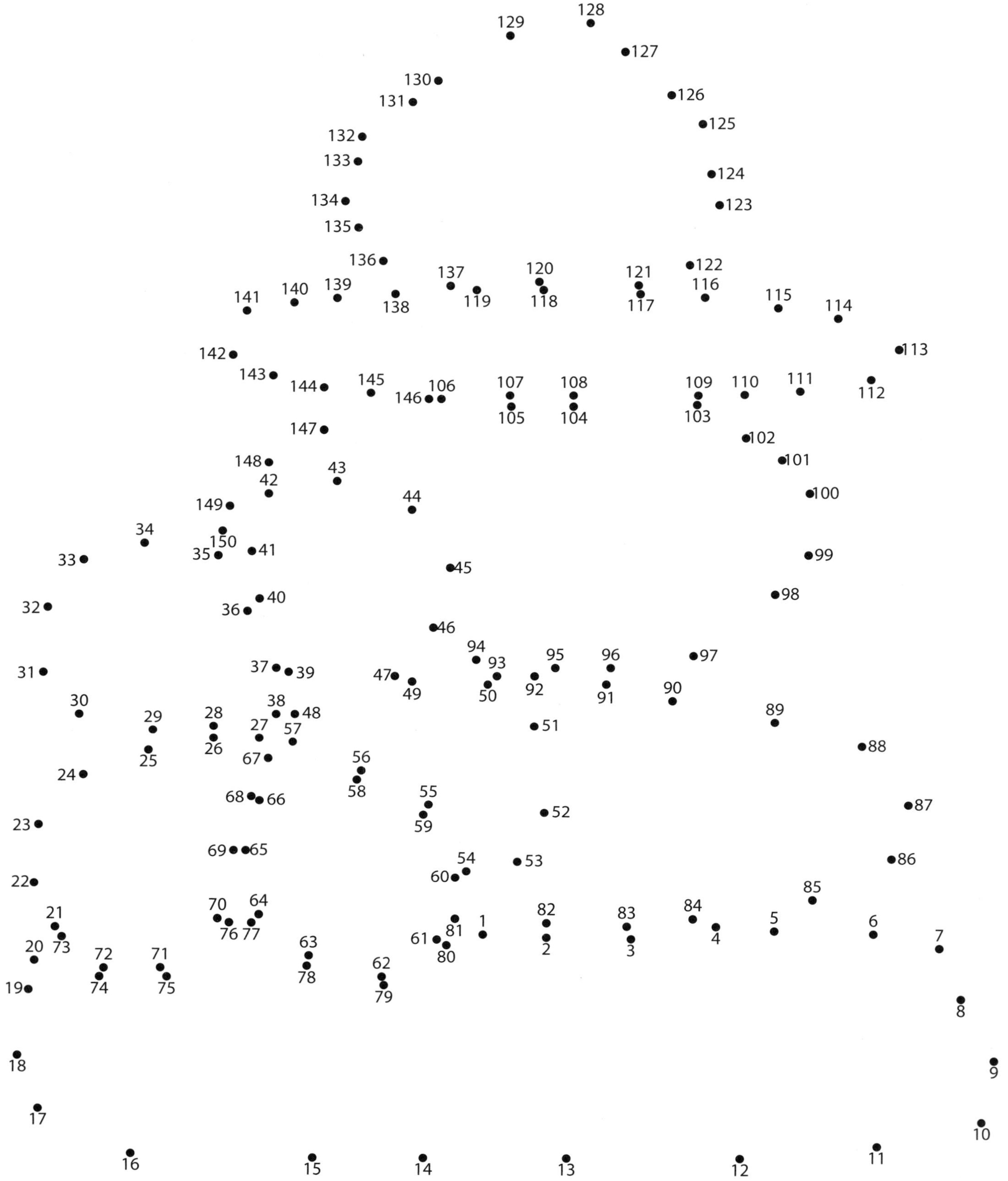

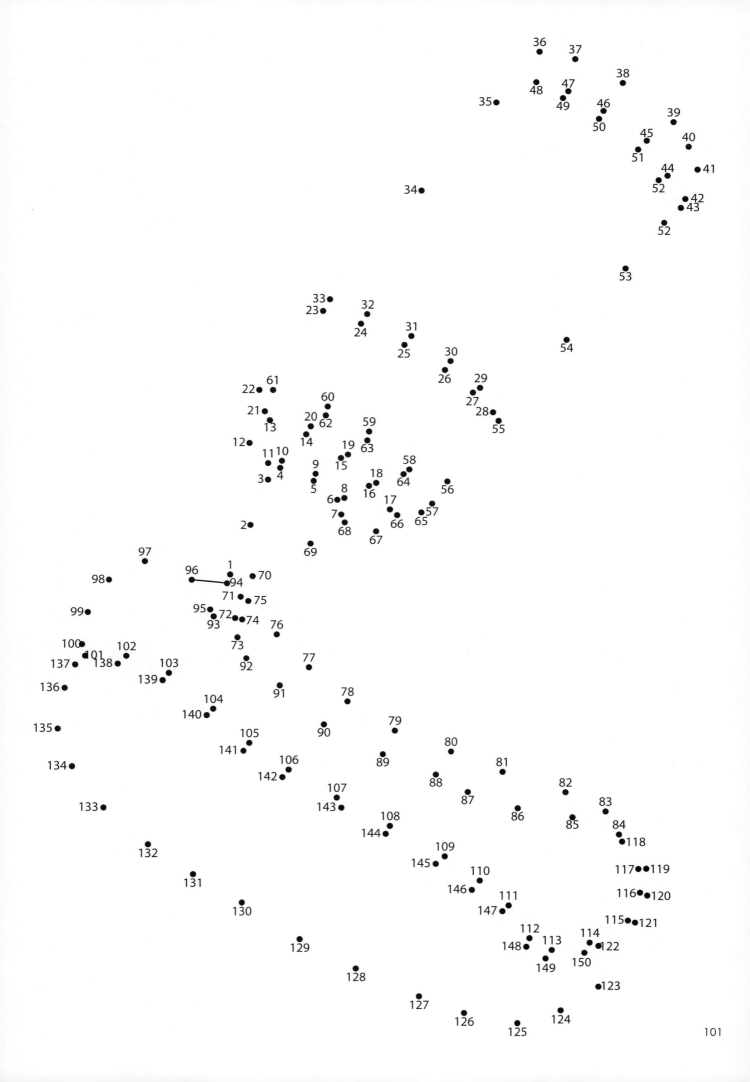

101

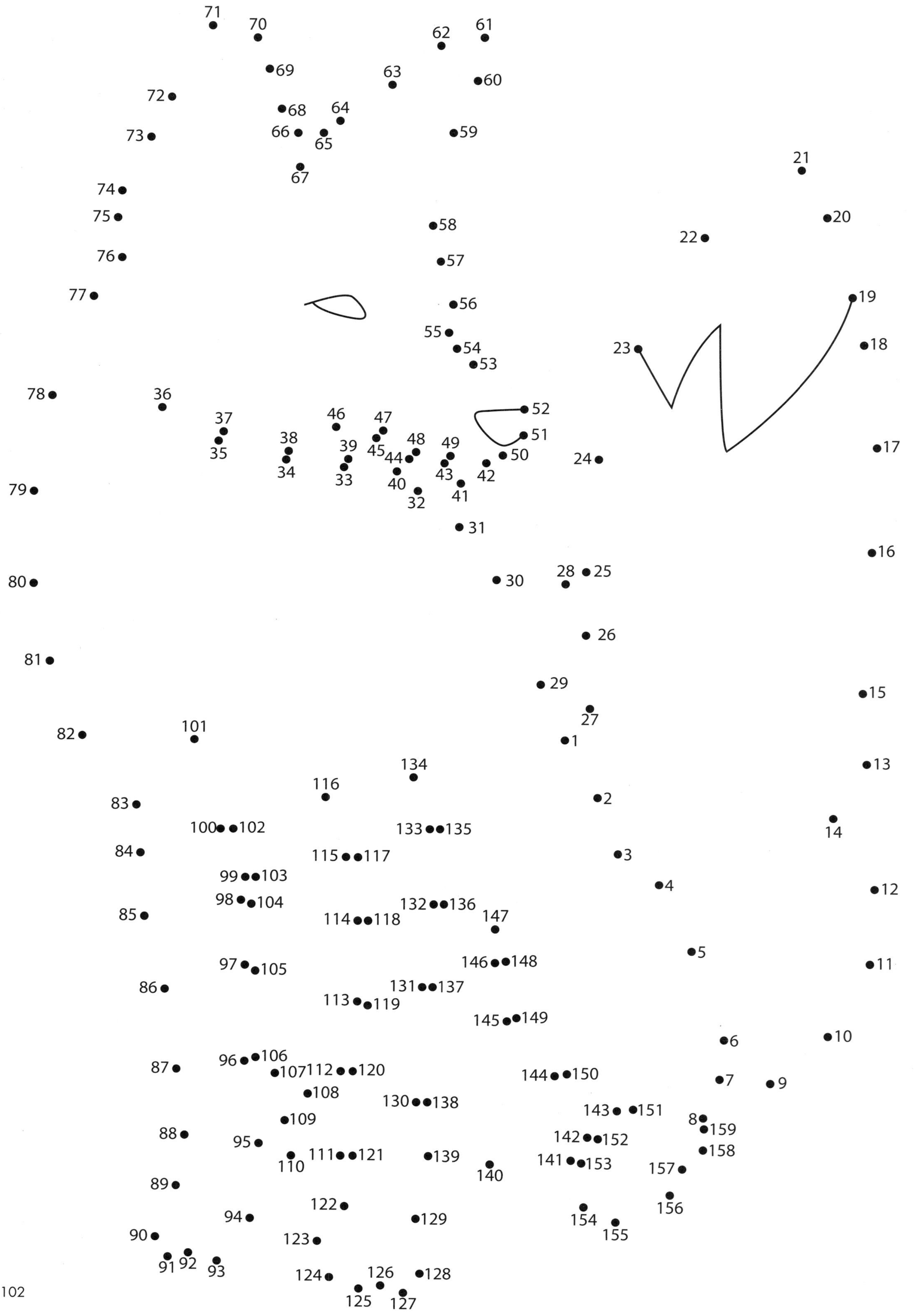

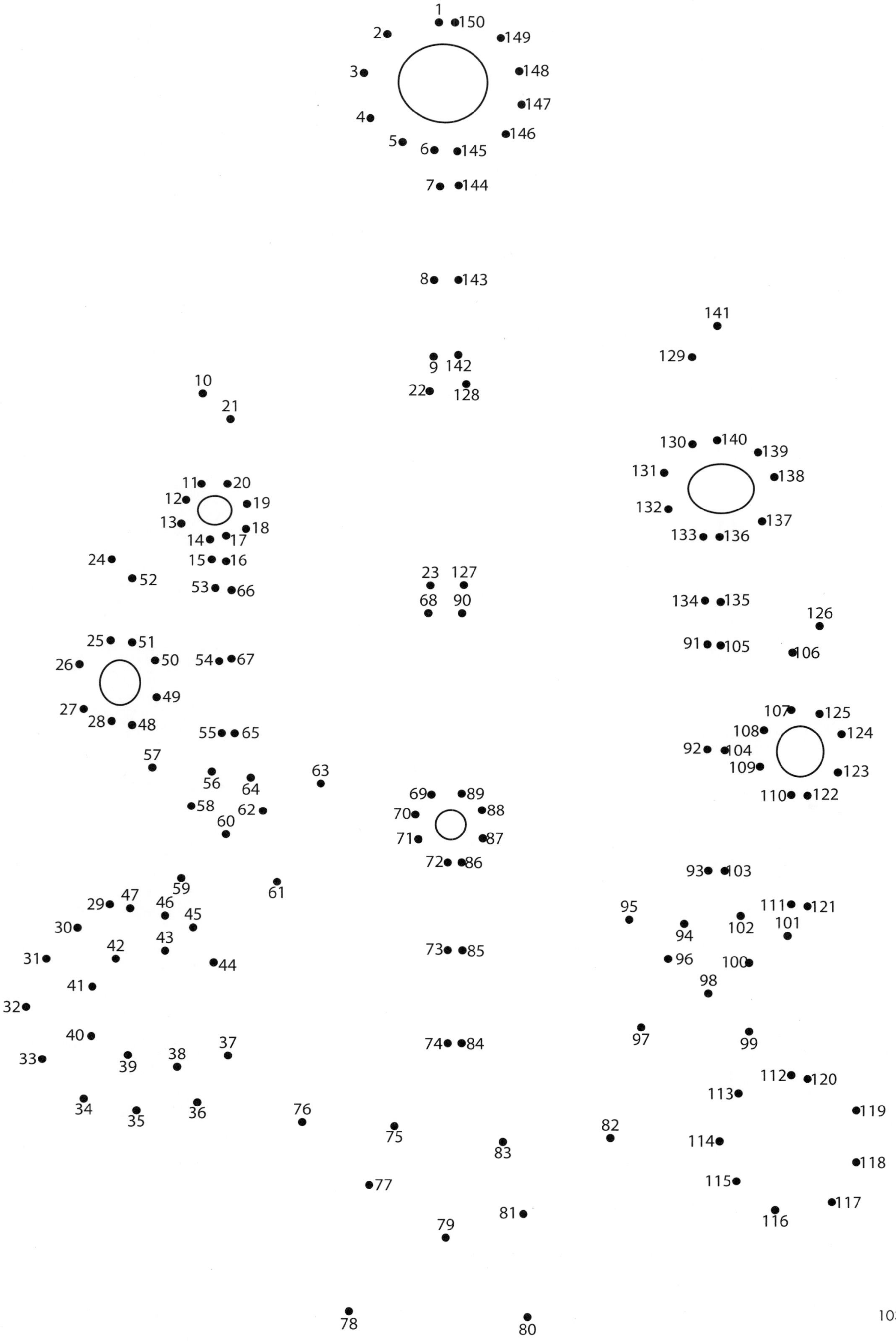

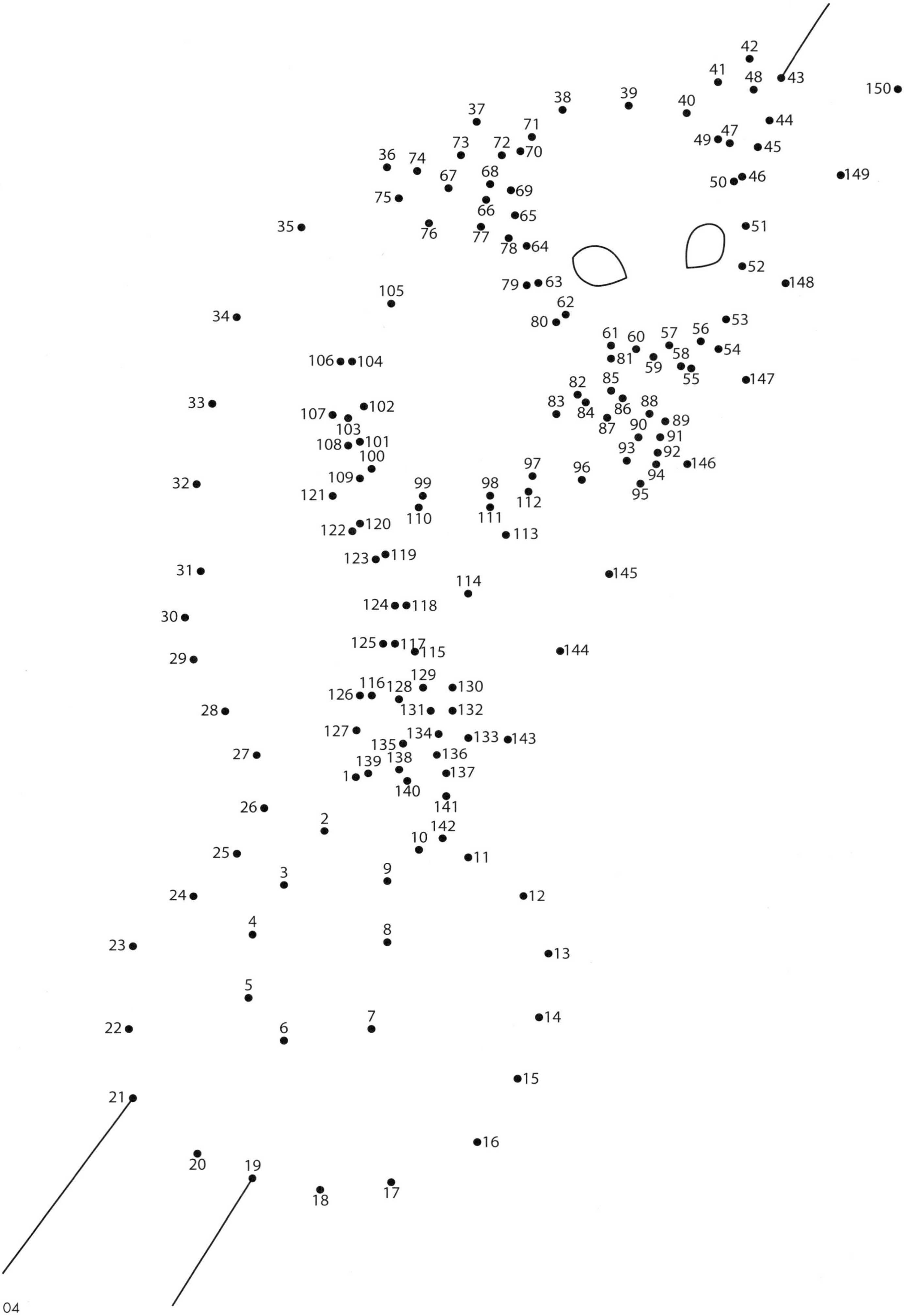

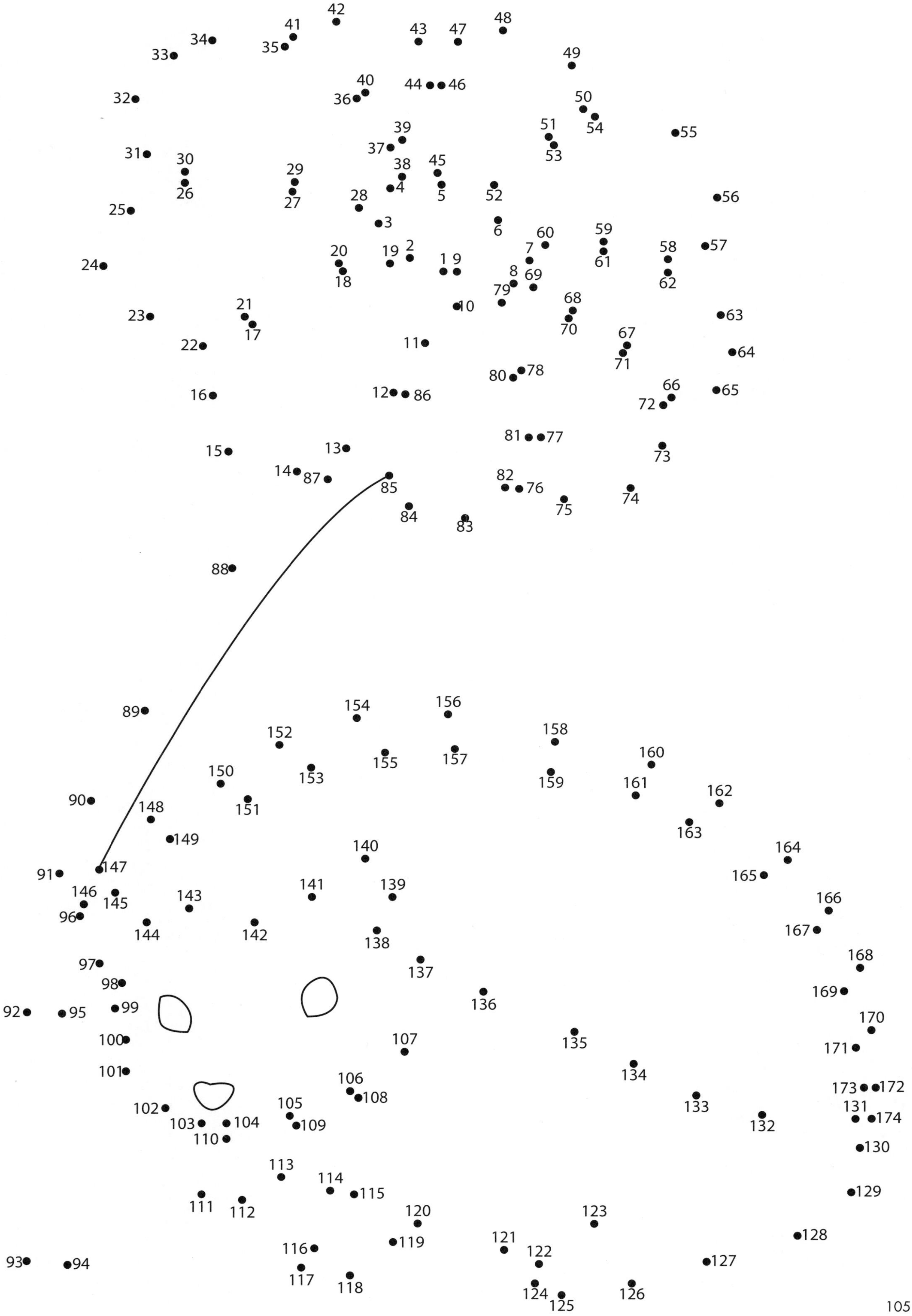

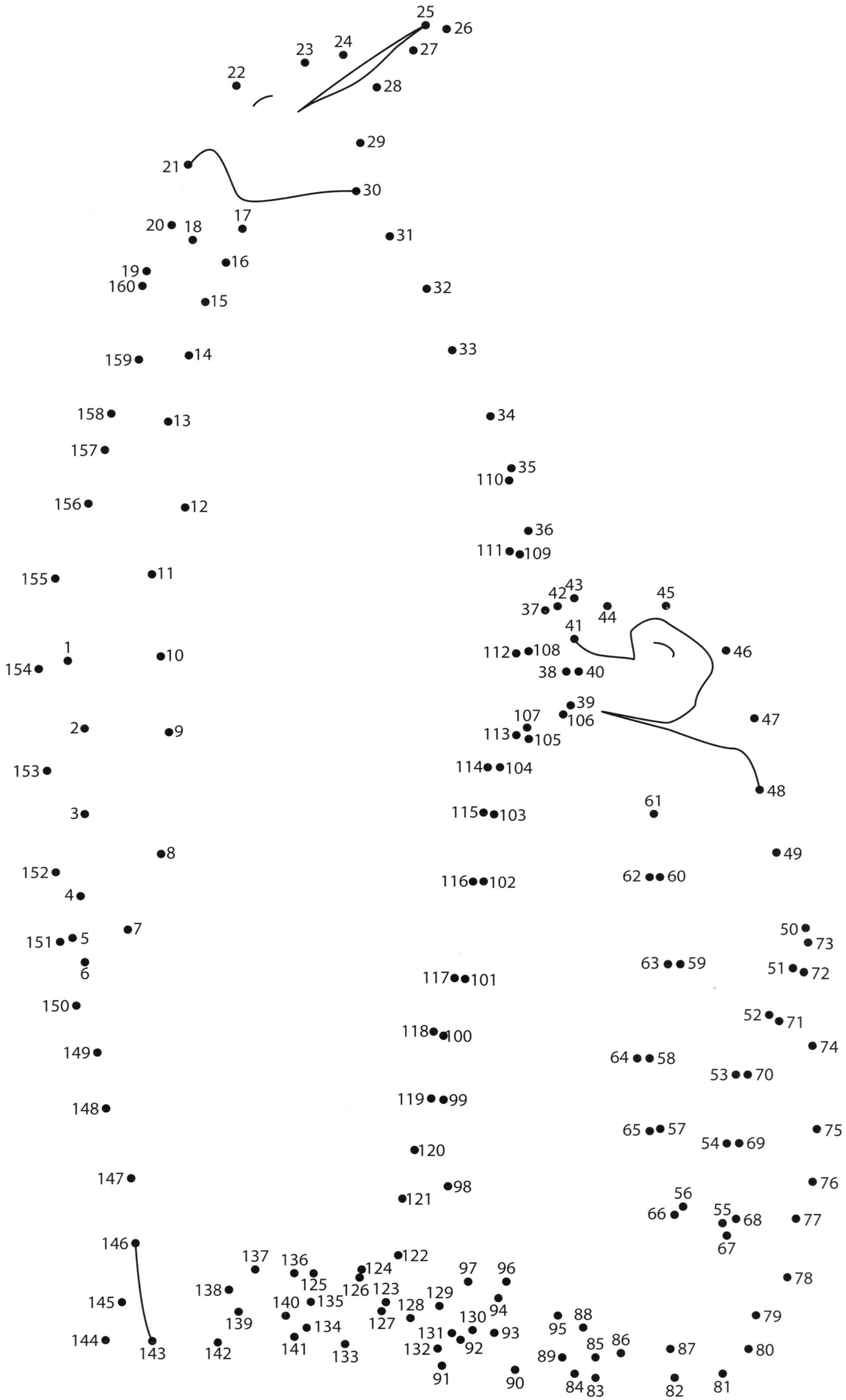

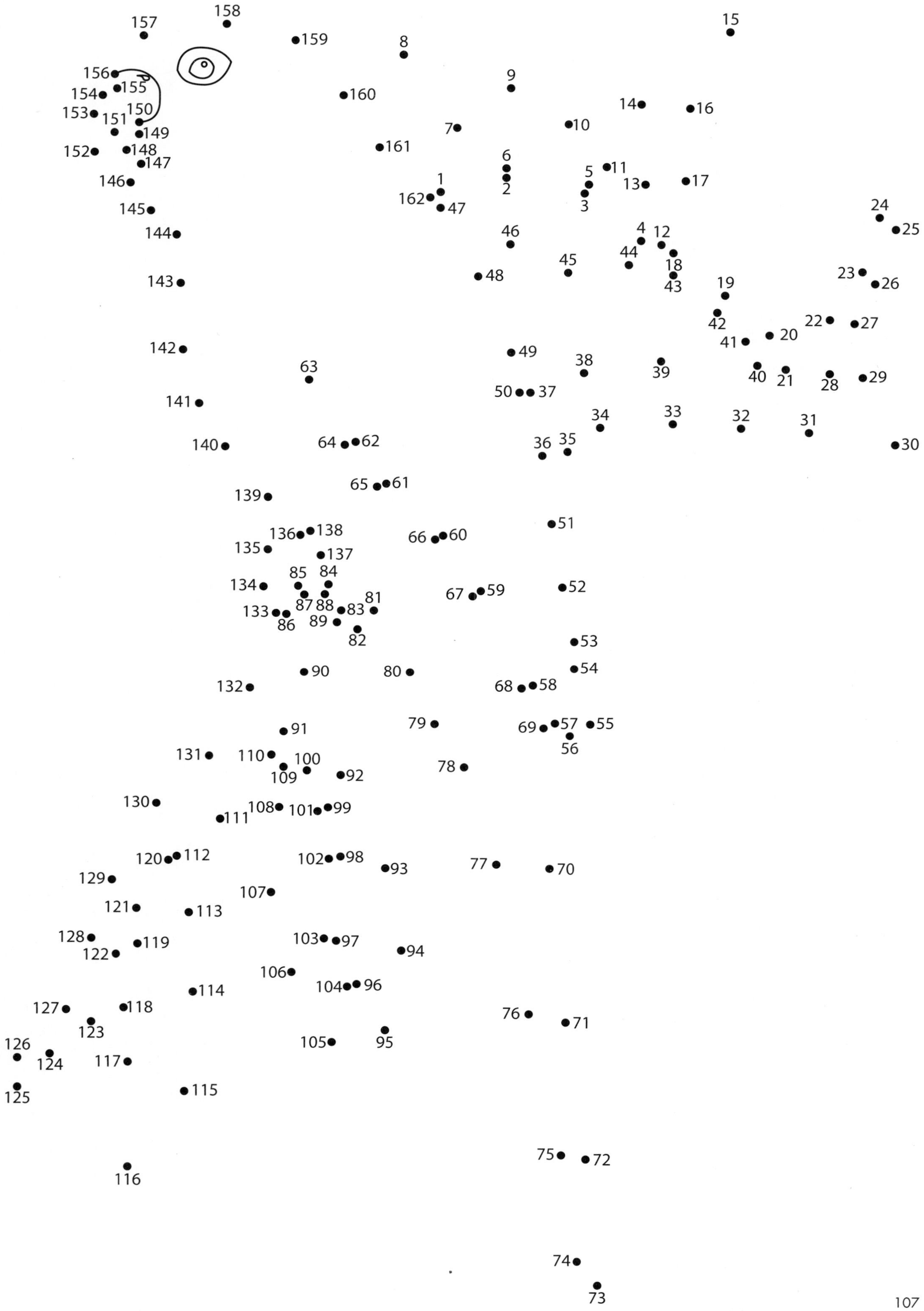

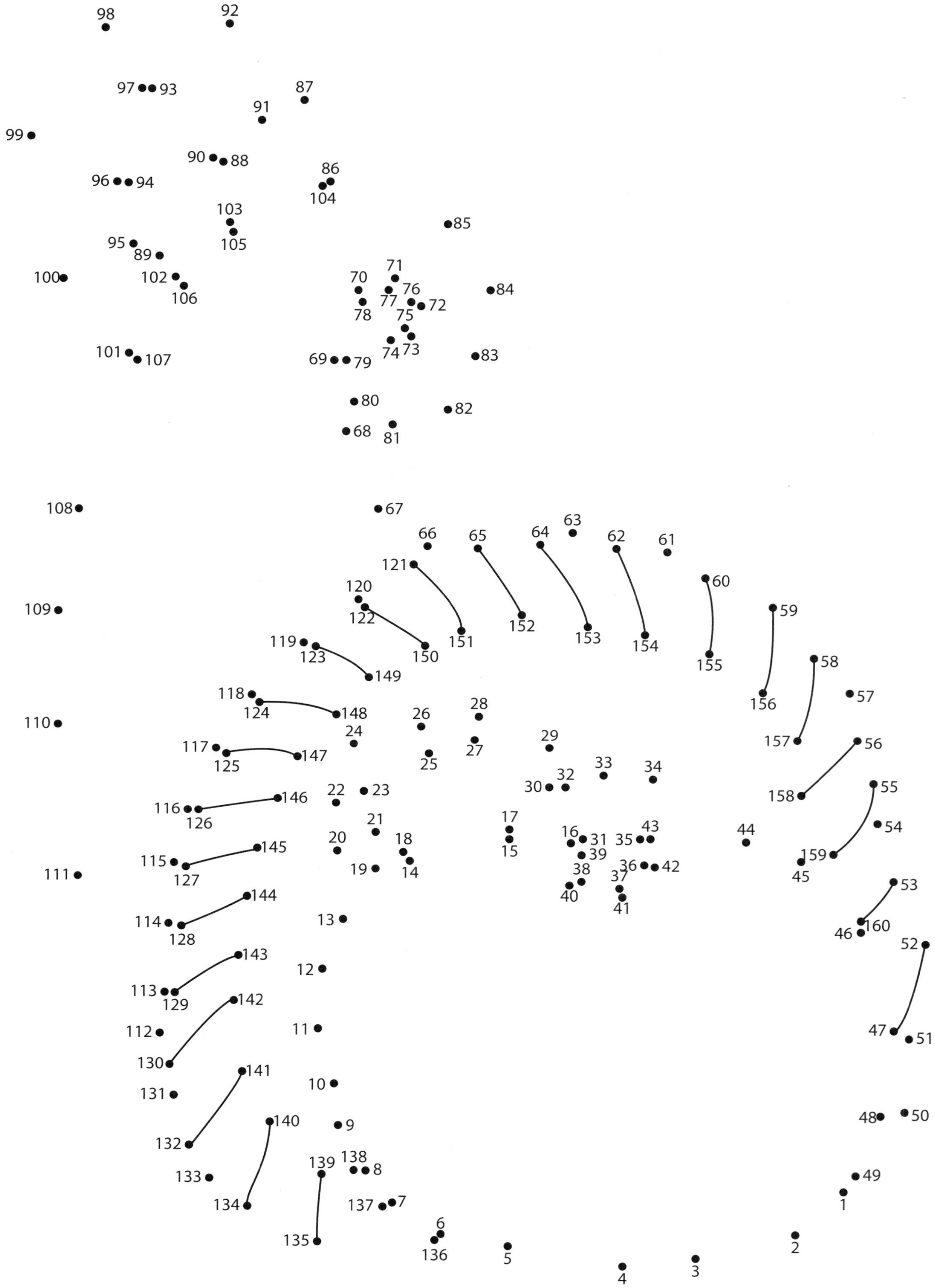

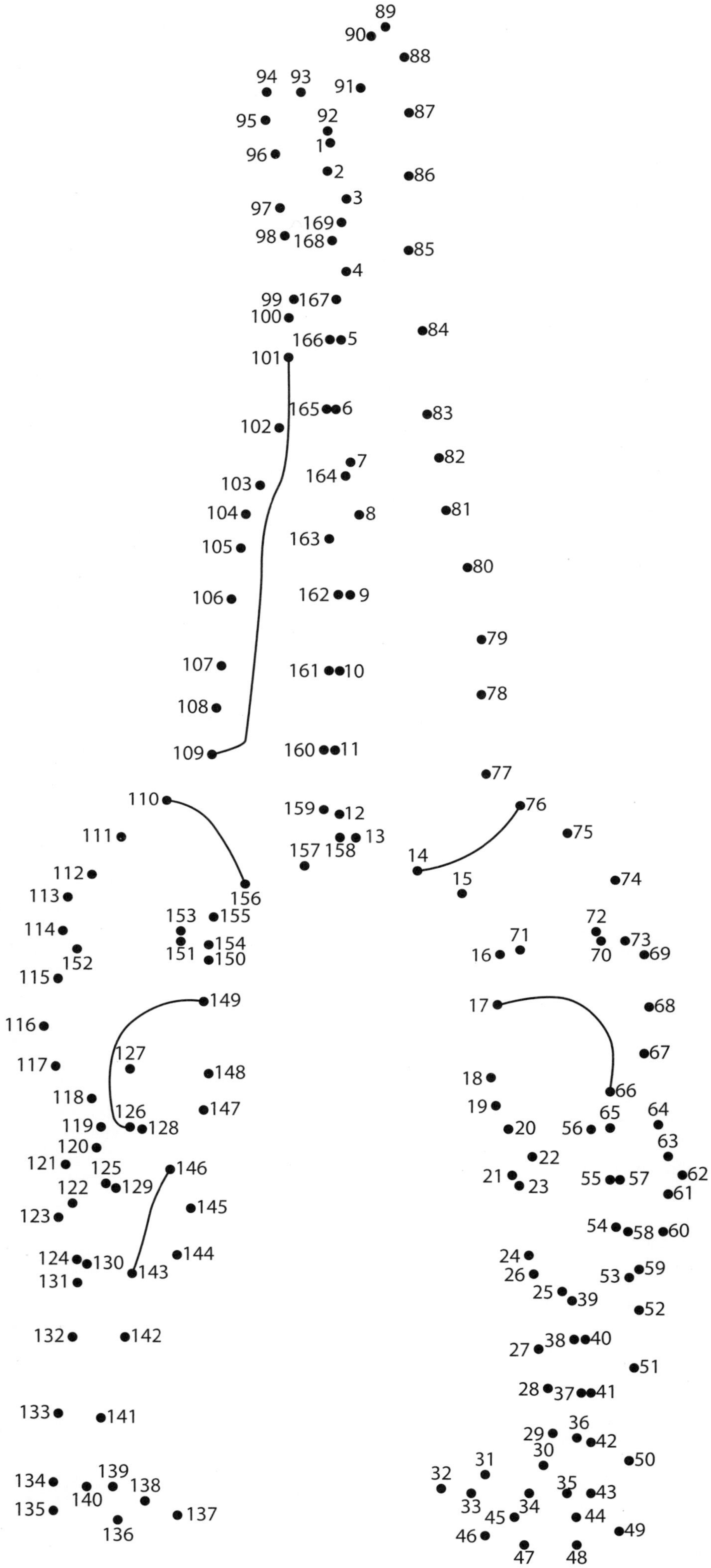

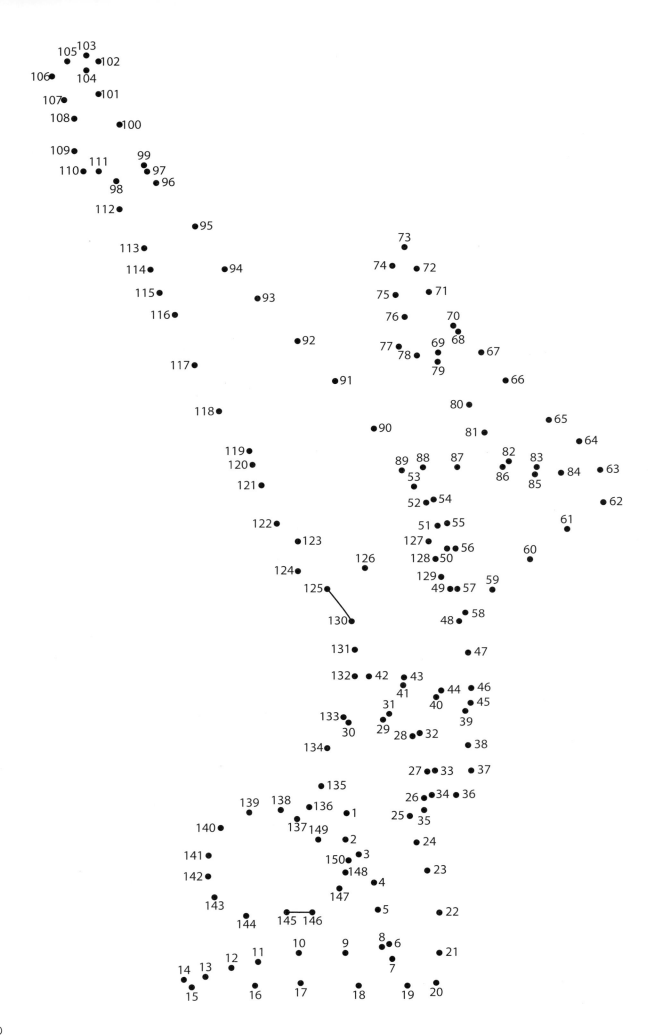

110

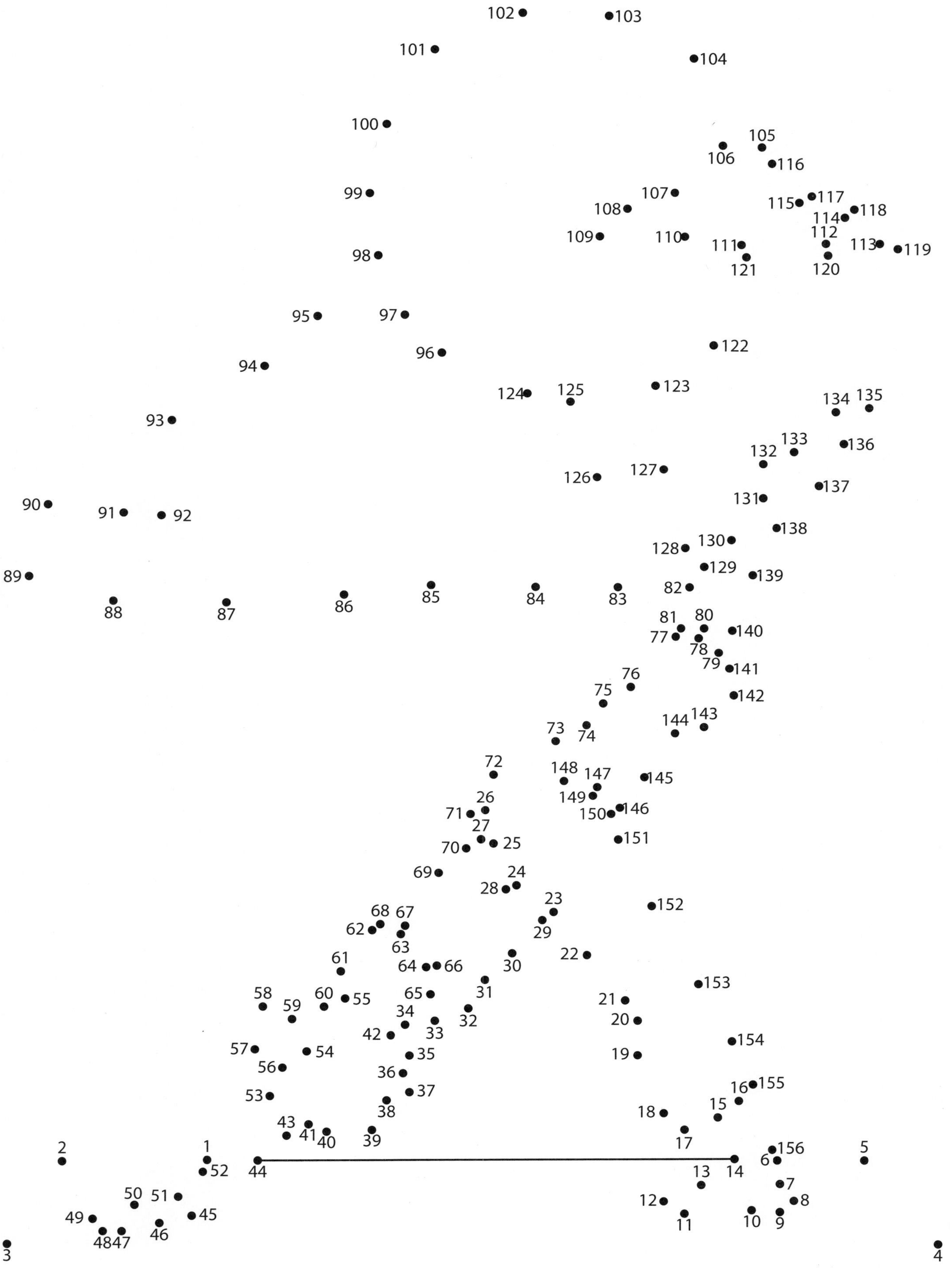

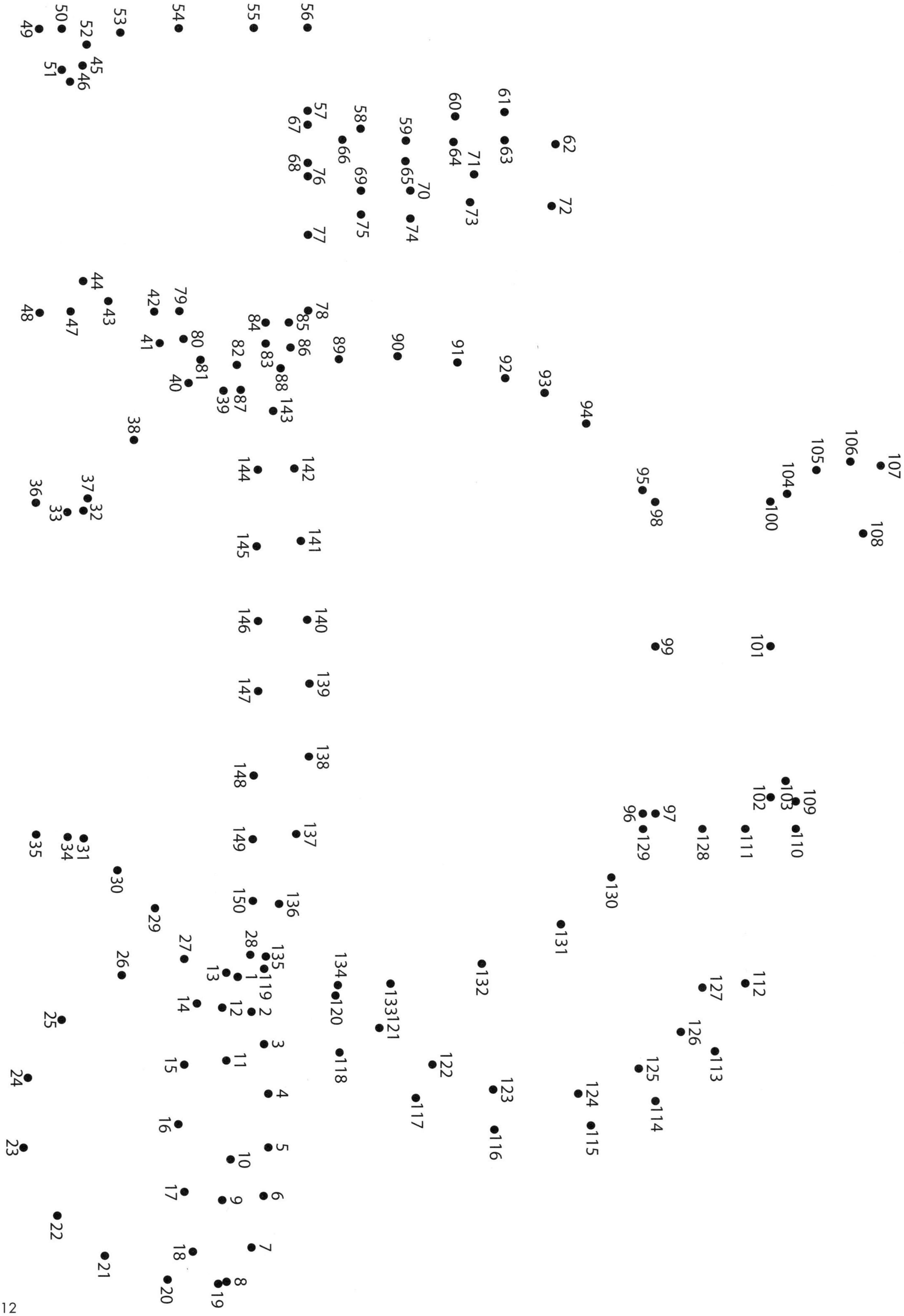

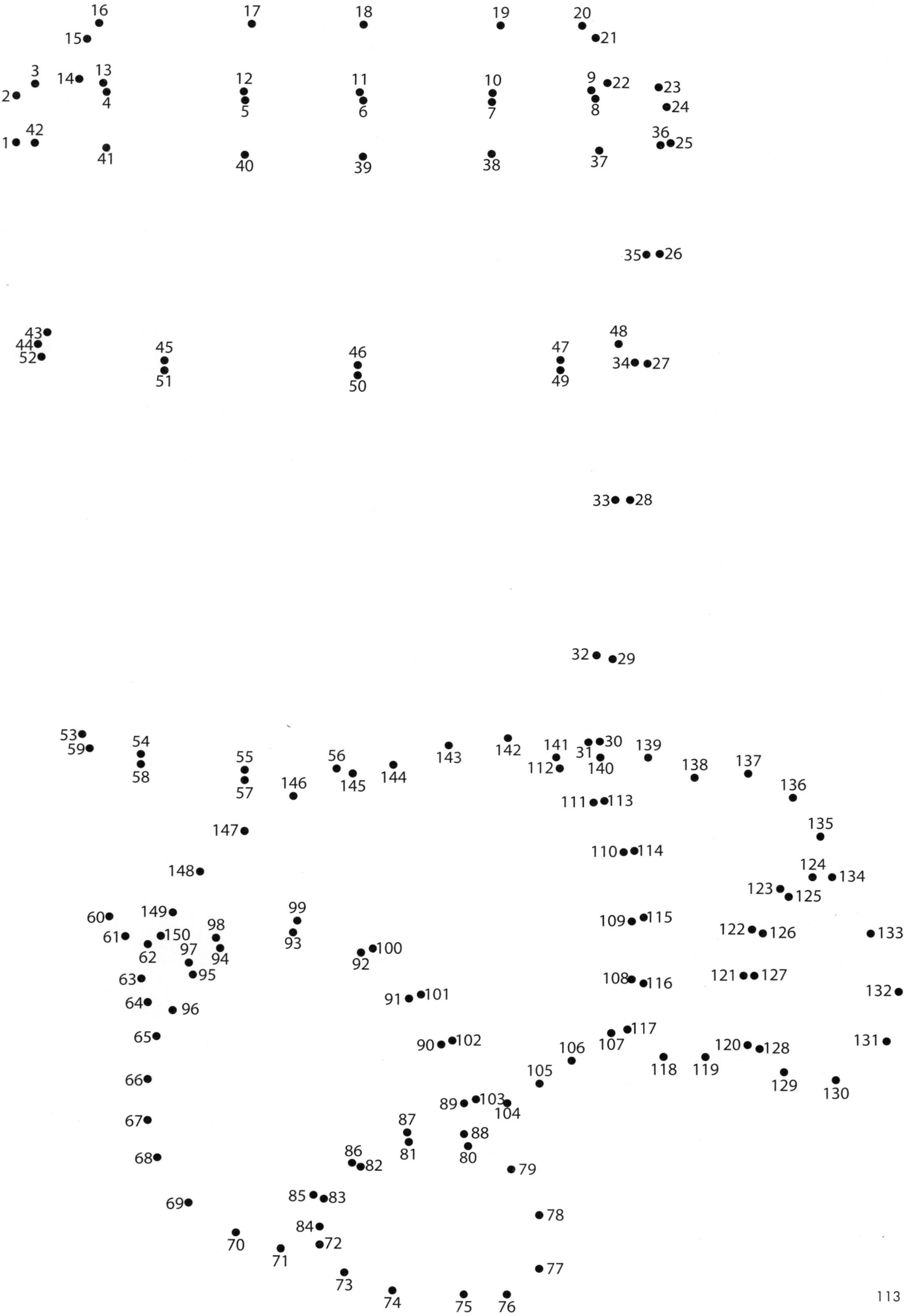

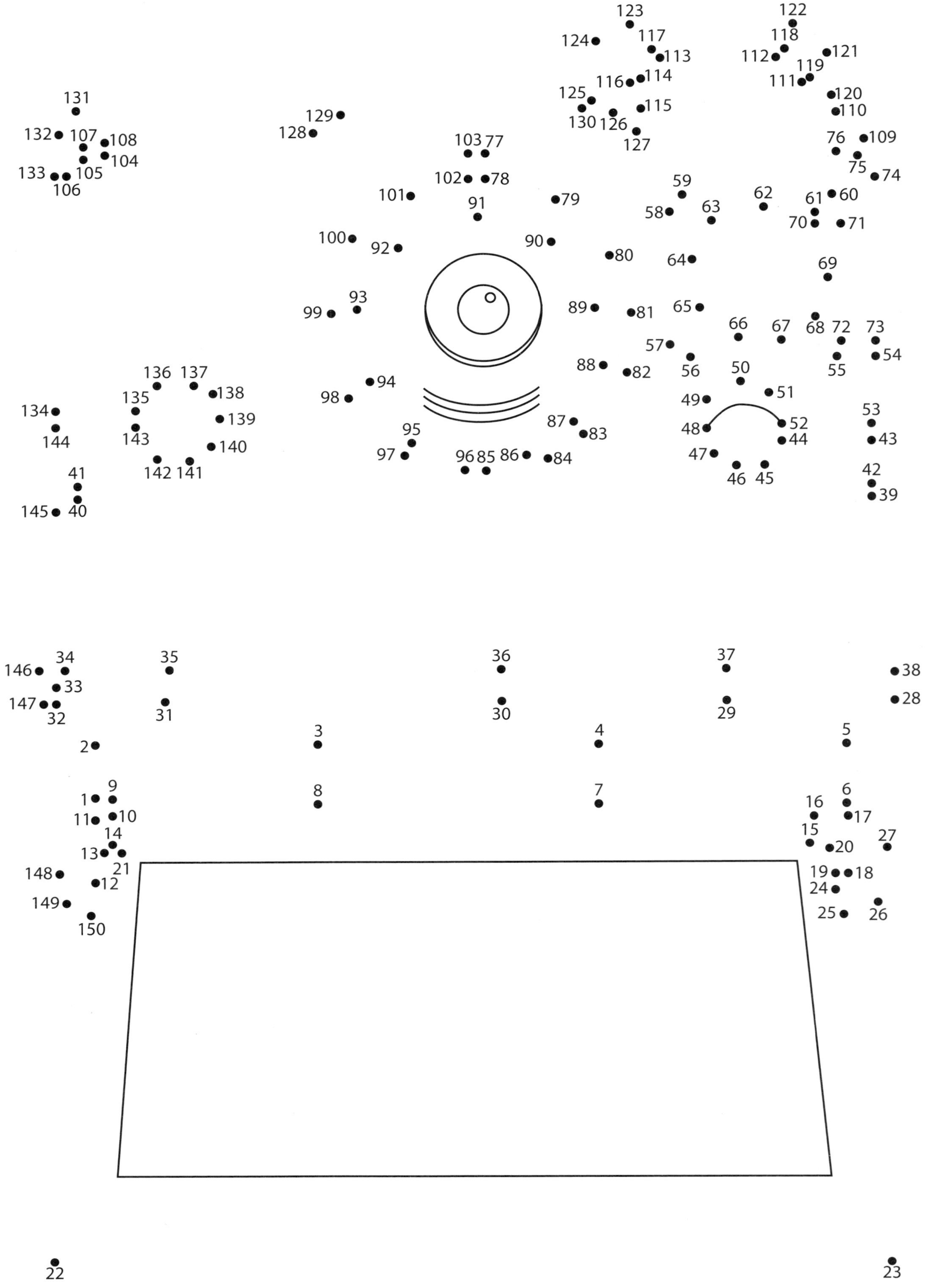

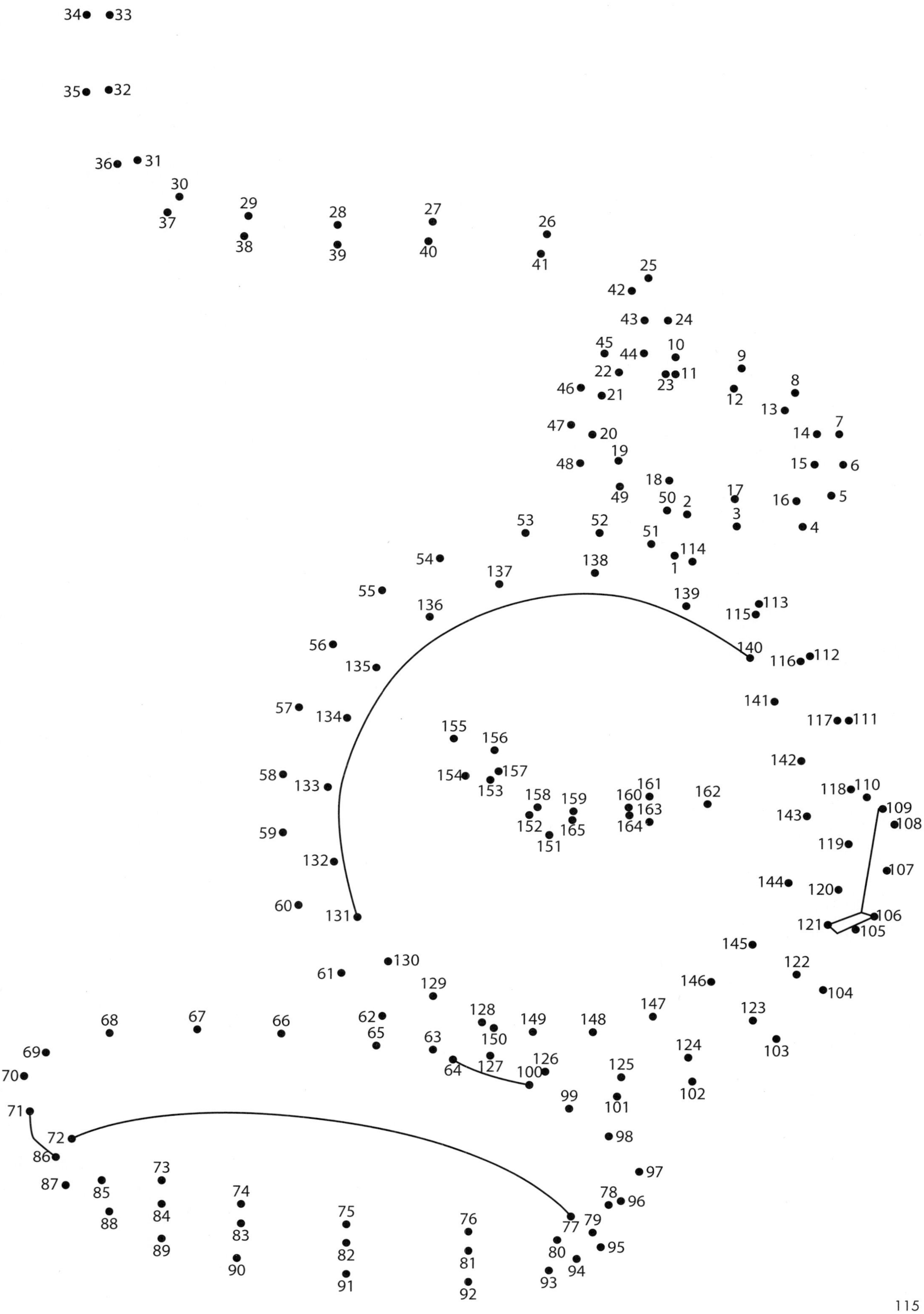

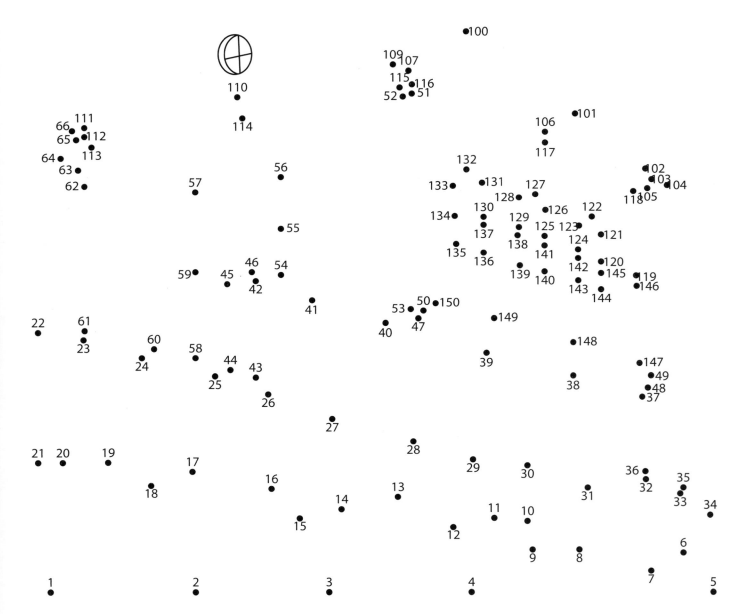

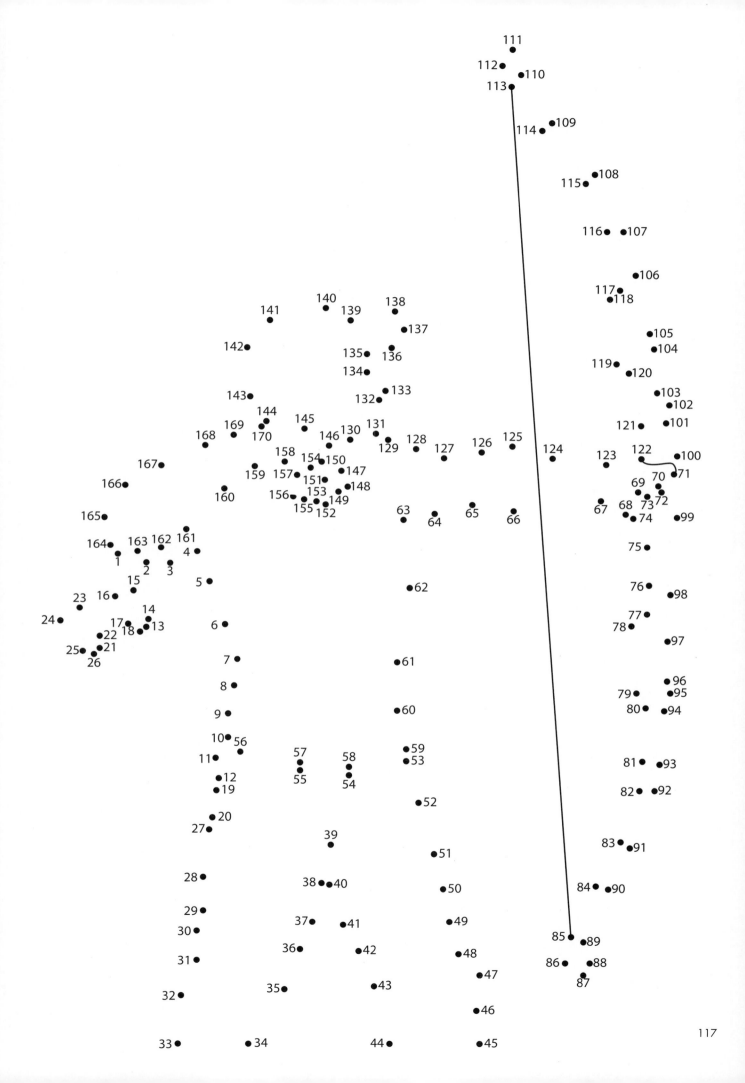

117

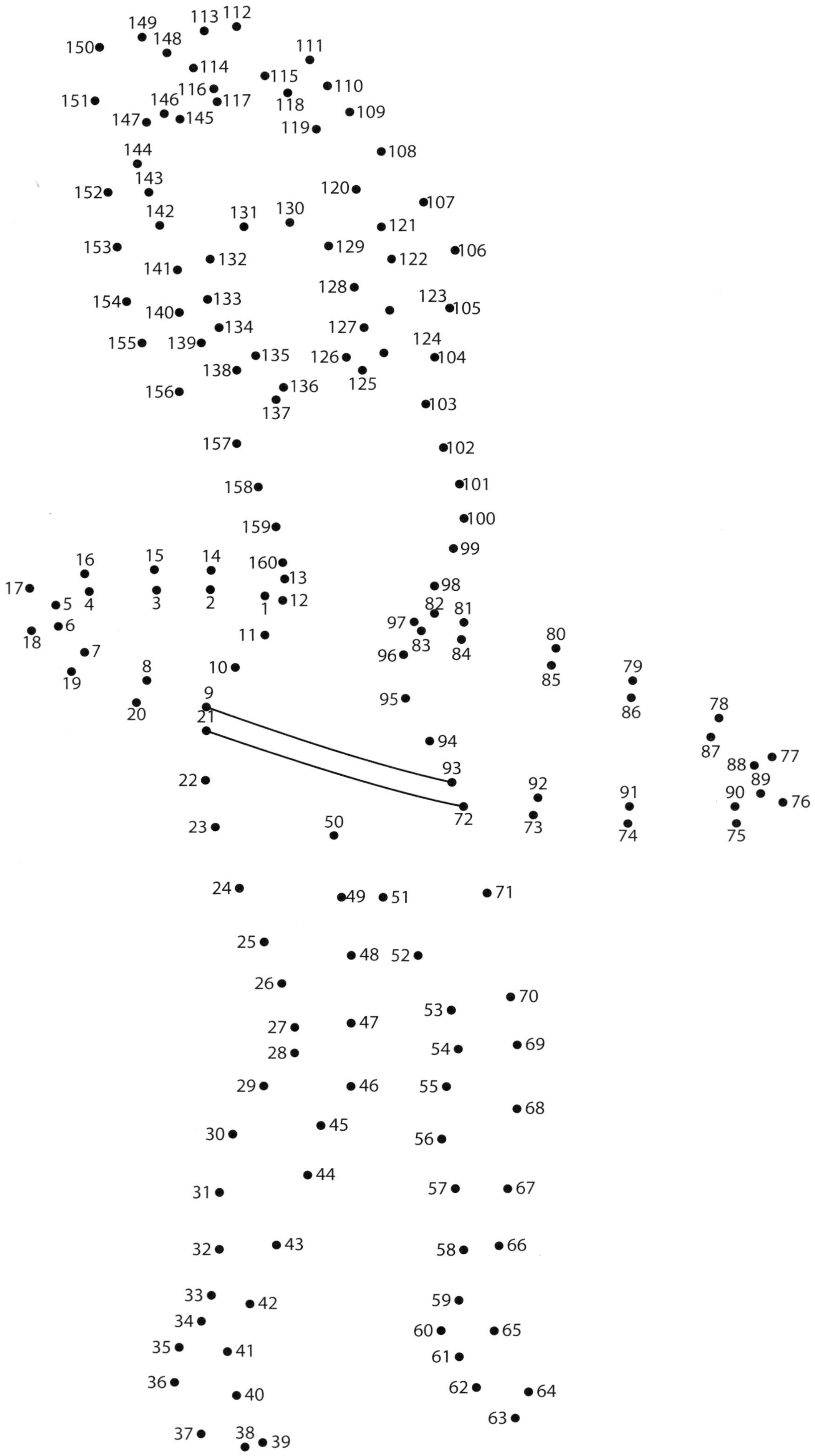

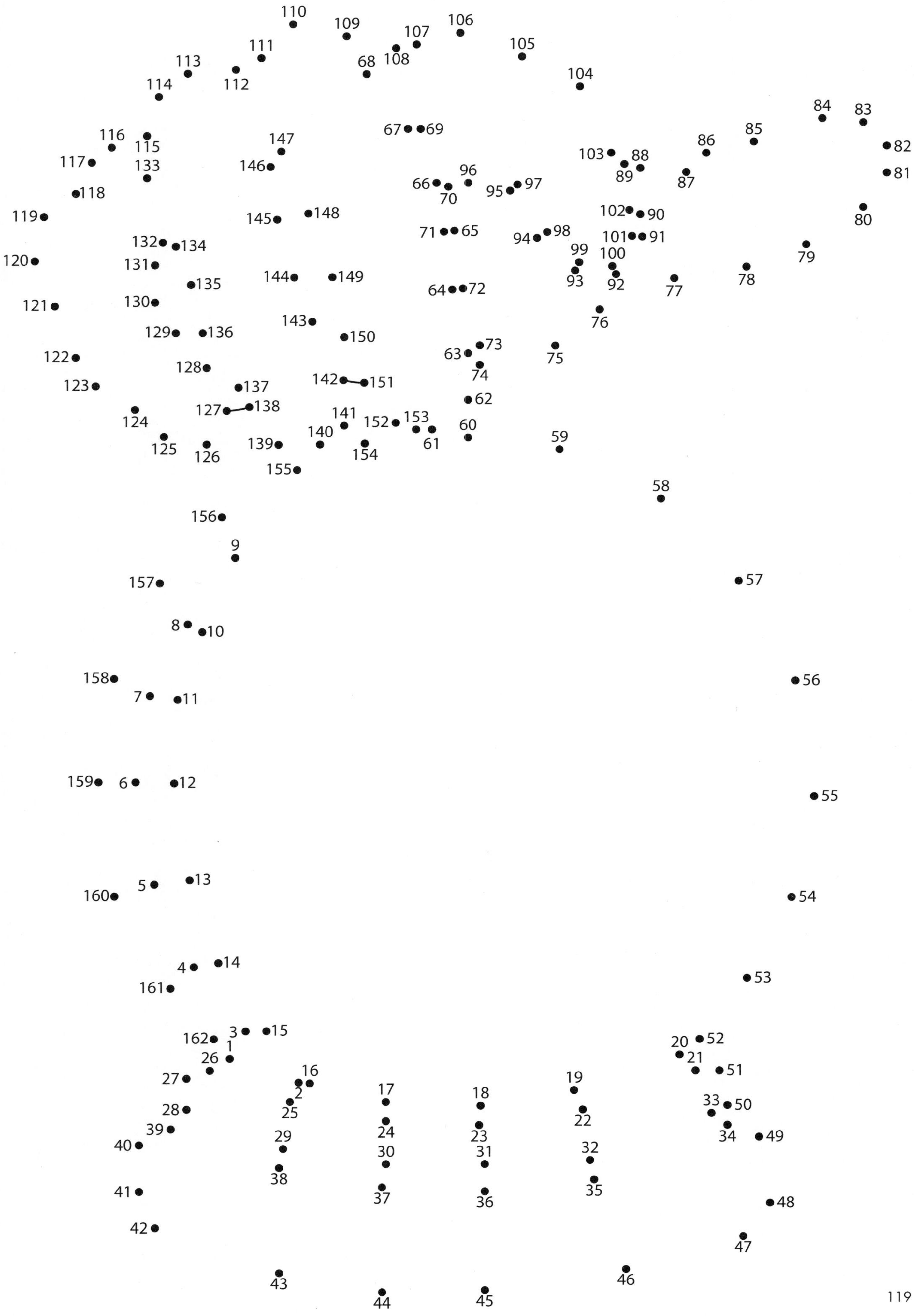

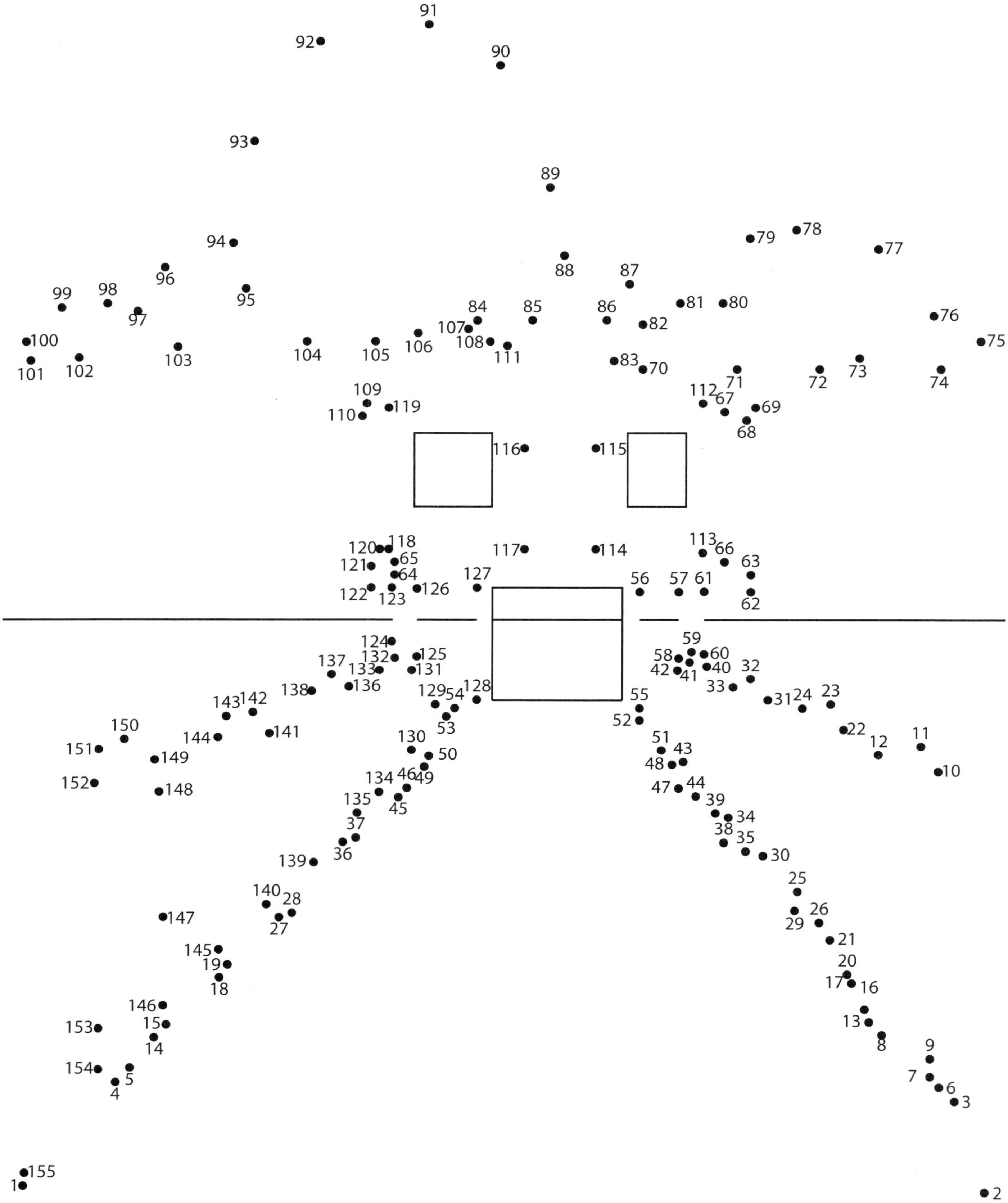

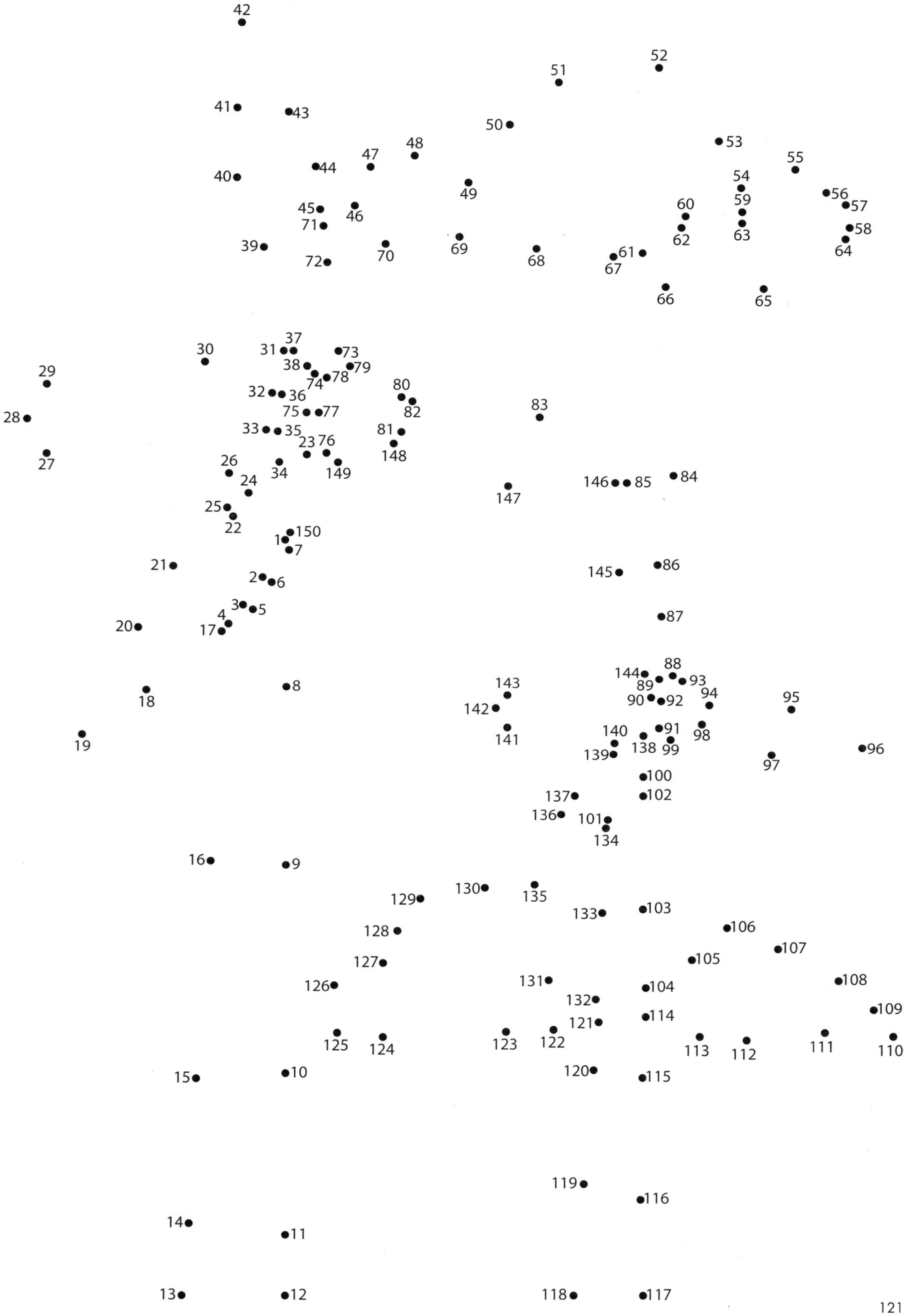

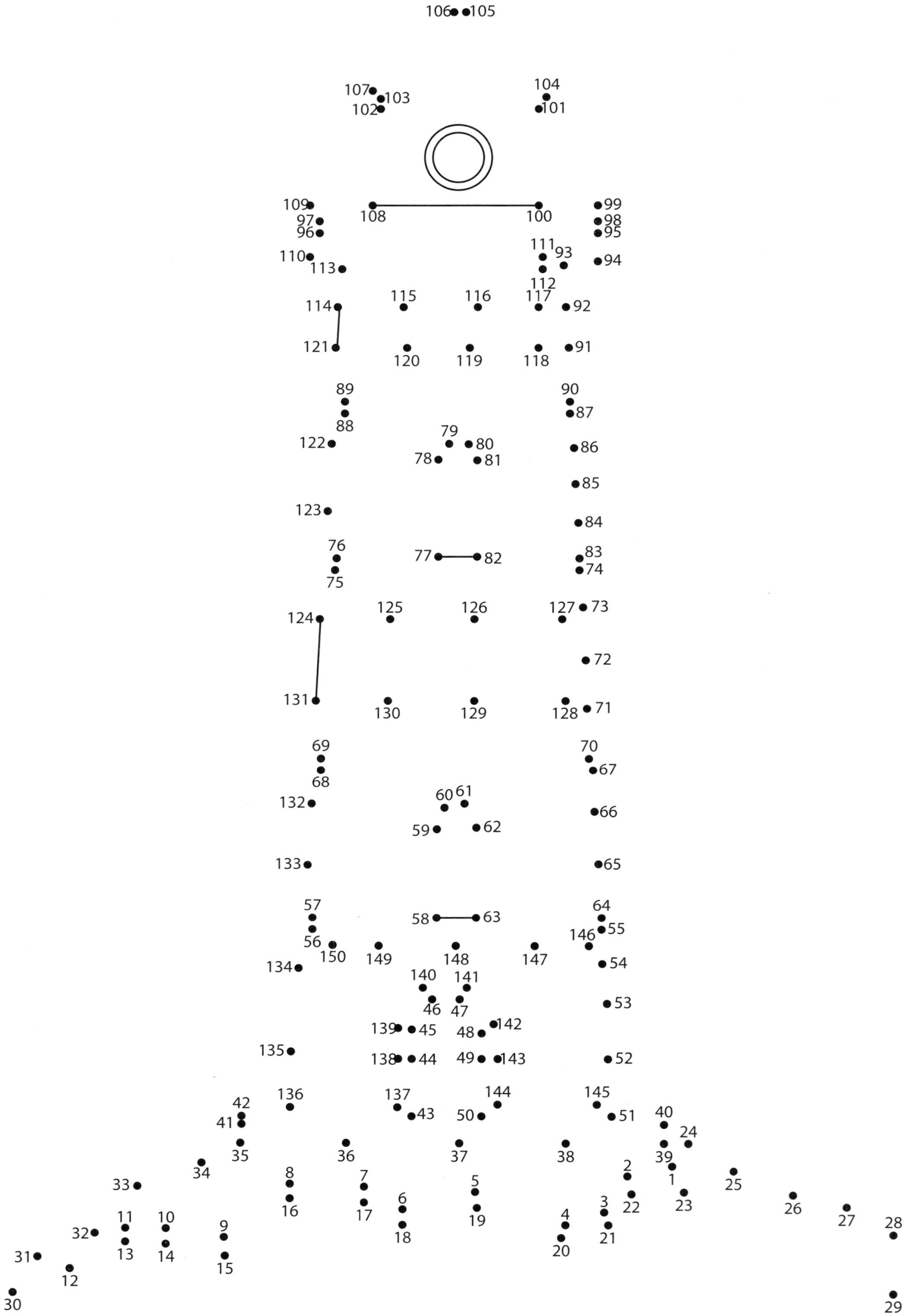

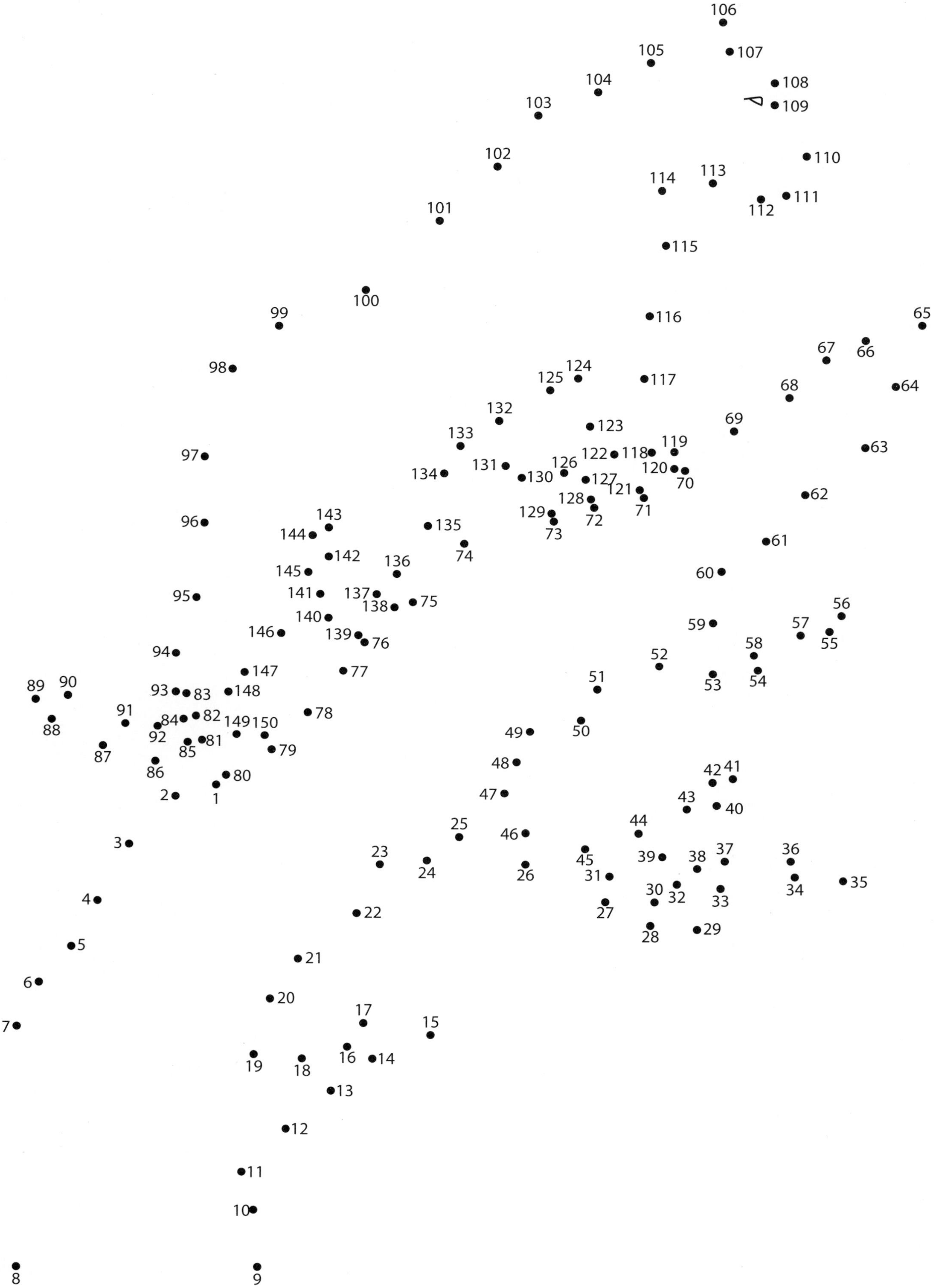

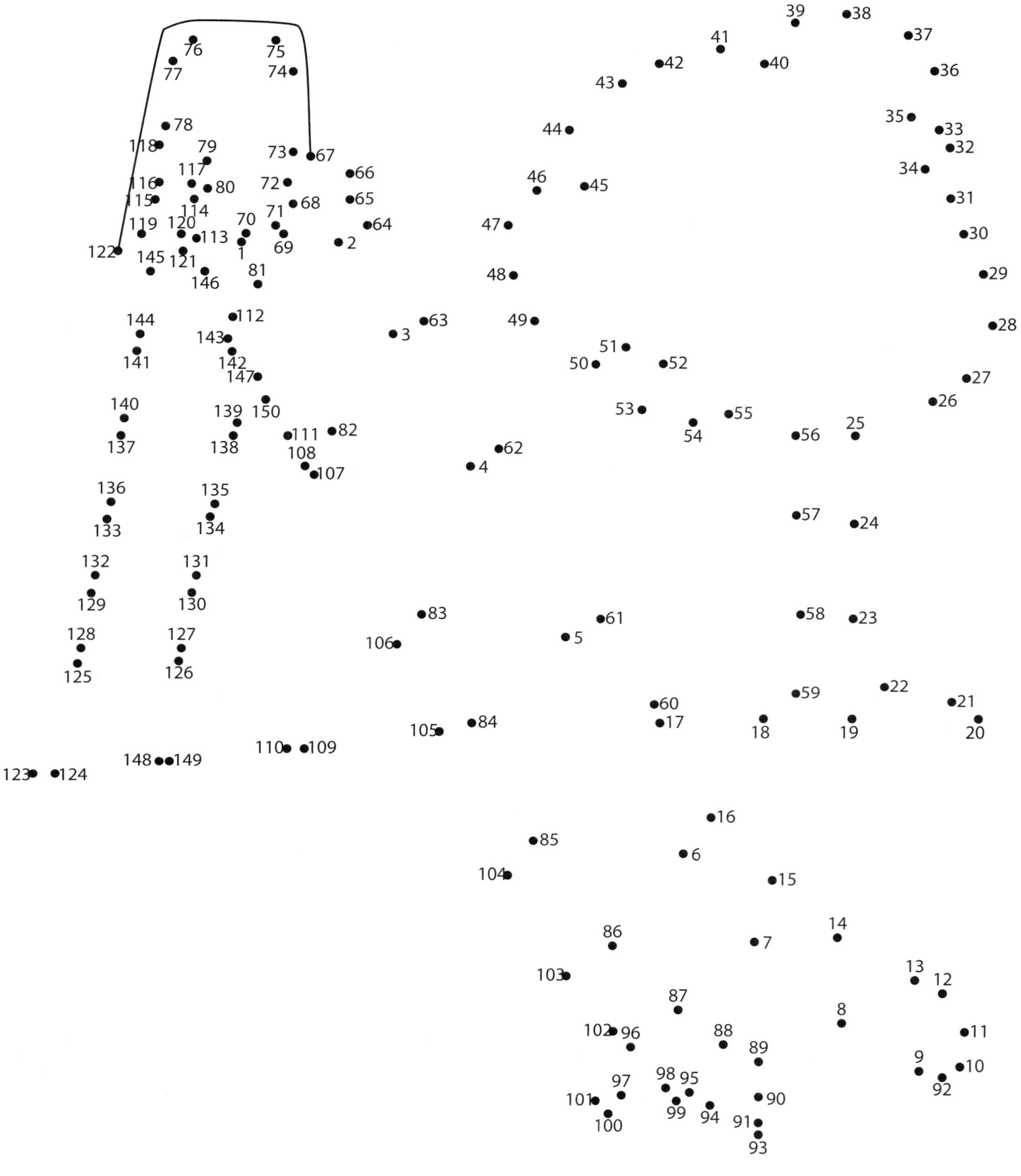

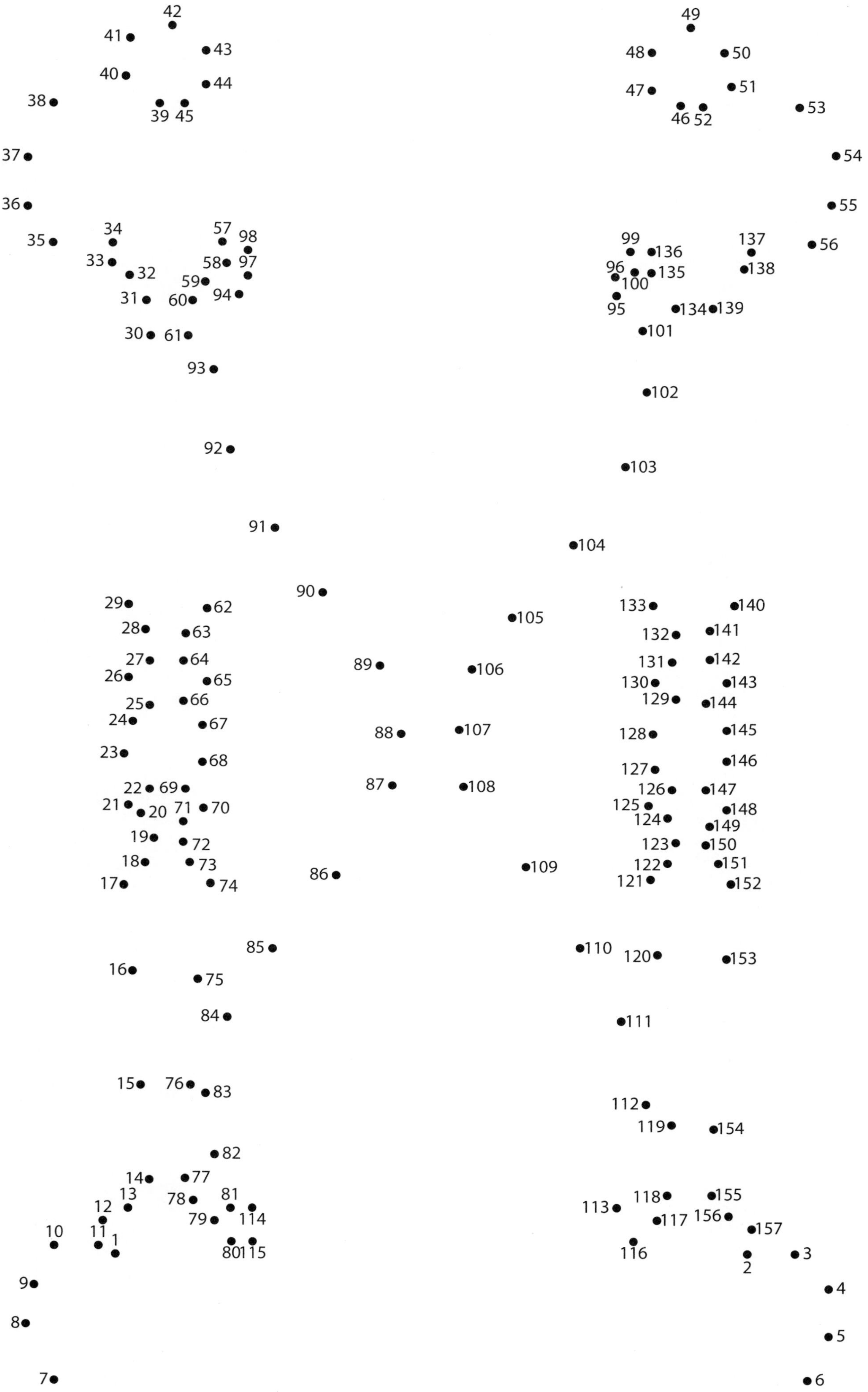

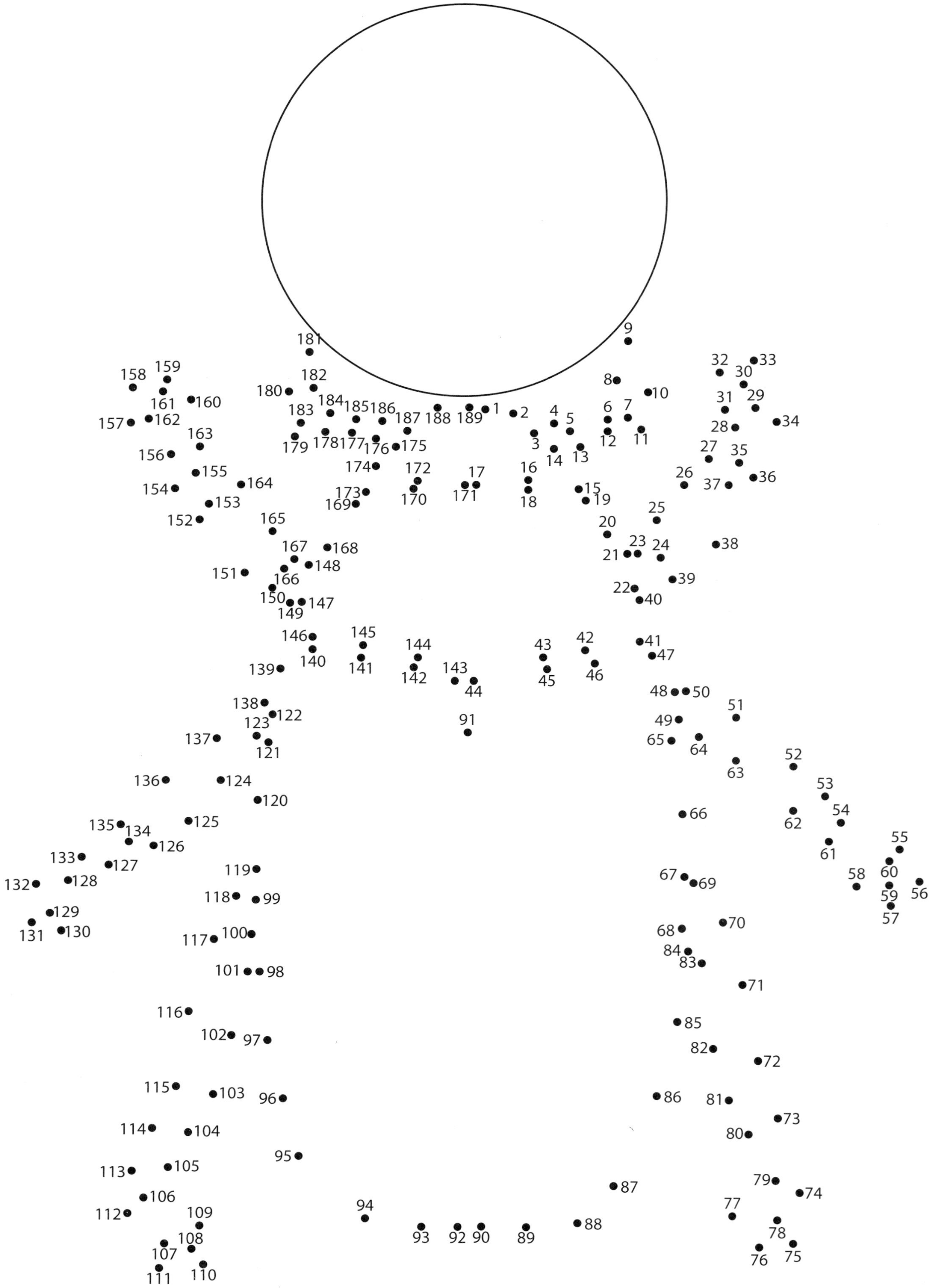

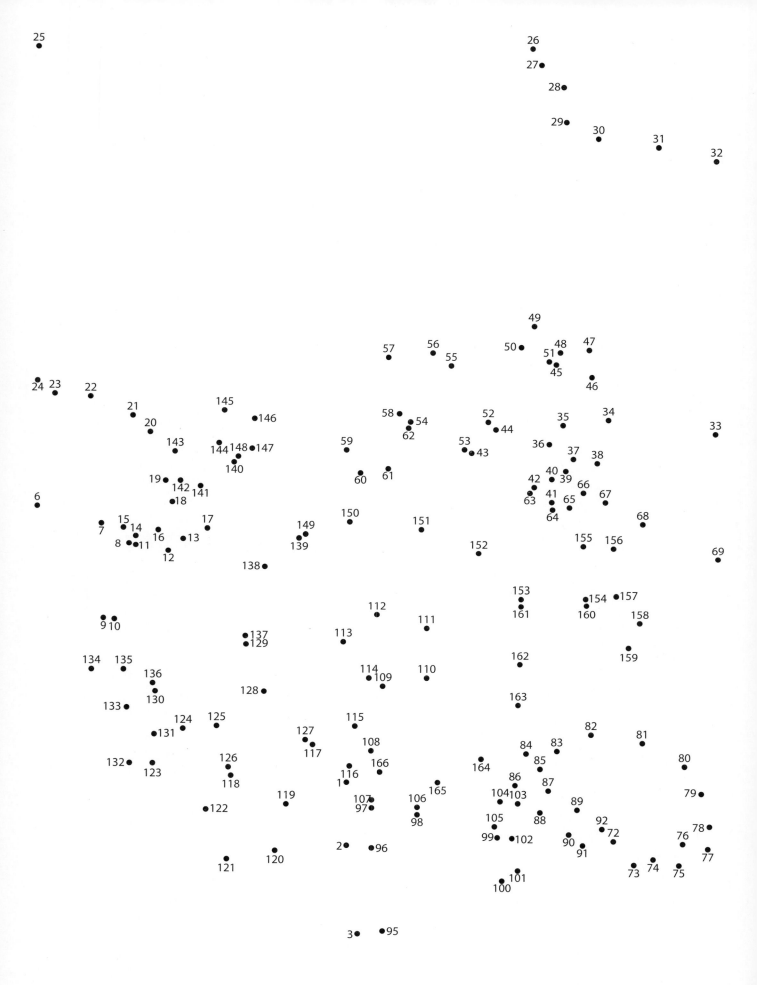

List of illustrations